The Picturesque and the
Later Georgian Garden

Genuine antique remains used to compose a picturesque tableau at Virginia Water, Surrey (print, 1828).

The Picturesque and the Later Georgian Garden

Michael Symes

 redcliffe

First published in 2012 by Redcliffe Press Ltd.,
81g Pembroke Road, Bristol BS8 3EA
www.redcliffepress.co.uk
info@redcliffepress.co.uk

© Michael Symes

ISBN 978-1-908326-09-6

British Library Cataloguing-in-Publication Data
A catalogue record for this book is available from the British Library

Typeset in Minion Pro 11.5pt
Design and typesetting by Mark Cavanagh
Printed by HSW Print, Tonypandy, Rhondda

Contents

Introduction

It may be thought that the 'picturesque' garden of the late eighteenth century is a subject that has received a great deal of attention. However, the term has given rise to much confusion and uncertainty. The Picturesque and the Sublime were recognised categories of the time – though their differentiation remains problematic, partly because they are conceptually mismatched – but a third label, 'romantic', has an important part to play, for although not an accepted category it was frequently used as an adjective during the century and afterwards, giving it a quasi-categorical status.

The whole subject is fraught with difficulties: it is a glacier on which one struggles to maintain a grip or foothold. There are no neat definitions, nor are there clear distinctions between one category and another – so much was subjective opinion at the time, so that what was sublime to one person was picturesque to another. The terms picturesque, romantic and sublime were often used loosely and without much thought. What is intended here is to set out some of the elements that so engaged and excited tourists of the day and try to provide an understanding of the sensibility that has largely come to determine our own responses to gardens and landscapes today. The Picturesque lasted no more than twenty years at its height, but its effects have reverberated ever since.

One problem is that the Picturesque and Sublime originally referred to landscape and natural scenery. Their application to gardens came only as a secondary step, and much of the general discussion of the terms has therefore to be translated into what is relevant within the parameters of a garden. However, what constitutes a garden is itself elastic, and this book will look at parks and designed landscapes that are sometimes on an enormous scale. 'Natural' scenery cannot be ignored either, since it can often be part of the Sublime (see especially the chapter on Scotland), and will therefore form part of the coverage here even though it may not be a garden.

That said, there is good reason for concentrating on gardens. It is a particularly interesting period for garden-making, reflecting the thinking and tastes of the age, and anticipating some of the aspects of the Romantic Movement. Gardens represent man's approach to controlling his immediate environment and moulding those elements, whether natural or artificial, that are deemed to be attractive or appealing in some way at the time of their creation. So, by studying gardens we can understand the tastes and *zeitgeist* of ages past. In this case, however, it is not an arid historical pursuit, but one which has shaped our own tastes for gardens and for scenery. Some of the denser arguments that raged over the Picturesque may be dead, but the legacy of the movement lives on.

The essence of the picturesque garden is that there should be some *frisson* or excitement about it. It should stir the feelings and imagination as well as appeal aesthetically. The gardens covered in this book tend towards the wild, in other words towards the Sublime, but those who sought to define categories at the time might sometimes include tamer works. Nor is there any attempt here to present a comprehensive picture or gazetteer of picturesque gardens: it is hoped, however, that the most outstanding examples and those that tell us most about themselves are described. Furthermore, nearly all may be visited. Some will be very familiar to garden historians, but others will be far less known or written about. The thrust of this book is *applied* Picturesque, gardens of the time that were, or can be, perceived to exhibit picturesque elements.

There will inevitably be some overlap and cross-over from one chapter to another. Accordingly, not all Scottish material will be confined to the chapter on the Scottish Picturesque: one or two gardens will appear elsewhere, as will some of the Scottish writers and theorists. Several gardens could have been included in one chapter rather than another, but where they have been placed it is to illustrate the main points of interest.

Although the title of the book relates the Picturesque to the later Georgian garden, there is no suggestion that all gardens of the later eighteenth century were picturesque – far from it. Indeed, the most popular of all forms at the time, the parkscapes of 'Capability' Brown and his followers, were usually judged non-picturesque by the pundits and critics.

Responses at the time are crucial to this study, so there are many contemporary quotations. For the same reason prints of the late eighteenth and early nineteenth centuries are used where possible as illustrations, which will give an idea not only of what the scenes looked like then but how they were perceived.

The language of the Picturesque is restricted, so a small range of adjectives continually repeated is generally encountered in writings of the day (and also subsequently). While this can be seen as a limitation, it also demonstrates a search for consensus, common denominators defining what constitutes the Picturesque.

The opening chapter, 'Approaching the Picturesque', attempts to identify the main strands of the subject. It is, however, a topic so large, convoluted and extensively written about that what is presented in that chapter is no more than a distillation of the principal points. Constrictions of space, apart from the risk of covering well-ploughed territory, forbid more. Particularly helpful sources for the reader to explore more deeply are indicated.

A word of explanation. The Picturesque and the Sublime (along with the Beautiful) will be given capital letters when used as nouns to indicate their status as a recognised aesthetic category, but lower case will be employed when they serve as adjectives. 'Romantic', however, will generally be used in lower case, since it did not form a category of its own. As to whether the Picturesque is a concept, a movement, just a category or all three, there can be no definite answers. Also, where a single umbrella term is required, 'picturesque' will be used, even though it often covers the Sublime, e.g. in the chapters on the Industrial and Scottish Picturesques. This is not to reduce the Sublime to a sub-set of the Picturesque but merely for simplicity and convenience. If Picturesque and Sublime are to be specifically differentiated, the text should make that clear.

CHAPTER ONE

Approaching the Picturesque

The Picturesque was a highly flexible concept impossible to pin down with precise definitions. In general, and in simplified terms, it was a way of viewing scenery (and by extension, gardens) and assessing it aesthetically as if it were a painting or series of paintings. However, the criteria by which a scene would be judged picturesque tended towards the natural and the wild – the essence of such scenery was that it should be broken in surface, irregular, varied and with contrasts of light and shade. Furthermore, the painting analogy was far from purely visual, and emotional and imaginative responses were called for.

The derivation of the word 'picturesque' is from the Italian *pittoresco*. John Dixon Hunt has traced the usage of the Italian term from being a technique of painting to an approach to composition that embraced asymmetry and boldness, together with stimulation of the imagination.[1] The English word literally means 'like a picture' or 'suitable for depiction', but that in itself implies both an active and a passive mode, suggesting the act of sketching or painting or, alternatively, looking at a painting.

The central problem of the Picturesque, and one which has caused confusion and misunderstanding at the time and subsequently, is that the term tries to do two distinct things that are by no means always compatible. One is the analogy with painting or pictures: the other is that it became an aesthetic category between the two established categories of the Beautiful (smooth, harmonious) and the Sublime (vast, frightening), nudging towards the Sublime end of the scale. But that in itself does not necessarily bear any relationship to paintings, and this dichotomy leads to absurd situations such as William Gilpin admiring the stunning views at Piercefield but declaring that they were not picturesque because they were mostly seen from too high a vantage point to admit of being satisfactorily painted (see p.56). Others saw the same views as eminently picturesque, taking the second sense of the word.

Another problem is the phenomenological one, i.e. treating the scenery as if it had intrinsically picturesque qualities. But many of those who discussed and thought about the subject preferred to regard the Picturesque as a way of seeing, so that the educated traveller and man/woman of taste would gain most from the experience. As we shall see, this difference was one of the issues in the 'Picturesque controversy'. In practice, however, even among those who took the 'subjective' view, written descriptions tended to slide towards giving the scenery itself picturesque credit. In this book, which is concerned largely with practical examples, the phenomenological approach will appear to be adopted, but, where scenery is described as picturesque, 'in the eye of the beholder' needs to be understood in parenthesis.

A further issue is how natural in appearance the scene should be. While most agreed that the more natural-looking the better, there was division when it came to admitting art (usually in the

1.1 Remains of Henry II's palace at Woodstock, Oxfordshire, as in 1714, print published 1799

form of buildings). Should art be allowed only insofar as it suited a rural scene? Or were some forms of architecture (notably ruins) picturesque in themselves and thus capable of enhancing the picturesque effect? Should new plantations be made only of species that would grow in that location naturally and traditionally?

The Picturesque is basically and essentially visual – but it cannot be confined to the eye in practice. Feelings and the imagination were often called into play, and associations might be evoked by features both natural and artificial. Other senses – sound, touch and smell – might well be engaged in experiencing an actual garden or landscape, and it is difficult to disentangle them from the purely visual impact. There is also the cultural heritage of ways to look at gardens, which might entail traditions of contemplation or melancholy.

In terms of time scale, the Picturesque flourished most in the last two decades of the eighteenth century and the first of the nineteenth in Britain. However, different strands can be observed to have developed at different times, some considerably earlier, and by the turn of the century (1800) there were advances in decorative gardens round the house that can be seen as counterpoint or complementary to the Picturesque or even as a new form of it.

The Picturesque as a subject

The Picturesque as a topic for discussion and explication has generated an industry of writing. Eighteenth-century authors would often cover aspects of the subject without specifically referring to the Picturesque by name, especially as it did not become recognised and established until late on in the century. From the 1760s or so a growing taste for the Picturesque can be detected, which is reflected in writings, though it was not really till the 1780s-90s that serious attempts were made to lay down precepts and principles. There was then a flurry of debate which died down in the early 1800s. Although the Picturesque continued to be mentioned, there is a long gap before Christopher Hussey's milestone work of 1927 revived interest, and the later years of the twentieth century saw the subject scrutinised closely in detail, implication and context.

To take the analogy between pictures and scenery, and also the art of painting and that of designing landscapes, first. Sir John Vanbrugh is said to have initiated the comparison when in 1709 he argued for the retention of the ruined Woodstock Manor in the park at Blenheim, claiming that it would make 'One of the Most agreable Objects that the Best of Landskip Painters can invent'[2] (Fig.1.1). Alexander Pope developed the notion further, not only asserting 'All gardening is landscape painting. Just like a landscape hung up,'[3] but suggesting that gardens should be composed on the principles of painting, principally perspective and light and shade. A few years later William Shenstone made one of his three categories of garden what he called 'landskip, or picturesque gardening', and followed Vanbrugh and Pope: 'I think the landskip painter is the gardiner's best designer.'[4] Philip Southcote, designer of the *ferme ornée* at Woburn Farm, agreed: 'Perspective, prospect, distancing, and attracting, comprehend all that part of painting in gardening.'[5]

The comparison came readily to mind when Horace Walpole talked about William Kent in his *History of the Modern Taste in Gardening* (1770), and indeed by mid-century it had become commonplace. Thomas Gray used it; and William Mason, in his long and largely unreadable poem *The English Garden* (1772-81), promoted the closeness of the two forms while elsewhere discriminating between them as no more than companion arts. It is to Mason that we owe the familiar phrase about designing gardens with a poet's feeling and a painter's eye.

William Gilpin's texts were often didactic, attempting to teach the tourist to view scenery as though it were a picture or sequence of pictures. Uvedale Price and Richard Payne Knight generally followed Gilpin though they did not always agree with him, and Price particularly was insistent on the need to study paintings before designing gardens or landscapes, while Payne Knight did just that with his collection of 273 Claude drawings. Their views, and the reactions of those who thought otherwise, form part of the Picturesque controversy (see pp. 21-2).

Apart from specifically comparing painting and gardening, there were many writers who appear to have developed a feeling for some aspects of the Picturesque – naturalness, irregularity, wildness – from early in the century. Some will be covered in the Literature section, principally the more descriptive works, but others will be mentioned here as impacting on the theoretical side of the subject. Naturalness and rugged scenes were admired by Anthony Ashley Cooper, Earl of Shaftesbury, as early as 1709, and French formality of garden design was subject to attack from such as Addison and Pope. In actual gardens irregularity often featured on each side of the main axial avenue – what Batty Langley called the 'artinatural' – and in Scotland Sir John Clerk of Penicuick composed *The Country Seat* (1727), which not only displayed a taste for wild scenery but advocated its harnessing and incorporation into the views from the house and grounds. He also includes a comparison with painting. Other descriptions and records show that this was put into practice in Scotland, together with appreciation and inclusion of old ruins.[6]

By mid-century a number of authors wrote in semi-didactic or theoretical ways about how gardens should be composed. Shenstone's posthumously published 'Unconnected Thoughts on Gardening' make an appeal for variety,[7] which covers the spectrum from the Beautiful to the Sublime (under the professed influence of Burke), with appropriate planting. Shenstone would have seen himself, like his contemporaries Walpole and George Mason, as an arbiter of taste. Mason, not to be confused with William, published his *Essay on Design in Gardening* in 1768, thus predating much of the Picturesque, with a revised edition put out in 1795 partly as a rebuttal of Price and Payne Knight, though he admitted he had not revisited the gardens described in the first edition. But even in 1768 it is clear that he admires most those properties that can be described as pictorial, looking ahead in several respects to the Picturesque.

Walpole's *Essay* was ready by 1770 though not published till a decade later. He exhibits a feeling for wilder scenery, though more in terms of planting than hard landscape, in his categorising of the forest or savage garden, of which Painshill was the perfect example: 'I mean that kind of alpine scene, composed almost wholly of pines and firs, a few birch, and such trees as assimilate with a savage and mountainous country'.[8] He was clearly harking back to the Alpine adventures of his Grand Tour in 1739.

Two Scottish authors are particularly relevant. John Dalrymple's *An Essay on Landscape Gardening* was not published till 1823, and was therefore unknown to readers, but the manuscript had been prepared for Shenstone and sent to him c1760. It reflects a fully-developed view of picturesque estates as they had already evolved in Scotland. Dalrymple divides gardens according to their location – (1) the grand, as in the Highlands, with rocks, mountains, lakes and rivers, e.g. Inverary; (2) the romantic, with sunk valleys, woods hanging over them, smooth rivers, steep but accessible banks, rocks and trees, as in the Lowlands – such scenes are suitable for painting and perhaps melancholic contemplation; (3) gently rolling countryside with verdure and cultivation, e.g. as often in England, with cheerful effect; (4) completely flat, causing no feelings.[9] It will be seen that (1) and (2) correspond to the Sublime and the Picturesque. He suggests that a Gothic castle or tower is appropriate for (1), and that natural features such as cascades can be artificially enhanced. A classical ruin, however, might be more suitable for (2) because it would further the sense of melancholy.

Dalrymple's concern with feelings and responses was taken up by Henry Home, Lord Kames, in his *Elements of Criticism* (1762) in which garden features such as ruins are examined for the emotions engendered by their appearance and associations. This fed in very aptly to the romantic side of the Picturesque, appealing to the imagination. Shortly afterwards William Mason's avowedly didactic poem *The English Garden* picked up both on the analogy with paintings and with following nature as far as possible but admitting art where it might 'improve' nature.

The most important and relevant contemporary contributions to the discussion of the Picturesque were, of course, by Gilpin, Price, Payne Knight and Humphry Repton, but they are discussed elsewhere in this chapter, in their own sections or under the 'Picturesque controversy'. The Romantics took some interest – Wordsworth visited many of the sites beloved of the Picturesque, such as Tintern Abbey, but he rejected what he saw as the 'tyranny of the eye' in favour of a closer engagement with nature and deeper reflections on what the features suggested to him. Garden writers and practitioners such as Loudon continued to refer to the Picturesque, usually with a view to proposing what they thought were superior and more modern approaches to garden design.

The Picturesque gradually faded, regarded as a quaint and finite movement that had had its day. But in the 1920s two publications revived interest, the perspective having changed from discussion of contemporary issues to historical consideration. One was Elizabeth Wheeler Manwaring's *Italian Landscape in Eighteenth Century England* (1925), which looked at the influence of Italian landscape painting on not only gardens and landscape but on the novel and poetry. Two years later came Christopher Hussey's seminal work, *The Picturesque,* which is still essential reading and an invaluable source book despite many advances in scholarship since and some critical disdain, founded mainly on Hussey's phenomenological approach. The book does, however, reveal a profound feeling for the subject and its cultural ramifications – architecture, the novel, English painting are included – and it brought the Picturesque centre stage once more.

Further interest grew in the second half of the twentieth century, alongside more serious study of garden history. W J Hipple's *The Beautiful, the Sublime, and the Picturesque in Eighteenth-Century British Aesthetic Theory* (1957) was concerned with theory rather than actual landscape or gardens, but was followed by Carl Barbier's *William Gilpin: His Drawings, Teaching, and Theory of the Picturesque* (1963), which drew together theory and practice. Some garden books had already declared the relationship of paintings to gardens – Christopher Tunnard's *Gardens in the Modern Landscape* (1938) and H F Clark's *The English Garden* (1948) – but more serious attempts to link the Picturesque and historical gardens came in the 1970s. Initially this was in a broader context of the continent – the Dumbarton Oaks publication of *The Picturesque Garden and its Influence Outside the British Isles* (1974) and Dora Wiebenson's *The Picturesque Garden in France* (1978), which made comparison between England and France and sought connections between the two countries. In the meantime John Dixon Hunt had examined particularly the literary and painting sources in *The Figure in the Landscape* (1976).

Nigel Temple's *John Nash & the Village Picturesque* (1979) considered one specific aspect of British Picturesque but included a helpful summary of the picturesque debate. A A Tait drew attention to the Scottish Picturesque in *The Landscape Garden in Scotland, 1735-1835* (1980), and soon afterwards David Watkin in *The English Vision* (1982) focused usefully (and primarily, as an architectural historian) on the Picturesque in architecture as well as in landscape and garden design. In the same year the catalogue *Humphry Repton, Landscape Gardener 1752-1818* devoted a section to the Picturesque controversy and Repton's relationship to it. But it was David Jacques' groundbreaking *Georgian Gardens* (1983) that first showed the full range and complexity of the garden from 1730, with many pertinent comments on, and examples of, the Picturesque. In the same year Christopher Thacker published *The Wildness Pleases,* showing how romanticism gradually grew, with special reference to France and Germany.

The best introduction to the subject as a whole is Malcolm Andrews' *The Search for the Picturesque* (1989). Art, literature and Gilpin's tours of the Wye Valley, Wales, the Lake District and the Scottish Highlands, are covered, though there is not a great deal on gardens. In 1991 Sidney K Robinson concentrated principally on Uvedale Price's theories in *Inquiry into the Picturesque.* The Welsh perspective was astutely summarised in *The Historic Gardens of Wales* by Elisabeth Whittle in 1992. The bicentenary of the two key publications by Price and Payne Knight brought forth a stream of scholarly responses, notably *The Picturesque Landscape: Visions of Georgian Herefordshire* (1994, accompanying an exhibition), a special issue of *Garden History* (22:2) that included an overview by Mavis Batey, and, in the wake of a symposium that year, *The Picturesque in late Georgian England,* published by the Georgian Group, looking at many facets of the subject. *The Politics of the Picturesque* (also 1994) took the opportunity to explore implications of the Picturesque and its legacy over a much longer subsequent time frame. Further, Nigel Everett brought out in this *annus mirabilis* of publications *The Tory View of Landscape,* which included consideration of 'the constitutional landscape of the Picturesque'.

In 1992 John Dixon Hunt brought together a collection of essays in *Gardens and the Picturesque* that were wide-ranging in theme and time scale, though all deriving from the springboard of the Picturesque. In addition to considerations of art, literature and 'reading' the garden, there is an important chapter on the theatrical nature of composed gardens and their connections with the theatre. A decade later the same author's *The Picturesque Garden in Europe* concentrated mainly on England and France, taking the concept of the Picturesque from an earlier date than in the present book. While it is a *sine qua non* for readers of the subject, not all significant aspects are covered.

Meanwhile, David Lambert considered literary connections 1794-1816 in *Garden History* (24:1) (1996). Writers on gardens of the eighteenth century, e.g. Tom Williamson's *Polite Landscapes* (1995) and Timothy Mowl's *Gentlemen & Players* (2000) have incorporated the Picturesque, with further insights into it. Mowl's series of county garden histories have thrown up a number of 'discoveries' of what he calls the Savage Picturesque. There have been, in addition, many individual articles in recent years on picturesque gardens, and more specialised works such as the Soane Museum's *Visions of Ruin* (1999). The books on Repton by Stephen Daniels and André Rogger (1999 and 2007 respectively) add considerably to our understanding of Repton's role in the Picturesque and its context.

The Sublime

The concept of the Sublime will forever be associated with Edmund Burke (1729-1797), who published the first edition of *A Philosophical Enquiry into the Origin of our Ideas of the Sublime and Beautiful* in 1757, with an amplified version two years later. But he did not invent the concept, though he may have been the first to conduct this sort of investigation. Burke was widely read and quoted by followers of the Picturesque, though not everyone swallowed his ideas unthinkingly and a number of critics have since found it unsatisfactory. Several authors, from Milton onwards if not earlier, had described scenes and episodes in the very terms of fear and awe that characterise Burke when he attempts to identify feelings attached to notions of the Sublime. Closer to Burke's time were the poets James Thomson and Mark Akenside, whose *Pleasures of the Imagination* (1744) includes descriptions and emotional responses that seem to prefigure Burke.

To Burke the Sublime was associated with feelings of pain engendered by terror. It could be vast, infinite, dark or dangerous. But in running a gamut from awe to dread, he does not seem to distinguish between them nor to take sufficient account of distance, although it is mentioned as a factor. A far-off range of bare mountains might well be awesome but it would not fill the viewer with horror. That would happen only when it was sufficiently close to threaten. Immediacy of danger is crucial, and so is scale: smaller cascades might well be considered picturesque, but the long, almost perpendicular falls along the Anza valley in the Italian Alps, for example ('White Fall', 'Milky Fall'), are definitely sublime. Sometimes the Picturesque is the Sublime on a smaller scale.

The importance of Burke, in fact, may not be so much as a thinker – he was surpassed by Henry Home (Lord Kames) and by Kant in the *Analytic of the Sublime* (1790) – but that he encouraged readers to think about the Sublime, particularly in relation to landscape, and thereby generated a quest for it. It may seem improbable to us today, but mountainous scenery took a long time to be established as something attractive and desirable – mountains had long been regarded as God's rubbish – but gradually (partly through experiencing the exceptional sublimity of the Alps on the Grand Tour) spokesmen arose on their behalf. A poem on the Lake District by Dr John Dalton and a letter about Keswick addressed to Lord Lyttelton of Hagley by Dr John Brown and subsequently published, both in the 1750s, encouraged Thomas Gray and Arthur Young to visit the Lakes ahead of Gilpin. The thrills of the Sublime were a strong part of the attraction.

The vocabulary of the Sublime, as with the Picturesque, spread to the continent. In Italian *orrido* as an adjective equates to our 'horrid', but as a noun it refers specifically to a turbulent river running between the steep sides of a narrow gorge.

By contrast the Beautiful was characterised as something to be experienced pleasurably. Its essence, according to Burke, was smoothness, smallness, delicacy, bright and clear colour, and gradual variation. But both Gilpin and Price muddied the water by conflating the Picturesque and the Beautiful under 'picturesque beauty'.

The romantic

Romantic is a notoriously difficult word to define, not only because it has more than one connotation but because in modern times it has tended to be used more or less entirely in the amatory sense. Historically there were two main senses, of stimulating the imagination and, more specifically, of evoking the romances of the Middle Ages in particular. The OED suggests extravagant, imaginary and relating to romance (fiction). A romance was a chivalric tale of a hero and adventure; or an improbable, unrealistic fantasy. One of the most influential, more than a century after it was written, was Spenser's *Faerie Queene*, which was illustrated by William Kent and contained a number of garden episodes.

Sir John Vanbrugh, who anticipated so many later developments of the landscape garden, bought a farm at Chargate, near Esher, Surrey, in 1709 which later became Claremont under the Duke of Newcastle. Vanbrugh gave his reason for purchasing Chargate as 'the situation being singularly romantik'.[10] By referring to the location and topography rather than to the existing scenery (which was not all that exciting), it would seem that he meant that it gave scope for imaginative landscaping, particularly, in Vanbrugh's case, the placing of buildings in the scene.

By mid-century the word was being used quite commonly to describe scenes in gardens, such as Resta Patching's perception of the cascades at The Leasowes in 1755 as 'rural and romantic'.[11] In the context of that poetic and associative garden it is evident that the sense of appealing to the imagination is intended. In general, as the century wore on, this sense is probably most frequently applicable, and it often comes to be treated as more or less synonymous with 'picturesque' although Gilpin tried to preserve a distinction. As will be seen, it was used regularly as an adjective. After 1790, however, there is an overlay of the Romantic Movement, implying freedom, nature and emotional response.

The whole question of the relationship between the Picturesque and the Romantic Movement is vexed. Some, like Christopher Hussey, have seen the former as a precursor to the latter, anticipating and fuelling it. While this would not generally be accepted today, because of fundamental differences between the two, it cannot be denied that elements of the Picturesque happen to coincide with romanticism, such as love of nature especially in its wilder aspects.

A lone voice from a later period was Gilpin's nephew William Sawrey Gilpin, who in 1832 published *Practical Hints upon Landscape Gardening.* He divided scenery into the Grand, the Romantic, the Beautiful, the Picturesque and the Rural. Grand equates more or less with the Sublime, with Romantic seen as being on a smaller scale,

> with more parts, and a greater variety and quickness of transition from part to part. It is marked by precipitous steeps; angular rocky projections forcing their way between the rugged stems that are rooted in their crevices, or rising out of the wild undergrowth at their base. Intricacy seems to be the leading feature of the Romantic.[12]

In short, what most people would have described as picturesque, which Gilpin reserves however for smaller and more abrupt folds of ground, few flat surfaces and with rough clothing of wood; his examples come from Kent and Surrey.[13] Gilpin's classification is idiosyncratic and there seems no reason to press for 'romantic' to form a category of its own, but rather to recognise its importance.

But on the continent 'romantic' became, in effect, an accepted category of garden. Claude-Henri Watelet's *Essai sur les Jardins* (1774) divides gardens into three types: the picturesque (related to paintings), the poetic and the romantic. The latter appeals particularly to the imagination, to 'produce a few moments of stimulating illusion'. The sort of scenes Watelet envisages are wild and thrilling (partaking of the Sublime) and bear a striking resemblance to those described by William Chambers, who was an obvious strong influence.[14] This was rather extreme, but 'romantic' came to be accepted widely as a description of a 'natural' landscaped park, though that did not preclude straight drives or other signs of formality. The word was applied particularly in the early nineteenth century, by which time the English landscape style was prevalent. A good example of such a park, naturalistic but with axial avenues, would be Maksimir Park in Zagreb (1838-43), described as a romantic park to this day.

William Gilpin

The Rev. William Gilpin (1724-1804), schoolmaster at Cheam and later Vicar of Boldre in the New Forest, is traditionally hailed as the father or pioneer of the Picturesque, though he was far from the first to consider treating scenery as though it were a picture. Brought up in the Lake District, he conceived a lifelong attachment to wild landscape, and his later tours encompassed the most rugged parts of England, Scotland and Wales, which were admirably suited to his ideas of the Picturesque. He started formulating these ideas early on, as can be seen from the originally anonymous *A Dialogue upon the gardens...at Stow* (1748), which presents two friends going round the gardens at Stowe, by then less formal and more naturalised than they had been previously, and assessing what they saw. There is discussion of ruins; of distant views; and, most tellingly, the painterly analogy: 'I am admiring the fine View from hence: So great a Variety of beautiful Objects, and all so happily disposed, make a most delightful Picture.'[15] This adumbrates what would become much more fully worked through in later years.

The tours started, locally from Cheam and short at first, becoming lengthier and further afield from 1768, though publication did not commence till 1782, the reluctant and modest Gilpin having had to be coaxed into print. He had, however, published *An Essay upon Prints* in 1768, which served to advance the cause since he defined 'picturesque' as 'a term expressive of that peculiar kind of beauty, which is agreeable in a picture'.[16] Although he had a tendency to conflate the Picturesque and the Beautiful by continual reference to picturesque beauty, his notions of what constituted a good picture tended towards the wild, broken and rugged, which clearly had much more appeal to him. Thus, although Gilpin is firmly in the 'picturesque = like a picture' camp, the most desirable picture is of the kind that the picturesque tourists of the late eighteenth century sought, and the type that Gilpin had experienced in touring the Wye Valley, North Wales and the Scottish Highlands especially. Writing to Mary Harley in 1789 he claimed that wild scenery put everything else out of his mind:

> For my own part, whenever I sit down with a pencil and paper before me, ideas of rocks, and mountains and lakes always crowd into my head. My pencil runs naturally into it; and I conceive no other ideas of landscape, but of this sublime kind, to be worth recording. Indeed no other ideas suggest themselves to me, but these, and such appendages as suit them.[17]

The publications of the tours included Gilpin's own illustrations, engraved by others for the purpose. During the course of his life Gilpin produced over 6000 sketches, using pencil, ink and wash, mostly of imaginary scenes but many of views he had experienced on the tours. In the latter cases he was not slow to 'adjust' scenery if he thought it needed improvement to make it properly picturesque: when readers complained that the images in his publications were not always accurate he said he was only trying to give an idea of the scene and how it struck him – and to make a good picture. If a tree obscured the view, for example, it would be removed. It is, accordingly, as much from the sketches as from the text that we can learn about what constituted the Picturesque for Gilpin.

Gilpin's texts were enormously influential in teaching visitors how to see and what to look for. They not only encouraged tourism but actually spread a taste for mountainous scenery that half a century before hardly existed. His theories emerge from the various tour publications but were encapsulated in *Three Essays* (1792) which embraced Picturesque Beauty; Picturesque Travel; and Sketching Landscape. He starts the first by distinguishing beauty, which pleases the eye and is essentially smooth, from the Picturesque, which is capable of being depicted in a painting and which is generally characterised by roughness or ruggedness. Such an artist would rather portray a ruin than a house, and broken ground rather than a smooth garden (Gilpin thought no manicured garden could be picturesque). Variety was of the essence, with contrasts and fractured surfaces.

When Gilpin moved to Boldre in 1777, the tours ceased, and although their publication was still to come he settled in to an appreciation of the surrounding New Forest, with its bushes and glades, the results of which appeared in his *Remarks on Forest Scenery* (1791), said to be his most popular work, in which new facets of the Picturesque surfaced. Trees, singly or in groups, were admired for their shapes and their effects in the view (see pp.101-2).

Thomas Gray

Thomas Gray (1716-71), though not as central a figure as Gilpin (and dying relatively young, before the Picturesque was in full swing), contributed significantly to establishing an appreciation of wild scenery for which he is not always given proper credit.[18] Poet, botanist and antiquarian, with a serious interest in genuine Gothic architecture, he anticipated Gilpin in some respects, and Hussey claims he first used the word picturesque in its full sense in 1740.[19] In 1739 he accompanied Walpole and experienced the sublimity of the Alps, which left its mark on him. He toured widely in Britain and after his death William Mason published Gray's inventory of the most significant places he had visited, which included particularly the Lake District. He encouraged Gilpin to undertake further tours, and

1.2 The Tower at Foxley, Herefordshire

shared Gilpin's views on the correspondence between painting and scenery. He also shared Gilpin's use of the Claude glass (see p. 48) to view scenery and cultivated his own variation of it, the 'Gray glass'. He had a keen interest in gardens, and his verse shows how important allusion and association were to him. Gray's continuing influence can be seen nearly 25 years after his death in Payne Knight's *The Landscape*.

Gray is most remembered for his *Elegy*, and that in its own way was instrumental in carving out a special niche in the overall Picturesque, introducing the elements of contemplation and melancholy which were part of its emotional carapace (see p.29). For a close and subtle examination of the ambiguities of Gray's reaction to gardens in his poems and correspondence, see *The Figure in the Landscape*.[20]

Uvedale Price and Richard Payne Knight

The two Herefordshire squires Uvedale Price (1747-1829), knighted a year before his death, and Richard Payne Knight (1750-1824) were at the very heart of the Picturesque. Gilpin may have been the pioneer, but Price and Payne Knight codified picturesque theory and practice more strictly in the 1790s. Though often considered as a pair, they differed both on matters of principle and as to how they managed their own properties. It was Payne Knight more than anyone else who attempted to demolish Price's theories.

1.3 Wood and cliff at Downton, Herefordshire

Uvedale Price inherited the estate of Foxley, in the central plain of the county, from his father Robert, who died in 1761 and grandfather Uvedale who died three years later. It was already well managed with regard to long-established woodland, but Price added more existing woodland through purchase and new woodland through planting, all with an eye to optimise the picturesque possibilities of the site.[21] In addition viewpoints were created, and many agricultural improvements were introduced: the land had to be productive as well as aesthetically pleasing, and much of the timber was managed commercially. It has to be admitted, however, that the landscape was rolling rather than dramatic, giving an overall impression of pleasant and well-farmed countryside. The one picturesque building, a castellated tower (Fig.1.2), was erected by Robert Price c1740, who was also responsible for the principal circuit ride. Robert was friendly with Gainsborough and was influential in inculcating the young Uvedale with relating painting to scenery.

Price approached the landscaping of Foxley via landscape painting, especially Dutch.[22] So he practised what he preached, namely that a study of paintings that led to a fashioning of landscape as a series of such was essential. He was the principal advocate for designing a picturesque garden. He defined the Picturesque in contradistinction to smoothness, harmony and beauty: 'I am therefore persuaded that the two opposite qualities of roughness, and of sudden variation, joined to that of irregularity, are the most efficient causes of the picturesque.'[23]

Price set out his stall in 1794 with the publication of *An Essay on the Picturesque,* in which he spoke of variety as the great and universal source of pleasure. And while he championed studying paintings, and would continue to do so, he did not think they should be exalted above nature. The *Essay* was revised and issued again in 1798 to take account of Repton's response to the original *Essay* and his own further rejoinder, which concluded that, despite what Repton said, the latter created pictures in his landscaping. Evidently Price thought his points had not been made with sufficient force, for he returned to print in 1801 with *A Dialogue on the Distinct Characters of the Picturesque and the Beautiful,* framed as a conversation between three friends in order to make it more congenial to the public. In 1842 Sir Thomas Dick Lauder gathered together all Price's relevant writings in a volume entitled *Sir Uvedale Price on the Picturesque.*

Payne Knight, rogue scholar and radical, took a somewhat different approach. He had been working on his house (castle) and grounds at Downton Vale, in the north of Herefordshire, since the early 1770s, and the landscaping would have been completed some time before the appearance of his verse treatise *The Landscape* in 1794. Unlike Price, Payne Knight did not attempt to define the Picturesque, nor indeed did he even use the word in the poem and only occasionally as an adjective elsewhere. His purpose was didactic, to expound the principles on which landscape should be composed – and to hammer the deceased Brown and the 'tasteless herd of his followers'. Perhaps surprisingly, Payne Knight valued harmony, order and proportion, qualities that would be more likely to come under the head of the Beautiful, but it is later clear that grounds should look as natural as possible (which does not preclude planting) with the minimum interference or presence of art. His stance is politicised, with some parallels drawn with the then current revolution in France.

With regard to viewing scenery as pictures, Payne Knight firmly believed in the need for an educated mind and eye: '[scenes] afford no pleasure, but to persons conversant with the art of painting'. This has to be complemented by the ability to appreciate associations.[24]

At Downton Payne Knight had the perfect setting, far more naturally picturesque than Foxley. The River Teme flows through a gorge with high cliffs on one side (Fig.1.3) and lower rock on the other. Woodland abounds on both sides. On a hill, set back from the water, stands the house, a Gothic castle on the outside, classically decorated within. The main path undulates each side of the river, one at water level, the other above the cliff. It is distinctly steep in places. Although the 'natural' look was cultivated, as can be seen in Thomas Hearne's series of paintings (1786), with a couple of simple 'Alpine' bridges, there was one elaborate building, the Cold Bath, some 'hovels' and several seats (noticed by Repton), and a number of signs of industry – ironworks and a mill. The ironworks had been the basis of the family fortune. Two caves were excavated opposite each other at the start of the gorge, and there is a tunnel cut through the rock, which has an unexpectedly architectural arch. The tunnel blocks the visitor off from the river visually for a moment, but also in terms of sound – the water is noisier and more turbulent as one emerges from one end. As at Hackfall and Hafod, sound is part of the picturesque experience.

Payne Knight was not always as radical as he seemed, or was made out to be (he outraged many of his contemporaries). Later on he expressed an interest in seeing the return of formal Italianate parterres near the house. The pair of engravings by Benjamin Pouncy after Hearne made for the poem (Figs.1.4 and 1.5) have often been misinterpreted as contrasting a picturesque landscape with a Brownian one: in fact Payne Knight's note makes clear that the first is an 'undressed' scene, i.e. before anything has been done to it, and the second is 'dressed in the modern style'. So the contrast, while still tendentious, is between nature and Brownian improvement rather than showing what is picturesque (except by implication). To modern eyes, as to Repton at the time, both seem manipulated.

William Chambers

Sir William Chambers (1723-96) has become notorious for his championing of a largely imaginary concept of Chinese gardens in an effort to unseat the then popular (and to him bland and monotonous) Brown park. His ideas, based partly on two heavily restricted visits to China in the 1740s, first saw the light of day in his *Designs for Chinese Buildings…*(1757), in which a section on 'the Art of Laying Out Gardens among the Chinese' was included and excited considerable interest. It was later substantially expanded into *A Dissertation on Oriental Gardening* in 1772, often thought to be an act of revenge against Brown, who had recently beaten him to the commission to build a house at Claremont for Lord Clive. In a way this was a preview of the full Picturesque controversy of twenty years later, with a polemical largely anti-Brown publication followed by response from others. In this case the *Dissertation* was answered within a year by the satirical poem *An Heroic Epistle* by William Mason, egged on by Horace Walpole. The *Epistle* ran to several editions and constituted one of the most successful satires of the time,

1.4 A house and grounds in natural or 'undressed' state, engraved by Benjamin Pouncy after Thomas Hearne, from Richard Payne Knight, *The Landscape*, 1794 [University of Bristol Library, Special Collections]

1.5 The same scene 'dressed' in Brownian style, as above [University of Bristol Library, Special Collections]

sending up Chambers' extremist notions of Chinese gardens by imagining elephants, tigers and snakes being introduced to roam and slither around Kew.

While there may be some kernels of truth in Chambers' account of Chinese gardens and their philosophical and cultural approach to the art of gardening, the examples given are undoubtedly exaggerated. Yet what he writes is consonant in many ways with the Picturesque. He claims that the Chinese take nature for their pattern, with art supplying its deficiencies. Gardens are classified under three heads, the pleasing, the terrible and the surprising. The first combines the most attractive features both natural and artificial that can be brought about, 'being combined and disposed in all the picturesque forms that art or nature can suggest…nothing is forgot that can either exhilerate [sic] the mind, gratify the senses, or give a spur to the imagination'.[25]

The second category, the terrible, is pure Salvator Rosa – gloomy woods, dark caverns, distorted trees, terrifying waterfalls, ruins, dangerous rocks and mock volcanoes. The signs of habitation are fearsome: 'Bats, owls, vultures, and every bird of prey flutter in the groves; wolves, tigers and jackalls howl in the forests; half-famished animals wander upon the plains; gibbets, crosses, wheels, and the whole apparatus of torture, are seen from the roads'.[26] This is the stuff of the Sublime. The third category, what Chambers calls the surprising or supernatural, appeals to the imagination by exciting strong and contrasting feelings. He says these scenes are of the romantic kind, and range from the sounds of animals and men in torment to 'beauteous Tartarean damsels, in loose transparent robes'.[27]

However lurid Chambers' accounts, the appeal to the emotions and to the imagination, especially in the endeavour to thrill, marks him out as being in the vanguard with regard to picturesque and sublime gardens. While he was derided in England, his books were translated on the continent and were generally taken seriously, encouraging the French to conceive of the landscape garden as *le jardin anglo-chinois,* though they also had more direct access to Chinese sources. And there were certainly some elements of real Chinese gardens that had their counterpart in picturesque gardens, notably rockwork, though it may not be appropriate to talk of direct influence (see p.86). There is also the matter of *chinoiserie* as exotic architecture in a garden, though the heyday for that was mid-century and it fades away towards the picturesque period.

The Picturesque controversy

There was no single controversy, but strong feelings were aroused by those who put forward their ideas on the Picturesque. Matters came to a head in 1794, with the publication of both Price's and Payne Knight's manifestos, which provoked an instant response. Repton defended himself against personal attack, though was saddened at having to do so, since it severed a friendship with both men. In particular he refuted Price's insistence on the closeness of the analogy between garden/landscape design and painting, maintaining that '*painting* and *gardening* are nearly connected, but not so intimately related as you imagine: they are not sister arts proceeding from the same stock, but rather congenial natures, brought together like man and wife'.[28] Later he spelled out in common-sense terms all the differences between the two – that a garden changes all the time through light, growth and the seasons, that one cannot paint a downhill view, and that views and spatial relationships constantly change. Other responses by Repton included a justification for his own professional need to rank convenience and pleasing the client along with seeking picturesque effect, together with a defence of Brown and some of his trademark devices (mainly the belt and the clump).

Another soon into the fray was John Matthews of Belmont in Herefordshire. The fact that Repton had recently laid out his grounds may have decided whose side he was on, but the situation of Belmont on the Wye was sufficiently picturesque for Matthews to regard himself as an expert. His poem *A Sketch from The Landscape* had a frontispiece illustration of Payne Knight throwing the contents of a chamberpot at Brown's tomb in a garden, which gives a good idea of the level at which the poem was pitched. It purports to be by Payne Knight, with footnotes of matching verses from *The Landscape*. In turn it was itself mocked and derided by Payne Knight in the second edition of *The Landscape* the following year. This was further responded to by Matthews in a second edition of his own, where he also took the opportunity to answer Price in a prose postscript, defending Brown and his employment of the Beautiful. He tells Price that the Picturesque should be reserved for the further reaches of an estate: 'In gardens, I conceive, we must only hope for the picturesque in the wilder parts of the scene.'[29]

In addition to considerable to-ing and fro-ing in print between Price, Payne Knight and Repton, there were rifts beginning to open up between Price and Payne Knight. Price believed that the Picturesque was a quality innate in scenery and that it legitimately formed a category between the Beautiful and the Sublime: Payne Knight thought that it was in the eye of the beholder and needed a trained and educated mind to appreciate it. For the same reason he did not believe in categories, including Burke's Sublime. Moreover, both Price's and Payne Knight's views had to be squared with the 'picturability' sense of the term, which they did in rather different ways. In later years, however, the two men were reconciled.

The year 1795 saw reinforcements arrive on the side of Brown and Repton. William Marshall reviewed the two 1794 publications adversely, not to say abusively. He saw Price and Payne Knight as dangerous and intolerant and promoters of bad taste. George Mason revised his *Essay on Design in Gardening* from nearly thirty years before to take on board these new developments, and criticised the supremacy of the painting analogy in Price, dismissing the belief 'that none should presume to garden, who have no previous knowledge of painting'.[30]

1.6 James Gibbs' Temple of Liberty at Stowe, Buckinghamshire

Both Price and Payne Knight continued to express their convictions into the new century, with Price's *Dialogue* of 1801 attempting to refute Payne Knight's note in the second edition of *The Landscape* which claimed that Price's distinction between the Beautiful and the Picturesque was imaginary. However, the debate was wearing thin and before long looked more and more like an old battlefield. By 1816 Repton could regard it with hindsight.

1.7 Sanderson Miller's ruined castle at Hagley, West Midlands

Gothic

How Gothic relates to the Picturesque requires a number of answers. For a start, architectural Gothic is only part of the story, but is in itself diverse and constantly changing. It is possible to discern half-a-dozen different Gothics during the course of the century, distinguished not only stylistically but in their purpose, implications and connotations. Three of these phases predated Horace Walpole's Strawberry Hill (from 1747), sometimes taken to be the birthplace of Gothic Revival. An early one is what Mavis Batey has termed collegiate Gothic, referring to the alcove at the end of the canal at Shotover, Oxfordshire, constructed by the mason William Townesend, who had been responsible for repairs to some of the old Oxford colleges and drew his inspiration from them. This seems to have been an isolated example, though it might well have shown the potentiality of Gothic for garden buildings.

Another early phase was Kentian Gothic, as practised by, but not confined to, William Kent. From the 1730s Kent produced a number of Gothic structures in gardens, notably at Rousham and Merlin's Cave at Richmond, and essayed Gothic on a larger scale for the house at Rousham and the extensive wings to Wayneflete's medieval tower at Esher Place, Surrey. This style was not particularly authentic, but it carried a new meaning and could also be described as political Gothic. For it flourished in the years after 1733, when Lord Cobham of Stowe broke away from government and in effect formed a Whig Opposition. They adopted Gothic as a style that supposedly harked back to medieval values and the championing of liberty. The most prominent example was James Gibbs' Gothic Temple (or Temple of Liberty) at Stowe itself, dating from 1742 onwards. This was particularly striking in the landscape, even among so many other garden buildings, by virtue not only of its architecture but by its unusual triangular plan and the rich ironstone of which it was built. And it made a strong statement about liberty.

Another category was castle Gothic, which had an early genesis in the work of Vanbrugh. At Castle Howard there were theatrical walls with turrets and bastions, and he created his own small castle

1.8 Gothic Temple at Painshill, Surrey

at Greenwich. Keenly alert to the impact of a castle or castellation in the landscape, he gave Kimbolton, Cambridgeshire, 'Something of the Castle Air', and had battlemented towers on the Belvedere on the mount at Claremont, Surrey. At Grimsthorpe his 'castle house' had four balustrade towers enclosing what remained of the old house. After Vanbrugh's death his style was carried on with the complete bailey and keep of Stainborough Castle in 1731 at Wentworth Castle, South Yorkshire. A later phase was exemplified by Sanderson Miller, from his own constructions at Edge Hill, Radway, from 1742 (see pp.75-6). Miller's castles were ruinous, which added further resonances, and though initially at least party political (notably at Hagley, 1748), the intention and effect were more dynastic (inventing a supposed earlier history) and for impact in the landscape. Party political implications died down from about 1750, but medieval concepts of liberty were not forgotten in the late realisation of Miller's castle at Wimpole in 1770.

'Strawberry Hill Gothic', as embodied by Walpole, was partly based on genuine medieval sources from all over Europe but in practice led to a proliferation of what might equally well be called rococo or pattern-book Gothick (with a 'k' to denote its fanciful nature), a playful use of Gothic forms that lent itself admirably to lightweight garden buildings. These abounded in mid-century pictorial gardens such as Painshill, where the Gothic Temple was of wood made to look like stone and the Gothic Tower and Ruined Abbey were of brick rendered to look like stone. The pattern-books of the period gave material assistance, since an architect did not have to be employed. As with Miller's castles, so mock ecclesiastical ruins would have an impact both visual and emotional in the landscape and often contributed to picturesque effect (see chapter on ruins).

Picking up on both ruinous and intact castles, there was a new momentum from the 1770s, first with Robert Adam and then with James and Jeffry Wyatt and John Nash. One can detect a new mood of romanticism and fantasy in their castellations, with Vanbrugh's plainness and solidity replaced by something more visually appealing. At the same time medieval church architecture reappeared in modern guise in James Wyatt's Lee Priory and the colossus of Fonthill Abbey.

Walpole is also traditionally known as the father of the Gothic novel. In his case, *The Castle of Otranto* (1764-5) was given a medieval setting, but the Gothic label soon attached itself to stories where architecture that was specifically Gothic played no part. The essence was the feeling of horror – thrills and chills – which chimed in with the growing taste for the Picturesque and the Sublime. It became very popular, especially among young, impressionable minds, as was illustrated by Jane Austen's Catherine Morland in *Northanger Abbey*.

Gothic, then, allies itself with the Picturesque both visually, in its asymmetrical and sometimes ruined forms, and emotionally, in both architecture and literature, where fear or horror is evinced, bringing it into the realm of the Sublime. It is part of the Picturesque but not a separate sub-category, and a taste for Gothic (changing and developing as it did) would often go hand-in-hand with a taste for the Picturesque.

Antiquarianism

Gothic, with its historical connotations, feeds into the great growth of interest in native antiquarianism in the eighteenth century. Prompted in part by the Grand Tour, which revealed the splendours of the past in Italy, scholars sought equivalent evidence of antiquity (medieval and earlier) in Britain – though what they discovered was sometimes given a fanciful provenance. The Society of Antiquaries was founded in 1717, and serious investigation was undoubtedly undertaken, but the more colourful figures, principally the eccentric William Stukeley (1687-1765), tend to be the most memorable. Stukeley, the first Secretary of the Society, was a romantic ahead of his time, and saw Druids everywhere. He conducted valuable surveys of Stonehenge and Avebury – but came to the wrong conclusion, attributing the upright stone formations to the Druids. He was nicknamed 'Chyndonax', after a supposedly so-named Druid priest.[31]

Despite his aberrations, such as identifying Jehovah with Bacchus, Stukeley showed remarkable prescience in introducing Gothic into his Lincolnshire garden at an early date (1726) and visiting the Lake District in 1725, fifty years before it became fashionable to do so.[32] The garden was conceived as a Druidic grove, and doubtless inspired that later follower of the Druids, Thomas Wright, who, however, adopted a more imaginative, rococo approach to his garden building designs.

Antiquarianism brought together a number of strands that were to affect the Picturesque: ruins, Gothic, past native civilisations (even if often imaginary), and an association of old oral poetry with wild landscape, notably the bards of the Welsh mountains and Ossian in Scotland (see pp.125-7). The bards, indeed, were seen as custodians of Druidic traditions.[33]

'Capability' Brown and the Picturesque

Were the landscape parks of Brown and his ilk picturesque? While the answer was an emphatic No from Price and Payne Knight (and several others besides), a significant number of contemporaries, through opinion and practice, professed otherwise. Taking 'picturesque' in its sense of being suitable for picture-making, there was an impressive body of paintings and prints of Brown's parks. Famous places such as Blenheim or Chatsworth were bound to be continually depicted, but a print of Chatsworth (Fig.1.9), is highly revealing, since it shows Brown's work as more predominant than it actually was – the grand formal cascade has been airbrushed out. Richard Wilson painted Croome Court, Moor Park (Hertfordshire) and Syon, and William Tomkins Audley End, while later on Turner immortalised the parks at Harewood, Blenheim and Petworth. Whether the parks so depicted were picturesque in the 'wild' sense of the word was, of course, a different matter.

Another aspect is the written description. There were some commentators who, either in prose or in verse, compared Brown's art to the work of the great landscape artists. In an age when fulsome flattery was common, one must expect a certain amount of exaggeration, but even so it is telling that writers should have reached for a comparison with Claude or Poussin. Thus the author of the 1767 poem on Temple Newsham, outside Leeds, brings in Rubens, Claude, Poussin, van Ruisdael and even Salvator Rosa in his encomium on Brown's efforts there and at some previous sites:

> And all around romantic scenes display.
> Delighted still along the Park we rove,
> Vary'd with Hill and Dale, with Wood and Grove:
> O'er velvet Lawns what noble Prospects rise,
> Fair as the Scenes, that Reuben's hand supplies!...

1.9 The park at Chatsworth, Derbyshire, engraved by William Watts after Paul Sandby, 1786

> But your great Artist, like the source of light,
> Gilds every Scene with beauty and delight;
> At Blenheim, Croome, and Caversham we trace
> Salvator's Wildness, Claud's enlivening grace.
> Cascades and Lakes as fine as Risdale drew,
> While Nature's vary'd in each charming view.
> To paint his works wou'd Pousin's Powers require,
> Milton's sublimity, and Dryden's fire:[34]

Brown is thus equated with the greatest of poets as well as artists. But the commonest comparison was with the paintings of Claude.[35]

There are good reasons, too, for regarding Brown as not always unpicturesque in practice. It is doubtful whether Price and Payne Knight were acquainted with the whole range of his *oeuvre*, and thus they were all too easily able to stereotype him, as had Chambers earlier. Brown demonstrated, in fact, a considerable degree of variety. He was responsible for ornamental shrubberies – Croome Court, recently replanted, is a fine example – and has in recent years been revealed to have had more interest in flowers and floriferous plants than was at one time imagined. He anticipated Repton's revival of flower gardens by his plan for radiating petal-shaped beds at Brocklesby, Lincolnshire. At Petworth, an early commission, he adapted existing specialised gardens into a 'wilderness' with winding paths lined with flowering shrubs, and this was followed by a circuit shrubbery at Syon.[36] He also designed shrubberies at Belhus, Essex, and probably elsewhere though sometimes the dating of the shrubberies does not coincide exactly with his presence. But in any case he must have visualised his designs as 'pictures' and even referred to composing with a painter's eye (see p.70 on Roche Abbey).

Painting

As the Picturesque was supposed to bear such a close relationship to painting (both act and product), it is to be expected that many well-known landscape artists would be invoked as models. It has become a commonplace that the seventeenth-century quartet of Claude Lorraine, Nicolas Poussin, Gaspard Dughet (Poussin's brother-in-law, often referred to as Poussin at the time) and Salvator Rosa were greatly influential in this respect. What they tended to portray was an imaginary classical or sometimes biblical world, with a landscape marked by distant hills, temples and ruins, with some episode of fable in the foreground. In the case of Rosa, the landscape was sometimes threatening – broken trees and bridges, impending rocks, bandits – and thus eminently amenable to demands of the wilder Picturesque. As Horace Walpole summed up his experience of the Alpine Sublime in 1739: 'Precipices, mountains, wolves, torrents, rumblings – Salvator Rosa!'[37] There was a great vogue for collecting Claudes (in particular), and many were engraved and sold as prints, thus ensuring a wide dissemination of what these paintings looked like.

Because so many of the paintings included buildings, the pictorial gardens of the mid-eighteenth century were often seen to derive some inspiration from them. Henry Hoare of Stourhead wrote in a letter to his daughter in 1762 that one particular scene he was devising in the gardens 'will be a charm[in]g Gasp[ar]d picture'.[38] As time went on, Rosa was more often invoked as being a romantic before his time: he was independent and something of a rebel, although, as an exhibition at the Dulwich Picture Gallery in 2010 showed, his *oeuvre* was far more extensive than unsettling landscapes, and included portraits and calmer scenes.

But the quartet, based in Italy, was not the only formative influence. The Dutch landscape school of the seventeenth century had also produced masters such as van Ruisdael, Cuyp and Hobbema, whose names also crop up from time to time in connection with eighteenth-century gardens. The very word 'landscape' is derived from the Dutch *landschap,* and the Dutch paintings were recognised as being more than representational, infused with a spirit, a nationalistic pride in converting the low-lying wet land of the Netherlands into productive agricultural and aesthetically attractive landscape. This transforming power of the Dutch over their own countryside, as registered in paintings, found its counterpart in the English transformation of extensive gardens. Another popular Dutch artist, Swanevelt, painted landscapes in Rome 'where he obtained the name of *the hermit,* from his solitary walks among the ruins of TIVOLI and FRESCATI'.[39]

The stock of landscape painting as a *genre* rose steadily, becoming ever more in demand in the eighteenth century as the love of landscape itself blossomed. From occupying a lowly place in the hierarchy of painting in comparison to history or religious paintings or portraits, it became both respected and popular, particularly through the fast-growing medium of prints. Garden and landscape art of the century reflected not only what was happening on the ground but the condition of some older gardens: furthermore it helped to spread taste and fashion. Thus the rococo French school, starting with Watteau at the beginning of the century, and continuing through Boucher, Fragonard, Pater and Lancret among others, promoted a pleasure-loving way of life often set in gardens that was exaggerated for effect. Some, like Fragonard and Hubert Robert ('Robert des Ruines'), portrayed Versailles in decline or Italian Renaissance gardens in decay. A gentle melancholy, fragility and sense of transience were much in evidence in rococo art.

Two artists in Rome in mid-century, Clérisseau and Piranesi, had a noticeable impact on Grand Tourists and on painters and architects (such as the young Robert Adam) who went to study under them. Their speciality was ruins, some imaginary but mostly depictions of classical Roman ruins in a manner calculated to heighten their emotional appeal by emphasising their decay, with weeds growing out of the cracks and so on. Both were astute enough to exploit the commercial possibilities of the English taste for 'pleasurable melancholy' (see chapter on ruins).

There were also Italian artists who came to England. Canaletto, famed for his evocations of Venice, stayed for several years in mid-century, during which time he essayed landscapes such as the park at Badminton and Alnwick Castle, together with more intimate views of the pleasure gardens of London. Francesco Zuccarelli visited London often between 1752 and 1771 and was known for his Arcadian style of landscape painting, carrying on the tradition of Claude and Poussin but with staffage of French-style rococo figures. Like Claude-Joseph Vernet, Zuccarelli made some attempt to combine the content of Claude with that of Rosa.

At home the visual arts were in the ascendant. In the field of topographical art, the Dutch and French painters and engravers who dominated in the first half of the century gradually gave way to British artists. Richard Wilson returned from Rome with his head filled with Italian light and colour which he proceeded to impose on his English garden and landscape canvases. Depiction of gardens surged, through such artists as William Tomkins and William Hannan, and began to reflect the change in taste from the pictorial to something more picturesque. There were artists who excelled in the portrayal of the Sublime – Joseph Wright of Derby (who had witnessed Vesuvius erupt) with his violent glimpses of industrial processes, and John Robert Cozens with his mountain landscapes that brought out the expressive power of watercolour. Cozens had accompanied Payne Knight on his second Grand Tour, and later did likewise with William Beckford. The young Turner visited Wales, and John Martin continued exploiting mountain views in the early nineteenth century, just as Caspar David Friedrich had on the continent. Thomas Girtin should also be mentioned in this context. Philip de Loutherbourg was a theatrical scene painter who could turn his hand to landscape – and did so with theatrical effect.

The English watercolour school expressed particularly well the colouring and shapes of the Picturesque. Mention will be made later of the topographical work of Paul Sandby, the founder of the school, Thomas Hearne, who painted sequences of estates such as Downton, and Repton for his Red Book illustrations. In oils, Thomas Gainsborough was pre-eminent, famed for his landscapes that brought out picturesque qualities, although he, like Hearne, also focussed on individual trees, as at Foxley (1760), where he was acquainted with the Price family. Michael Angelo Rooker forsook oil for watercolour in a career that embraced landscape with a predilection for ruins. Such paintings were often engraved, and of the engravers William Woollett, François Vivares and Luke Sullivan stand out as a trio, though there were many others deserving of note. They all depicted gardens, though as they were active in mid-century some of the sites were still formal. Finally, the gifted amateurs such as Coplestone Warre Bampfylde, owner of Hestercombe, should be recognised. Not all were great artists, but they understood the appeal of the Picturesque.

Literature

Apart from the theorists and those who promoted particular approaches to landscaping, there was a body of literature of various kinds, especially verse, which is relevant to any study of the Picturesque. One category was the topographical poem: by no means a new *genre* it stretches back at least as far as Ben Jonson's *To Penshurst* (1616). But in the eighteenth century it became suffused with a sense of place and response to scenery, thus working towards a picturesque sensibility. Associations, historical and otherwise, might play a part, as in Alexander Pope's early pastoral *Windsor Forest* (1713). John Dyer, author of *Grongar Hill* (1726), in the Towy Valley, South Wales, was both poet and artist, and in some ways his descriptive approach is indicative of both, but he moralises on what he sees. The most popular poem of the century was James Thomson's protracted *The Seasons,* produced over a period of nearly twenty years, which contains some descriptive passages, most famously of Stowe, Richmond Vale and Hagley. It is far from mere word-painting, and Thomson directs the reader to mental and emotional response and (in the case of Hagley) to the release of the imagination. Richard Jago's *Edge-Hill* (1767) ambled through geology and creation theory as well as describing the hill and laying down instructions to garden designers.

There were many verse descriptions of individual sites, notably Stowe. While some were little more than lists of features, many would have an agenda of some sort, whether to praise the owner, draw parallels with painting, or to derive a moral from the scene or from features within it. This would all be in the interest of educating the eye and sensibility and of creating taste for gardens and landscape. Others spoke in more general terms about colourful, varied and natural scenery, such as Joseph Warton in *The Enthusiast* (1744).

One particular development in mid-century, but looking towards the Picturesque, was the so-called 'Graveyard School' of poetry. As the name suggests, it was to do with dark and morbid thoughts, and fitted in both with the deep-seated feeling for melancholy and with Gothic horror, still to come but partly at least triggered by it. The most well-known example is Thomas Gray's *Elegy in a Country Churchyard* (revised, 1751), with Robert Blair's *The Grave* (1743) and Edward Young's *Night Thoughts* (1742-5) both finding great popularity right across Europe. A precocious example of the *genre* was Thomas Parnell's *Night Piece on Death* (1722).

Gray was also responsible for spearheading the next identifiable poetic movement, the bardic. *The Bard* (1757), representing Celtic tradition and the spirit of defiance in the rocky fastnesses of North Wales, was not only popular as a poem but was painted by several artists, most memorably by Thomas Jones (1774), who gave his old prophet a background of 'Druid stones' and mountains. The Celtic Revival merged Druids and Celtic fable, and can be seen as a heavily romanticised antiquarianism. While Thomas Percy's *Reliques of Ancient English Poetry* (1765) was scholarly, it was imagination and invention that dominated. James Macpherson, purporting to have used old Gaelic sources, published various 'translations' between 1760 and 1765 which enjoyed great success and for the most part were accepted as genuine ancient poetry though now discounted as forgeries (see p.125). This 'Ossian' corpus was paralleled a few years later by Thomas Chatterton, dead before he was eighteen, who invented a medieval Bristolian, Thomas Rowley, with a number of supposed poems by him. A memorial was raised by the controversial Philip Thicknesse in the latter's garden outside Bath which combined antiquarianism, romanticism and the Picturesque (Fig.1.10). It was close to the site of Saxon and Roman coffins

Monument to the Memory of Chatterton.

1.10 The memorial to Thomas Chatterton, near Bath, print published in the *Ladies Magazine*, 1784

that had been dug up, and comprised a cave scooped out of the hill beneath an ash, with a primitive arch set in front and a relief of Chatterton's head above, surmounted by an urn.[40]

Some poetry might point to a light-hearted examination of landscaping issues, such as William Whitehead's *On the Late Improvements at Nuneham,* where Brown and Dame Nature meet and each tries to claim credit for what has been accomplished. But, as the arguments grew stronger and more heated, so their seriousness was pricked by satire. William Mason's (originally anonymous) *An Heroic Epistle* answered Chambers' work on oriental gardening, as we have seen, by sending up Chambers' already exaggerated notions of Chinese gardening. Matthews' *Sketch from The Landscape,* mocking Payne Knight, was at a far less elevated level of verse. No better, poetically, was William Combe's Dr Syntax, modelled on Gilpin, who has ludicrous adventures in *In Search of the Picturesque,* pointedly illustrated by Rowlandson, though Combe's satire may have been given an edge by the wrongful accusation that he had been stealing at Foxley when staying with Price some years before. Later satire tended to be in prose: Jane Austen has quiet fun at the expense of Repton in *Mansfield Park* and exploits Gothic horror in *Northanger Abbey,* while Thomas Love Peacock combines a satire against Repton (in the person of Mr Milestone) with mockery of the Picturesque itself in *Headlong Hall.* It has to be said, though, that, however witty, Peacock's work was on the brink of being out-of-date when published (1815).

The politics of the Picturesque

Most followers of the Picturesque were tourists, and those who sought the thrills of the Sublime have been likened to those who enjoy horror films. But it is in that very purpose of pleasure-seeking that the problem for political commentators lies. For when the human element enters, the danger is that the overriding importance of visual spectacle obliterates other concerns: a gipsy, for example, might appear picturesque but that would shut off consideration for his or her condition. This is illustrated most starkly in Nathaniel Wraxall's comment in 1813 that the elderly Scottish women he encountered were sublime in their hideousness: 'The old women far exceed in Ugliness, our English Hags. It is not easy to conceive the sublime extent of their Ugliness, augmented by the Effects of the Weather, Climate, Rags, & Poverty.'[41]

A nineteenth-century critic of the Picturesque was John Ruskin, who in his day found the contemporary Aesthetic Movement ('Art for Art's Sake') equally reprehensible in not addressing moral or social concerns. But the lack of concern has been primarily remarked on by those modern commentators[42] who see the Picturesque as a detached, essentially leisured-class indulgence that treated all scenery, alive or inanimate, as objects to be enjoyed, admired or judged aesthetically. Socially the movement accepted the *status quo* and thus fitted in with the Whig ascendancy of the greater part of the eighteenth century. There were not many who shared Payne Knight's hope for a happy outcome to the French Revolution, especially after the excesses of the Terror in 1794. But he saw the Revolution originally as a liberation from tyrannical power, and made connections between the Picturesque and political freedom: his own plantings bore some political symbolism.[43]

Detachment may reveal a key difference between the Picturesque and the Romantic Movement. The latter, spearheaded by Wordsworth and Coleridge, on one hand sought inspiration and subjective emotion among the mountains but on the other showed an interest in, and championed freedom for, the ordinary person. And Wordsworth echoed Payne Knight's thoughts about what was happening in France in the 1790s. Payne Knight's position, however, was somewhat ambivalent. For all that he was against the Establishment and liked to stir things up, he favoured the retention and conservation of ancient forests, old houses and old structures, and, as we have seen, went on to promote a return to Italian parterres and formal gardens. He might well, of course, have seen that as radical for his time.

1 John Dixon Hunt, *The Picturesque Garden in Europe* (London: Thames & Hudson, 2002), p.13.

2 Quoted in Kerry Downes, *Sir John Vanbrugh: A Biography* (London: Sidgwick & Jackson, 1987), p.348.

3 Joseph Spence, *Observations, Anecdotes, and Characters of Books and Men*, ed. JM Osborn (Oxford: Clarendon Press, 1966), Vol.I, p.252, #606.

4 *The Works in Verse and Prose of William Shenstone, Esq.* (London: R&J Dodsley, 1764), Vol.II, p.129.

5 Spence, *Observations*, I, p.425, #1130.

6 See Christopher Dingwall, 'Gardens in the Wild', *Garden History* 22:2, 1994, pp.133-56.

7 Shenstone, *Works*, II, p.147.

8 Horace Walpole, *The History of the Modern Taste in Gardening* (New York: Ursus Press, 1995, orig. 1770), p.52.

9 John Dalrymple, *An Essay on Landscape Gardening* (Greenwich: Bolton Corney, 1823), pp.6-7.

10 Quoted in *Claremont Landscape Garden* (London: The National Trust, 1984), p.6.

11 Resta Patching, *Four Topographical Letters* (Newcastle, 1757), p.58.

12 William Sawrey Gilpin, *Practical Hints upon Landscape Gardening* (London: T Cadell/Edinburgh: W Blackwood, 1832), p.6.

13 *Ibid.*, pp.7-8.

14 Claude-Henri Watelet, *Essay on Gardens: A Chapter in the French Picturesque*, ed. and trans. Samuel Danon (Philadelphia: University of Pennsylvania Press, 2003), pp.44-5.

15 William Gilpin, *A Dialogue upon the Gardens...at Stow* (London: B Seely, 1748), p.14.

16 William Gilpin, *An Essay upon Prints* (London, 1768, second ed.), p.x.

17 Quoted in Carl Barbier, introduction to *The Reverend William Gilpin and the Picturesque* [exhibition catalogue] (London: London County Council, 1959), p.5.

18 Gray's interests and contributions are discussed in David Jacques, *Georgian Gardens: The Reign of Nature* (London: Batsford, 1983).

19 Christopher Hussey, *The Picturesque: Studies in a Point of View* (London and New York: GP Putnam's Sons, 1927), p.32.

20 John Dixon Hunt, *The Figure in the Landscape: Poetry, Painting, and Gardening during the Eighteenth Century* (Baltimore: Johns Hopkins University Press, 1976, republished 1989), pp.145-65.

21 Charles Watkins, Stephen Daniels and Susanne Seymour, 'Picturesque Woodland Management: The Prices at Foxley', *The Picturesque in late Georgian England*, ed. Dana Arnold (London: The Georgian Group, 1995), pp.29-30.

22 Stephen Daniels and Charles Watkins, 'A Well-connected Landscape: Uvedale Price at Foxley', *The Picturesque Landscape: Visions of Georgian Herefordshire*, ed. Stephen Daniels and Charles Watkins (Nottingham: University of Nottingham Press, 1994), p.40.

23 Uvedale Price, *An Essay on the Picturesque* (London: J Robson, 1794), pp.44-5.

24 Richard Payne Knight, *An Analytical Inquiry into the Principles of Taste* (London: T Payne and J White, 1805), p.142.

25 William Chambers, *A Dissertation on Oriental Gardening* (London, 1772), p.36.

26 *Ibid.*, p.37.

27 *Ibid.*, p.40.

28 Uvedale Price, *Essays on the Picturesque* (London: J Robson, 1798), Vol.II, p.17 (Repton's letter to Price).

29 John Matthews, *A Sketch from the Landscape* (London: R Faulder, 1794, second ed, no date), p.26.

30 George Mason, *An Essay on Design in Gardening* (London: B&J White, 1795, revised ed.), p.205.

31 Stuart Piggott, *William Stukeley: An Eighteenth-Century Antiquary* (London: Thames & Hudson, 1985), p.53.

32 *Ibid.*, p.74.

33 Malcolm Andrews, *The Search for the Picturesque* (London: Scolar Press, 1990), p.128.

34 *The Rise and Progress of the Present Taste in Planting Parks, Pleasure Grounds, Gardens, &c.* [1767] (Newcastle-upon-Tyne: Oriel Press, 1970, facsimile ed.), pp.29-30.

35 Jacques, *Georgian Gardens*, p.69.

36 Mark Laird, *The Flowering of the Landscape Garden: English Pleasure Grounds 1720-1800* (Philadelphia: University of Pennsylvania Press, 1999), pp.133-44.

37 *The Yale Edition of Horace Walpole's Correspondence*, ed. W S Lewis (New Haven and London: Yale University Press, 1948), Vol.XIII, p.181.

38 Kenneth Woodbridge, *The Stourhead Landscape* (London: The National Trust, 1982), p.25.

39 Gilpin, *Essay upon Prints*, p.158.

40 See *From Gothic to Romantic: Thomas Chatterton's Bristol*, ed. Alistair Heys (Bristol: Redcliffe Press, 2005), pp.68-9.

41 Quoted in Andrews, *Search for the Picturesque*, p.210.

42 See, for example, *The Politics of the Picturesque*, ed. Stephen Copley and Peter Garside (Cambridge: Cambridge University Press, 1994).

43 Andrew Ballantyne, *Architecture, Landscape and Liberty: Richard Payne Knight and the Picturesque* (Cambridge: Cambridge University Press, 1997), pp.199, 220.

CHAPTER TWO

From Pictorial to Picturesque

The idea of looking at scenes in a garden as a series of pictures spread widely from the 1730s. We have seen that the analogy of garden views and paintings had arrived early on, from Vanbrugh trying to persuade an unconvinced Duchess of Marlborough in 1709 that the ruinous old Woodstock Manor should be retained. This implied two things, first that the visitor should view the scenes in terms of painterly composition, and second that the designer should base the layout on the principles of painting, or even on known paintings. That would not mean an exact or close copy, but adopting the artist's approach to composition. Following on from these ideas the concept of the circuit garden evolved, to reach its peak in the mid-century. The circuit was devised to show the visitor a number of views or set-piece tableaux in a certain sequence. This could be a subtle, if manipulative, process, revealing the scenes in an order that had a cumulative effect and reached a climax. Going round the circuit in the wrong direction might ruin the carefully-contrived experience, as William Shenstone discovered at The Leasowes: 'It is said of the elegant Mr Shenstone, that nothing created in his mind greater vexation than the perverseness or malice of those who passed thro' the walks of The Leasowes in a contrary direction to that which he originally designed.'[1]

The circuit depended on a path or drive that the visitor could follow. Seats or benches might be placed strategically to cause the visitor to pause and savour the view at that particular point. On foot, the 'stations' would encourage definite stops, whereas the later carriage-drives, such as Repton's (see p.157), would proffer changing scenes viewed mostly in motion, with less frequent stops. Above all the circuit presented the garden as a journey – the path itself might undulate and range from easy to difficult and steep, and the scenes encompassed could vary in cultural or historical associations and in mood. In the greatest and richest of the mid-century gardens the scenes were far from just visual and compositional, and the circuit would provide a well-rounded experience, to be appreciated on several levels. The idea of the circuit as analogous to a spiritual journey or pilgrimage to find Eden has been explored by Max F Schulz, who concluded that the pictorial garden 'contained a complete and ordered world comprehended by the associative turns of mind of its participants alike in the symbolic actions of the circular walk and in the allegorical encounters along the way'.[2]

The concept of the garden as a series of set compositions found early and sharp focus in the work of William Kent, himself an artist. He did not draw up plans for designing gardens but sketched different views in the garden, showing proposed buildings and (usually rather vague) plantings. His approach was pictorial, and recognised as such by Walpole years later, who spoke of Kent in painterly terms:

> At that moment appeared Kent, painter enough to taste the charms of landscape…Thus the pencil of his imagination bestowed all the arts of landscape on the scenes he handled. The great principles on which he worked were perspective, and light and shade…His buildings, his seats, his temples, were more the works of his pencil than of his compasses.[3]

So in Kent (according to Walpole, at least) we find not only the garden seen as pictures but the elements of the landscape – trees, buildings – controlled and guided by the principles of painting that an artist would employ.

As John Dixon Hunt points out, soon after Kent's death there were many who, with hindsight, perceived a strong and direct connection between garden design and painting in his work. Apart from Walpole, Joseph Spence, Shenstone, Lord Kames and William Mason all testified to his prominent part in practising painting in gardening, involving the artist's armoury of perspective, 'prospect', distancing and bringing nearer.[4]

Rousham

In the majority of gardens Kent worked on, the set-piece or picture effect would normally be centred on a building, often backed by trees. These might be isolated, in an open area, and not directly connected to other buildings or 'pictures'. His temple out in the park at Holkham, Norfolk, is particularly isolated. In such cases the building may be effective as something unexpected, but it is not integrated into a unified plan or design. But in the case of Rousham (his best surviving work) the circuit reveals a coherent scheme of moving from one picture to another. It starts with the formality of a bowling green at the back of the house – niches in the walls of the house contain copies of classical sculpture that relates to figures to be encountered in the gardens. There is an outward view, to rising ground outside the owner's (General Dormer's) property, yet he established a distant eye-catcher in a field there, a façade of an arch. It has been pointed out that the views outward are of medieval-style features (the arch and the closer mill by the Cherwell, which Kent Gothicised), while the internal are classical, as if to suggest a cultural world within, set in a surrounding of native history and value.

Rousham is limited in area, and the circuit makes subtle if convoluted use of it. A helmeted term of Minerva stands at the entrance, suggesting battle (a theme of the top level of the garden), opposite a term portraying Minerva in her other role of wisdom, with the emblem of an owl, at the end of the circuit. The violent figure of the Lion attacking the Horse stands at the edge of the bowling green to set the tone of the upper garden. Further along the top walk, divided from the paddock by a ha-ha, there is a figure of the Dying Gladiator to carry on the theme. This, the term and the Lion and Horse, are all of stone, which contrasts with the lead sculpture on the lower levels. On a short balustrade are two terms, Hercules and Pan. These represent the boundary and cross-over between the heroic and the rural (Hercules is associated with both, so is an apt link-man). The twin themes of the garden thenceforward are love and the countryside, with a Palladian gateway exhibiting Flora and Plenty; Antinous at the end of the Lime Walk, usually taken at the time to be Apollo, god of the sun and overall of the natural world; Venus's Vale, where the goddess is accompanied by Pan and Faun looking out to the fields beyond; and in what remains of Bridgeman's amphitheatre Ceres and Bacchus, standing for the sources of food and drink, are united by Mercury, perennial messenger and servant of the gods.[5]

2.1 Vale of Venus at Rousham, Oxfordshire

Quite apart from the iconography of the sculpture – and the figures all make the visitor pause to contemplate them – the pictorial circuit at Rousham unwraps many memorable scenes, each reached with a sense of the unexpected. At the top level there is a feeling of the *ferme ornée,* looking back to the house across a field with cattle or horses, and the Gothic seat does double duty as a cowshed on its hidden side. There is a serpentine rill through a wood, with a cold bath half-way along (originally called the Cave of Proserpina, daughter of Ceres) and a classical temple built by William Townesend (normally a Gothicist) which produces an echo. The Lime Walk leads to the *coup de théâtre* that suddenly bursts on the view – Venus's Vale, with its pool and twin cascades. The Cherwell winds round the bottom of the hill but affords views across. Kent's 'Praeneste' terrace, an arcade very loosely modelled on the classical complex at Palestrina (formerly Praeneste) in Italy, serves to lead the visitor below the bowling green and to the amphitheatre and then to the Pyramid at the top of another small slope. Each of these buildings constitutes a tableau with its own character, making a chain of visual experiences with cultural connotations.

As a model of how to make the most of a restricted space Rousham is unmatchable, given that most of the effects are in fact large enough to allow for standing back to admire. But precisely because it is so compact it differs from the generally much larger-scale landscapes of the picturesque period. The *tableaux* tend to be self-contained, even if three-dimensional (Venus's Vale), and it is only in the outward-looking views that there is a sense of panorama and extent. Kent's 'pictures' are thus discrete, and confirmation can be found in several of John Rocque's surveys of gardens in which Kent had a hand. Rocque, surveying (or at any rate publishing) from 1734, often embellished his maps with vignettes of buildings round the borders. So, for Chiswick, Richmond Gardens, Claremont, Kensington Gardens, Esher Place (Fig.2.2) and Wanstead, Rocque portrayed garden features mainly by, or attributed to, Kent. Others, such as the survey of Wrest Park, contained cameos of earlier buildings. The vignettes are revealing in two ways:

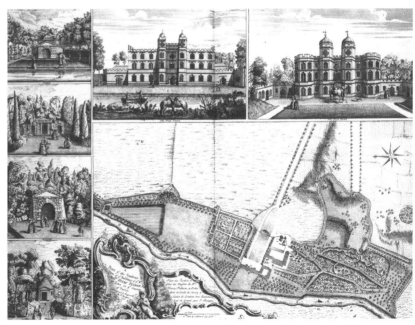

2.2 Plan of Esher Place, Surrey, by John Rocque, 1737

2.3   View from top of amphitheatre at Claremont, Surrey

first, they show what the buildings looked like, at a time when other illustrations of them might be scarce, and, second, they indicate a way of regarding the scenes as pictures. Often the building is depicted with a backing of trees and at the head of a slope or lawn bordered by plantings, which further indicates Kent's characteristic method of set-piece construction, a building in a setting. Although he is best known for his surveys (which included detailed and painstaking maps of London and Dublin) Rocque was able from time to time to expand his taste for vignettes by drawing a larger image of a garden scene for engraving.

One facet of perspective that became commonplace in gardens was the use of foreground, middle ground and distance. It could be argued that this had been the case in formal gardens, where the parterre near the house was generally succeeded beyond by a wilderness of groves cut through with paths, but in the landscape garden it became the basis for nearly all design, up to Brown's use of a lawn as the foreground, a lake in the middle and a park (perhaps a deer park) beyond the lake or ha-ha. Kent was well aware of this painterly approach, and from the top of the amphitheatre at Claremont (Fig.2.3) there is a perfect 'picture' with the grass slopes of the amphitheatre in the foreground, the lake in the centre, and the rising hill behind (the hill was brought into the estate by Brown, and the main road turnpiked the other side of it).

A more subtle control of perspective was shown in some gardens where the configuration of foreground, middle ground and distance changed as one went round, so that elements in one division would move to another. Joseph Spence explained how this worked at Woburn Farm, for instance.[6] The same can also be perceived in the circuit at Painshill.

Painshill and Stourhead

In all Kent's projects there remained some degree of formality, such as straight walks, often inherited from

2.4   Reconstructed hermitage at Painshill, Surrey

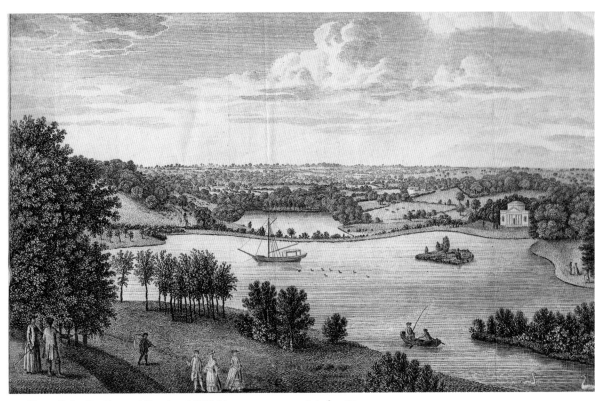

2.5   View of lake, Pantheon at Stourhead, Wiltshire, anonymous print of c1780

an earlier layout (usually Bridgeman's). In the case of the two great amateur gardens of Painshill and Stourhead, created by their owners, Charles Hamilton and Henry Hoare, there was much more naturalism and an evolving response to the Picturesque. The two gardens were roughly contemporary, with most work carried out in mid-century, and there was interchange between the two owners, including Hamilton borrowing heavily from Hoare's Bank.

In the case of Painshill, the early emphasis was on plantings: decoration by buildings, together with a growing awareness of the Picturesque, came after 1750. Hamilton approached design very much with an artist's eye, and is thought to have studied painting, as well as amassing a large collection of paintings, especially landscapes. He created a varied landscape using theatrical and painterly techniques of perspective and illusion, and was adept at changing mood by a mixture of buildings and their surrounding plantings. Some of the buildings fitted in particularly well with a picturesque agenda – two ruins (Abbey and Mausoleum), a hermitage (Fig.2.4) and the grotto. The sheer range and amount of artificial rockwork, on Grotto Island and on and around the cascade, also pointed to the Picturesque. As regards plantings, they gave a different flavour to separate areas of the gardens, but were at their most picturesque on the wooded hill and 'Alpine Valley' in the western part of the grounds. Here a predominantly evergreen wood of firs and pines mingled with old oaks and birch to produce what Horace Walpole referred to as the perfect example of a forest or savage garden, with an Alpine feel to it.[7] For an expanded account of the Picturesque at Painshill, the reader is referred to the author's chapter on the subject in a recent book on Hamilton and Painshill.[8]

At Stourhead developments were rather different though Hoare gradually brought it closer to the spirit of Painshill. It appears that Hoare's initial vision was to create a classical paradise around a central lake, dotted about with classical buildings that possibly carried some allegorical purpose. The circuit has been taken to represent Aeneas's journey to found Rome, as in Virgil, or, more loosely, an allegory of life from youth (the Temple of Flora) through tribulation (the grotto or underworld) to wisdom (the Temple of Apollo), reached at the top of a steep path. Henry Hoare alluded to Virgil's account of the underworld in a letter to his daughter, and also showed that Gaspard Dughet was in his thoughts when speaking of a proposed scene in the gardens as forming a charming Gaspard picture.[9]

However, the purity of the classically-inspired landscape began to dissolve as discordant elements were introduced, bringing with them, nonetheless, a far greater range of associations and resonances, as at Painshill. Exoticism arrived in the shape of the ephemeral Turkish Tent and Chinese Umbrello (the former a modest version of that at Painshill) and a Chinese bridge, while the Bristol Cross, erected in 1765, provided a native, medieval presence in front of the church as viewed from across the lake. Medievalism was continued by the Gothic Convent in the woods (1760s), a rustic cottage with pinnacles and spires, and rusticity by the hermitage (1771), constructed from old tree trunks and branches. Its positioning, on a steep zig-zag path which ran through its centre, was suggested by Hamilton, who had perched his own hermitage above a sharp drop at Painshill twenty years before. A cascade, based on the model of Bampfylde's at Hestercombe (see below), and indeed designed by him, was fashioned in 1766 to take Stourhead a further step towards the Picturesque.

Woburn Farm, West Wycombe and Hardwick Park

In this trio of gardens, there is a strong sense of circuit, and hence a sequence of scenes, though the wilder side of the Picturesque is not present. They are (or were) of a more pictorial nature and studded with buildings. Woburn Farm, near Chertsey, Surrey, was famed as perhaps the greatest example of the *ferme ornée*, where the ornamentation of pleasure grounds was integrated with the agricultural parts. But in order to appreciate the integration, a circuit would conduct the visitor through and alongside the fields, and the walk itself was decorative – sometimes lined with trees, sometimes with hedges that contained colourful climbers, and sometimes with a tiered border of planting. Woburn Farm was developed from 1735 and became celebrated through Europe. The buildings included a (mock) ruined chapel, a Gothic cottage and an octagon summerhouse poised above a slope down to the diminutive river Bourne. There were also several small bridges and a minute grotto.

At West Wycombe there is no obvious circuit, and the situation was somewhat muddied by the entrance drive being altered in the 1760s. Nonetheless, the buildings are to be experienced as a sequence and are linked by several pairings through architectural similarities (the Round Temple and the Temple of Music) or by association (Temple of Apollo and Daphne's Temple). Furthermore, virtually all the buildings in the pleasure grounds and in the park to the east are unified by the application of flintwork, obtained locally. Although obscured in places now, the view from all parts extended to the church with the golden ball on the hill, built by the owner, Sir Francis Dashwood, who thereby controlled the views, which served as a constant reminder of the activities within the hill (the Hell-Fire Caves). Conversely, the view from the top of the hill back down to the grounds revealed their layout, with the lake assuming the form of a swan, the emblem of High Wycombe.[10]

2.6 The Temple of Minerva at Hardwick Park, County Durham

Hardwick Park, County Durham, is a much underrated landscape garden, dating from 1750 onwards, that deserves recognition as one of the great pictorial compositions. We owe its creation to John Burdon, who purchased the property in 1748 and had a dam constructed soon thereafter so that the centrepiece, a lake of about sixteen acres, could be formed. Round the lake was a circuit walk encompassing (in anti-clockwise sequence) a Gothic Seat with high ogee arches, fronted by a small pool; a classical Bath House with Doric portico, round bath and changing rooms; a small cascade in front of a bottle-shaped pool which was headed by the Bono Retiro, a rough Gothic construction of two storeys, the upper of which was a library with stained glass windows; the architectural showpiece, the Temple of Minerva (1754-7), set on a hill with a square colonnade around a richly ornamented room with an octagon dome (Fig.2.6); a Gothic Bridge over the serpentine river that curled round the east and south of the lake; Neptune on a plinth on an island; the Gothic Ruin (a sham castle); a grotto viewed across the river, comprising a cave of rocks; and a Palladian Banqueting House (now completely vanished) that represented the final point of the tour, where refreshment would be provided. On the other side of the river, away from the circuit, were not only the grotto but a cascade from the river feeding the lake under a rock bridge.[11] So there were plenty of incidents and tableaux, with some small-scale effects of picturesque rockwork, a ruin, and a balance between woodland and open ground, with a great deal of cultural presence, painted and sculptural, in at least three of the buildings. The quirky and unusual architecture is attributed mainly to James Paine.

Enville, Hagley and The Leasowes

These gardens, the West Midlands 'trinity', evolved over many years, but the prime advances were from the late 1740s and show a distinct tendency towards, or anticipation of, the Picturesque. The circuit was most marked at The Leasowes, where the set route was expected to be followed exactly. With the other two, the walks were more diffuse and often over open ground without a defined path, but the visitor was nonetheless intended to see all the points of interest. Being within a few miles of each other, the outward views were shared, and stretched over the Shropshire hills as far as the Welsh mountains in the distance. Each was on hilly and sloping ground, which enabled the owners (all their own designers) to devise some telling water effects.

At Enville there were several buildings of different character – 'Shenstone's Chapel', a Gothic summerhouse, a Gothic gateway, a rococo boathouse, a Gothicised farmhouse, a rustic cottage, a Gothic seat, a rustic/classical portico, an old building refurbished (the Shepherd's Lodge), a grotto, a turning-seat and a rotunda. Many were specifically to provide a 'station' from which to obtain a particularly splendid view and were accordingly at a height. Sanderson Miller's summerhouse was, however, on flat ground near the house but is of most visual and architectural interest (Fig.2.7). The most picturesque feature was the series of cascades which ended by boiling into the lake with a tremendous roar.

2.7 The restored summerhouse or museum by Sanderson Miller at Enville, Staffordshire

2.8 General view of The Leasowes, West Midlands, including ruined priory, engraved by Benjamin Pouncy after Evans, 1792

Water was always a problem at Hagley, where there were two stepped cascades or linked pools, one smaller than the other. But the pools sometimes ran dry, and water did not play as prominent a part as it did at many other estates. Hagley did, however, afford magnificent views, and its most celebrated building, the sham castle (Fig.1.7), was romantic Gothick, pointing unwaveringly towards the Picturesque.

The Leasowes (Fig.2.8), the most prominent of all circuit gardens, with nearly forty pauses for viewing (and reflecting), usually marked by an alcove or bench, had fine internal vistas as well as outward views plus a visual and emotional climax in the gloom of Virgil's Grove. It had two cascades, one described by Arthur Young in 1770 as 'astonishingly romantic'[12] (Fig.6.7). Among many Gothic buildings the Ruined Priory was the most substantial. It was a heavily literary garden and depended on the visitor having a classical education and a strong imagination. But in its naturalism and incorporation of all kinds of scenery from agricultural to industrial it looks forward as well as slightly back to Pope and the Augustan age. These three gardens are covered in detail in *Enville, Hagley, The Leasowes: Three Great 18th-Century Gardens* (Redcliffe Press), by the present author and Sandy Haynes.

Croome Court, Hestercombe and Shugborough

Brown's parks were not normally considered picturesque – and certainly not by Price and Payne Knight – for their impact was serene and unhurried, smooth rather than lively. However, some contained variety enough to make for something pointing towards the Picturesque, though in the case of Croome Court, Worcestershire, such elements were emphasised by others on the scene and later. Robert Adam and Sanderson Miller were around at more or less the same time, and James Wyatt made significant additions later. Brown's great triumph was hydraulic, draining a swampy morass and enabling a major landscape to arise in its place. While responsible for some buildings (the rotunda and the original Dry Arch, later modified by Wyatt), Brown would have had to defer to his fellow-architects for the most compelling, Adam's Temple Greenhouse and island temple, the grotto and a 'Chinese' bridge taken from a pattern-book by Halfpenny. He was not even responsible for the lake (the New River), which pre-dated him. But the most distinguishing feature at Croome was its ring of distant follies, ever drawing interest outwards (though some were barely visible) and accessible from a long, tortuous outer circuit. Beginning with Adam's Dunstall Castle (1766-7), the ring comprised Panorama Tower, Pirton Tower, the Owl's Nest, Broadway Tower and Baughton Tower, stretching chronologically past 1800. The idea of the distant ring was not unique, but certainly distinctive: the other contemporary example would be Wentworth Woodhouse, South Yorkshire, with its rather bizarre collection of triangular Hoober Stand, the Needle's Eye arch, the tall Mausoleum and Keppel's Column.

Hestercombe, Somerset, has a slight feeling of Painshill about it (plus a little of Stourhead, which the owner, Coplestone Warre Bampfylde, knew well) though it was developed slightly later (1750-86) and the topography is very different. It is, again, a circuit garden with contrast of open and wooded scenery, an array of different architecture and changes of mood. The buildings provide unexpected internal peeps and vistas or panoramic views over the Vale of Taunton, and in the magnificent cascade – the heart of the garden – the pictorial nature of the circuit gives way to the picturesque. It is said that Bampfylde was inspired as a result of seeing the cascades at The Leasowes. All this richness is contained in the relatively small space of thirty-five acres, making the circuit more intense. One building comes hard on the heels of another of totally different type – the Gothic Alcove, the classical Temple Arbour, the

2.9 Robert Adam's Dunstall Castle at Croome Court, Worcestershire

2.10 The Mausoleum at Hestercombe, Somerset

Mausoleum with a pyramidal finial, an octagon summerhouse and a rustic Witch's House of tree branches complete with accoutrements of a figure of a witch and a painted owl and cat.

Shugborough, Staffordshire, was developed in a number of waves over the years from about 1740. The home of Thomas Anson, it was funded by his brother Admiral George Anson, who circumnavigated the globe and became extremely wealthy. The first wave saw a number of classical-style features – a ruined colonnade, the Shepherd's Monument in its original form and a collection of busts, terms and urns, some pieces of which were genuinely Roman – plus an attempt at real Chinese architecture in the pavilion and bridge. There was also a monument to Kouli-Khan, a Persian cat brought home by the Admiral. The second saw the Greek revival buildings of James 'Athenian' Stuart in the 1760s: the Doric Temple, with some similarities to that at Hagley, the Choragic Monument, Hadrian's Arch on a hillside and the Temple of the Winds. All were based on Greek originals found by Stuart and Revett on their expeditions. The final phase included Samuel Wyatt's kitchen garden and model farm.

2.11 Temple of Ancient Virtue at Stowe, Buckinghamshire, among overgrown plantings, print c1820

It was considered a fine landscape, but not necessarily a picturesque one. It did, however, show a move from an emphasis on a complex of buildings to a more dispersed approach, so that the landscape seems more natural. It must be borne in mind, however, that several buildings have been lost, some as a result of a disastrous flood in 1795: contemporary illustrations indicate quite an amount of *chinoiserie* to augment the authentic Chinese House (a pagoda, trelliswork and a seat, as well as a Chinese boat kept in a *chinoiserie* boathouse), together with a pigeon house with a Gothic tower.

As the eighteenth century progressed, some gardens became more picturesque willy-nilly, simply through becoming more heavily wooded or even overgrown. The most famous of all, Stowe, was a good case in point. Some of the features that harked back to the baroque layout took on a picturesque hue as they were gradually occluded by plantings. Fig.2.11 is one of a set of early-nineteenth-century views of buildings at Stowe surrounded by plantings that had far outgrown their original neatness.

In the second half of the century taste and design moved on, and wilder gardens came into being. Several will be discussed in the ensuing chapters, but a few not otherwise dealt with in detail may be mentioned here.

Croft Castle

In some ways Croft, in a part of Herefordshire not far from the Welsh border, was a cradle of the Picturesque. On the core of a medieval castle with corner turrets the residence was re-modelled in eighteenth-century Gothick, which included a separate curtain wall and gateway (1790s). There was a series of magnificent ancient avenues, which have to a greater or lesser degree suffered over time – oak, lime, beech and Spanish chestnut. To one side are woods containing a chain of pools in a valley that is distinctly steep in places. The combe may be more dark and wooded than it was, but its eighty acres were landscaped in the later eighteenth or early nineteenth century to provide a rich and rough picturesque (occasionally sublime) experience. A touch of rusticity was introduced by the grotto, composed of large blocks of limestone from the quarry nearby, and it was apparently built partly as a picnic and viewing spot. The pumphouse, intended to raise water to a reservoir, was probably constructed a few years later.

But although the Fish Pool Valley represents a significant exercise in the Picturesque, it is more for family reasons that Croft assumes such importance for our purposes. For the family links included two of the key players of the Picturesque, Richard Payne Knight and Thomas Johnes, and a number of their relatives demonstrate some impressive garden networking. Richard Knight of Downton purchased Croft in 1746, having already acquired some parts of the estate earlier. In that year his daughter Elizabeth married Thomas Johnes (senior), and their son, also Thomas, was born in 1748.[13] Thomas junior grew up at Croft, where in his formative years he may well have acquired a taste for the Gothic/medieval as well as seeing the possibilities of picturesque landscaping. He left Croft in 1785 in order to concentrate on the vast project at Hafod, though the property may not have been sold till 1800.

The Knight family was both distinguished and had many garden ramifications. Its background was iron, with works at Coalbrookdale and at Downton itself. At Wolverly, Worcestershire, they were in partnership with Sir Thomas Lyttelton of Hagley. Richard Knight was a lawyer and left his younger brother Edward to run the ironworks at Wolverly. Edward's son (also Edward) was particularly interested in gardens and architecture, visiting and commenting on places such as The Leasowes, Radway Grange and Hestercombe, and often striking up friendships with the owners. Richard Payne Knight, and his brother Thomas Andrew Knight, a leading horticulturist, were also nephews of Richard Knight.[14] A taste for gardening was evidently in the family genes.

Moccas Court

Also in Herefordshire, on the Wye, Moccas was the seat of the Cornewall family. A new house by Anthony Keck was completed by 1785, enabling the Cornewalls to move in 'properly', since they had been living in an old house nearer the church at Moccas. However, Brown had already been consulted in 1778, and Repton was brought in later, though it is difficult to ascertain how many of their proposals were implemented. The glory of Moccas was its park and its trees, particularly old oaks (Fig.7.7), but the location, on the river, was what really made it picturesque and, in a way, comparable to Downton. Jane Bradney has pointed out that Belmont (seat of John Matthews), where Repton was involved, also showed some similarity from its position on a great bend of the river. As at Downton, the cliffs the other side of the river were within the ownership of the family, and the outward view from Moccas showed the winding Wye and the cliff face with some rock exposed (Fig.2.12). The view back to the house from the rock would be equally impressive, with the cliff alongside. Repton advised on the walk beside the Wye and was responsible, at least, for opening up a view of the river: 'it is wonderful how great an effect may be produced by a very trifling removal of the ridge only; thus at MOCCAS COURT a very small quantity of earth concealed from the house the view of that beautiful reach of the river Wye which has since been opened'.[15] As we shall see in the chapter on Repton, he was always anxious to obtain the optimum view from the house.

Ilam Hall

Just on the Staffordshire side of the boundary with Derbyshire, stands Ilam, an outstanding feature even among the many wonders of Dovedale and the Peak District. Part of its uniqueness relied on a geological freak, the confluence of two rivers that poured out of the rock near each other after running underground for several miles. One of the rivers was the Manifold, which, as its name suggests, wound its way in folds through Dovedale. The mouths in the rocks are known as the 'Boil Holes'. The riverside walk includes caves cut out from

2.12 View of River Wye and cliff from the garden at Moccas Court, Herefordshire

the hill possibly as early as the latter years of the seventeenth century, anticipating the Picturesque considerably. Congreve (later to be commemorated at Stowe) is supposed to have written his first play, the Restoration comedy *The Old Batchelor* (1689), in one of the caves, and Dr Johnson wrote his novel *Rasselas* at Ilam. When he took Boswell there, the latter admired the wooded hills, the rocks, the Boil Holes and the path under the rock face.[16] Johnson thought that Ilam had grandeur tempered with softness, and that as the visitor looked up to rocks his thoughts were elevated, whereas when he gazed on the valleys he was composed and soothed. In comparing Ilam with the power and might of Hawkstone, Johnson felt that Ilam should be described by Parnell (Thomas Parnell, early eighteenth-century Irish poet, famed for the contemplative *The Hermit*) and Hawkstone by Milton.[17]

Even if some of the layout had already acquired a picturesque flavour, it took the later eighteenth century to appreciate it fully. Johnson and Boswell are a case in point: Whately also commented on the outward scenery in particular:

> It is not unusual to see a conical hill standing out from a long, irregular, mountainous ridge, and greatly improving the view: but at Ilam such a hill is thrown into the midst of the rudest scene, and almost fills up an abyss, sunk among large, bare, misshapen hills, whose unwieldy parts, and uncouth forest, cut by the tapering lines of the cone, appear more savage from the opposition; and the effect would evidently be stronger, were the figure more complete: for it does not rise to quite a point, and the want of regularity seems a blemish.[18]

This criticism seems rather at odds with Whately's normal approval of the Picturesque and irregularity, and was not shared by Gilpin and others. Whately continues to describe this hill and then the two rivers gushing from the Boil Holes:

> It certainly at first sight rivets the attention; but the conical hill is the most striking object; in such a situation it appears more strange, more fantastic, than the rude shapes which are heaped about it; and together they suit the character of the place, where nature seems to have delighted to bring distances together; where two rivers, which are ingulphed many miles asunder, issue from their subterraneous passages, the one often muddy when the other is clear, within a few paces of each other; but they appear only to lose themselves again, for they immediately unite their streams, just in time to fall together into another current, which also runs through the garden.[19]

2.13 View of the 'conical hill', the flat-topped Thorpe Cloud near Ilam, Staffordshire, anonymous print c1780

Gilpin, though disapproving of the flat-topped Thorpe Cloud hill (Fig.2.13), declared that he had seen few situations 'so pleasingly romantic' as at Ilam: the hill, the lawn, the bank, the river and the views 'bring together such a variety of uncommon, and beautiful circumstances, as are rarely to be found in one place'.[20]

Badger Dingle

If some of the attractions of Ilam had existed for some time, the developments at Badger Dingle, Badger, Shropshire, can be dated to the 1780s, at the height of picturesque fervour. The owner, Isaac Hawkins Browne, brought in James Wyatt to design Badger Hall (1783) and the landscape designer William Emes to shape the Dingle as a self-contained picturesque precinct, linked to the Hall by a carefully planted grove, some of which survives. The grove is about 500 yards in length, but the Dingle sits in an east-west combe nearly a mile long. It consists of a gorge between red sandstone cliffs down which the Snowdon stream winds westwards. Nature had clearly provided the setting, but it was exploited in terms of walks, plantings, water features and vistas. Even the cliffs appear to have been extended by workings (perhaps quarrying) at the time, and the caves may date from then. The southern bank of the gorge is particularly steep, and has no continuous path, but the northern side has a walk along its entirety, with minor paths leading to viewing points, forming two miles of walks in all. The main walk is towards the lower level of the cliffs. Small valleys and brooks punctuate the rocks on the northern side.[21]

Snowdon stream was dammed to form three pools, the uppermost (to the east) being nearly half a mile long. The upper dam, at the west end of the pool, was built across naturalistically to create a forked cascade. The plantings in the Dingle include a boundary line of yews on the south side, pines and various hardwoods. At the time alpines, together with rhododendrons and camellias, were grown, and the plantings deliberately allowed vistas and snapshots through the trees.

At the eastern end, above the large pool and the cascade, stands the Temple (at one time known as the Bird House), attributed to Wyatt c1781 and recently restored (Fig.2.14). A semicircle of Tuscan Doric columns surround a rectangular core: it was built as a banqueting room with kitchen. A boathouse further along the upper pool is probably an original feature as well. There is a short artificial tunnel leading to the top of a dam, and beside the path which goes through the tunnel there is an icehouse, a shaft cut into the rock. Above a second boathouse, on the second pool, is a cave which affords a good view back to the cascade. Further down the valley, keeping on the same path on the northern side, a larger cave is encountered, which appears to be deliberately gouged and is set on a stone ledge. Beyond is the third pool and a third boathouse, partly cut from the rock but fronted

2.14 Temple by James Wyatt, and cliff above upper pool at Badger Dingle, Shropshire
[photo: courtesy, Jochen Müller]

by brick on a stone foundation. The path above continues through a tunnel fifty feet long, and the Rotunda now meets the eye. Again possibly by Wyatt, its Doric columns mirror those of the temple. It is set against the sandstone bank and is composed partly of brick and partly of stone.[22] Although not at the far western end of the gorge, the Rotunda marks the final viewing station, and thus makes a pair with the temple.

1 Humphry Repton, *Red Book for Shardeloes* (1794), quoted in John Phibbs, 'The View-Point', *Garden History* 36:2, 2008, p.221.

2 Max F Schulz, 'The Circuit Walk of the Eighteenth-Century Landscape Garden and the Pilgrim's Circuitous Progress', *Eighteenth-Century Studies* 15:1, 1981, p.24.

3 Horace Walpole, *The History of the Modern Taste in Gardening* [1770] (New York, Ursus Press, 1995), pp.43-4.

4 John Dixon Hunt, *The Picturesque Garden in Europe* (London: Thames & Hudson, 2002), p.26.

5 Michael Symes, *Garden Sculpture* (Princes Risborough: Shire, 1996), pp.47-9.

6 Joseph Spence, *Observations, Anecdotes, and Characters of Books and Men*, ed. J M Osborn (Oxford: Clarendon Press, 1966), Vol.I, p.413, #1085.

7 Walpole, *Modern Taste in Gardening*, pp.52-3.

8 Michael Symes, *Mr Hamilton's Elysium: The Gardens of Painshill* (London: Frances Lincoln, 2010), pp.134-143.

9 Kenneth Woodbridge, *The Stourhead Landscape* (London: The National Trust, 1982), pp.19, 25.

10 For an account of West Wycombe, see Michael Symes, 'Flintwork, Freedom and Fantasy: The Landscape at West Wycombe Park, Buckinghamshire', *Garden History* 33:1, 2005, pp.1-30.

11 See booklet, *The Reawakening of Hardwick Park, Sedgefield*, published by The Friends of Hardwick, 2002.

12 Arthur Young, *A Six Months Tour Through the North of England* (London, 1770), Vol.III, p.343.

13 *Croft Castle, Herefordshire* (London: The National Trust, 1996), p.9.

14 *Ibid.*, pp.9-10.

15 Humphry Repton, *Observations on the Theory and Practice of Landscape Gardening* (London: J Taylor, 1803), p.10.

16 Timothy Mowl and Dianne Barre, *The Historic Gardens of Staffordshire* (Bristol: Redcliffe Press, 2009), p.138.

17 *Boswell's Life of Johnson*, ed. G B Hill and L F Powell (Oxford: Clarendon Press, 1950), Vol.V, p.434.

18 Thomas Whately, *Observations on Modern Gardening* (London: T Payne, 1793, fifth ed.), p.23.

19 *Ibid.*, pp.23-4.

20 William Gilpin, *Observations, Relative chiefly to Picturesque Beauty, Made in the Year 1772, on Several Parts of England; particularly the Mountains, and Lakes of Cumberland, and Westmoreland* (London: R Blamire, 1786), p.234.

21 Much of this information comes from an unpublished report by the architect Kenneth Major, 1990.

22 *Ibid.*

CHAPTER THREE

The Outward View

Looking out from a garden might furnish distant views of picturesque or sublime scenery: but does that make the garden itself picturesque? This chapter will explore how, in several cases, the overall picturesque effect was achieved by a combination of external views and internal features. In other words, the distant landscape acted as an inspiration to create something complementary within the garden.

A wide-angled view – often called 'prospect' at the time but what we would call panorama now – was well-established as desirable from a garden. Even in Roman times, views of the open countryside from a villa were valued, and Renaissance paintings often show a broader landscape beyond the confines of what might be a walled garden. At the turn of the eighteenth century the bird's eye views by Kip and Knyff show geometrically laid out estates within a background of countryside that might be hilly or wooded. The idea developed of 'calling in the country', making it part of the garden scene in effect. The widespread introduction of the 'ha ha' facilitated this, because the visible boundary between the garden and the park, fields or landscape beyond was removed. As Horace Walpole rhapsodised:

> But the capital stroke, the leading step to all that has followed, was…the destruction of walls
> for boundaries, and the invention of fosses – an attempt then deemed so astonishing, that
> the common people called them Ha! Ha's! to express their surprise at finding a sudden and
> unperceived check to their walk…I call a sunk fence the leading step for these reasons. No
> sooner was this simple enchantment made, than levelling, mowing and rolling, followed. The
> contiguous ground of the park without the sunk fence was to be harmonized with the lawn
> within; and the garden in its turn was to be set free from its prim regularity, that it might assort
> with the wilder country without.[1]

Calling in the country is, accordingly, linked indissolubly to the rise of the landscape garden.

Making the countryside appear to be part of your garden was one thing: views of distant landscape were, however, something else. An undoubted part of the appeal of the West Midlands trio described in the previous chapter was the far-away mountains of Wales, which were patently not part of the estates. So, parallel to calling in the country, a backdrop of 'other' scenery was an important constituent in a number of mid- or later-century gardens.

Mountains or hills would be the most obvious and striking of objects in the distance. The taste for mountains, and their potential sublimity, was encouraged by the Grand Tour, with its experiences of French, Swiss and Italian Alps. The pleasing 'discovery' that Britain could field a good number of competitors, if not quite so awesome in height or drama, fuelled a desire to make the most of them as spectacle or as backcloth to a garden (see especially the chapter on Scotland and the section on Claife and Belle Isle in the Lake District, pp.145-6). A panorama including hills was quite common – a superb example would be Wentworth Castle, South Yorkshire – although the overall effect might not be picturesque in the wilder sense.

The sea lent itself particularly well to distant or panoramic views. Repton worked at Sheringham and Holkham, both in Norfolk, which commanded views of the sea from the higher points in the park, and commented that the most celebrated places with such views were Mulgrave Castle, Yorkshire, Tregothnan and Mount Edgcumbe, Cornwall, 'and various places in Sussex and the Isle of Wight'.[2] While comparing the view of the sea at Sheringham to that of the south coast and even the bay of Naples, Repton admitted that the north-facing coast brought cold winds, especially in winter, and that those who had experienced the chill blasts 'will pity the bad taste of any one who should recommend a Site for a Mansion looking towards the Sea'.[3] So, although the view to be obtained from the house was always to be prized and cultivated, sight of the sea might well preferably be reserved to a vantage point somewhere in the garden or park.

Other features which might form a picturesque background to a garden were rivers and cliffs in combination. The perfect example is Piercefield, Monmouthshire, and there were comparable scenes further up the Wye, into Wales, and various rivers in Scotland such as the Esk or the River Manifold in Derbyshire. Some owners might be fortunate enough to have river and cliff within their property, as at Downton or Moccas Court. In some cases the view of a town or city might be considered picturesque: the sweep of Bath seen from the sloping combe at Prior Park would be an instance.

Part of the process of looking at scenery with a picturesque eye was the framing of part of the view as a picture. There were mechanical aids to this, chiefly the Claude glass, which was compact and could be used on the spot. It could be circular or rectangular in shape, but when opened up it was simply a convex mirror a few inches in diameter. Viewers would stand or sit with their back to the landscape and see its reflection in the mirror, in miniature. That would thus reduce the scene to a manageable size for encapsulating and for sketching. The foreground would stand out, but, as Malcolm Andrews points out, the background was generalised and lost detail.[4] The mirror was sometimes given a grey tint which would colour the reflection accordingly, and tinted glasses could be used to look directly at a landscape with the same effect (they also might be termed Claude glasses). But, either way, the 'real' image was being manipulated so as to resemble a painting. Gilpin, as we might expect, was particularly interested in the possibilities.

The *camera obscura* was more elaborate, though it was still portable. It was primarily used indoors, mostly in an artist's studio. It consisted of a box which, by lenses and mirrors, would project a miniature image of the scene viewed on to an inner wall of the box. This was taken round by some tourists, but the Claude glass was much more manageable.

'Framed' views could also focus attention on distant points. Just as the eye was concentrated by high hedges on an object at the end of an *allée* in a formal garden, so trees could conceal, then reveal, or otherwise determine, a view of landscape. The view would thus be partial, a vista rather than a prospect: a panorama would of course not have the constriction of a frame. Frames would tend to work best within a garden, with limited distances, but could on occasion be used to telling and special effect as in the 'surprise' view of Fountains Abbey from the gardens of Studley Royal (Fig.3.1).

3.1 'Surprise' view of Fountains Abbey from Studley Royal, North Yorkshire

3.2 Bastion terrace walk at Goldney, Bristol

One feature that acted as facilitator and encouraged the taste for looking outwards was the terrace walk. This dates back to formal gardens, when there might be a walk adjacent to the house from which one could look down upon and across the parterre. Bridgeman's long terrace walk at Oatlands (1727-8) was part of a geometrical layout but was subsequently made more natural, with a grass walk, in the mid-century. The views it commanded were of the flat Thames valley, though by an optical illusion the Oatlands lake, the Broadwater, appeared to continue as the Thames flowing under Walton bridge. Bridgeman also designed other such walks, such as the embankment at Sacombe, Hertfordshire. His contemporary Switzer laid out a walk with arrow-head bastions overlooking the countryside at Grimsthorpe, Lincolnshire. At Clifton, Bristol, Thomas Goldney built an extraordinary raised walk of grass with stone walls and parapets and ending in a bastion (Fig.3.2). The view was over the port of Bristol and to its Channel, where Goldney could witness his ships sailing in from the West Indies. Even in the late eighteenth century straight terrace walks were still being constructed, as at Polesden Lacey, Surrey.

The terrace walk became more naturalised as the century wore on. The three-quarter-mile uphill curving walk at Farnborough Hall, Warwickshire, looks out over rolling country, the site of Civil War battles, as reflected in the military-style bastions along the walk (Fig.3.3). It is itself decorated with buildings – an Ionic temple and a rococo oval pavilion by Sanderson Miller. In the same decade, the 1750s, the Rievaulx Terrace, Helmsley, North Yorkshire, followed the natural curve of a flattened hill top overlooking a vast valley. Rievaulx is perhaps the only example that deserves the epithet picturesque, and that is because of the view of the abbey below (see p.71). This can be compared with the earlier terrace walks, two at right angles to each

3.3 Terrace walk at Farnborough Hall, Warwickshire, with bastion viewing bays on left

other, at Duncombe Park nearby, where the views, though attractive, lack the same picturesque focus. So, although a terrace walk does not imply that either the garden itself or the view from it is necessarily picturesque, its popularity demonstrates a habit and taste for external scenery.

What has not always been fully recognised is how the view of the landscape changes. Not only might this be because of the season or the weather but, as Repton pointed out, the changing light as the day progresses can have a transforming impact. He observed, in considering the view of the Thames from the grounds at Purley, Berkshire:

> In the morning, when the sun was in the east, the landscape appeared to consist of wood, water, and distant country, with few artificial accompaniments; but in the evening, when the sun was in the west, objects presented themselves, which were in the morning scarcely visible. In the first instance, the Wood was in a solemn repose of shade, the Water reflecting a clear sky was so brilliantly illuminated, that I could trace the whole course of the river, the dark Trees were strongly contrasted by the vivid green of the meadows, and the outline of distant Hills was distinctly marked by the brightness of the atmosphere. I could scarcely distinguish any other objects; but these formed a pleasing landscape from the breadth or contrast of light and shade.

> In the evening the scene was changed; dark clouds reflected in the water rendered it almost invisible, the opposite hanging wood presented one glare of rich foliage; not so beautiful in the painter's eye, as when the top of each tree was relieved by small catching lights: but the most prominent features were the Buildings, the Boat, the Path, the Pales, and even the distant town of Reading, now strongly gilded by the opposite sun.[5]

The conclusion Repton draws, which not all would agree with, is that natural objects look best with the sun behind them and artificial objects appear best with the sun on them.

The outward view might well be sketched, by the tourist if the viewing station was on open ground, and by the owner's family, friends or visitors if the vantage point was within the estate. This might affect the end-product, for the view from a garden would tend to be from a point of comfort, whereas the tourist in a landscape might him or herself be already in a wild spot, thus giving the view more emotional and atmospheric immediacy. Treating the Picturesque as a purely visual experience serves to distance it: the full picturesque experience involved close contact. However, the process of producing a finished drawing or painting in itself reduced immediacy and introduced thought and judgment, since the on-the-spot sketch would usually be worked up later at leisure by the artist, as Gilpin did.

Mount Edgcumbe

Mount Edgcumbe, on the coast just inside the Cornish border and overlooking Plymouth Sound, is a breathtaking location and one where the natural topography has bestowed every conceivable picturesque favour. It evolved as a landscaped park through the eighteenth and early nineteenth centuries, and further areas within it are still being created today. It is rare among gardens in being extensively sea-girt, and the sea, together with the Sound and the mouth of the Tamar, provides the stunning outward views, experienced from a height. Standing on the front at Plymouth and looking across the water, one is drawn irresistibly by the siren lure of Mount Edgcumbe, waiting there to reveal its splendours.

Thomas Badeslade's plan of 1737 shows dense and broad blocks of trees, and this in itself would have screened many of the views. It was only from 1742, when Sir Richard Edgcumbe retired from politics and was created 1ˢᵗ Baron Edgcumbe, that the push towards landscaping truly began. During the 1740s the Ruined Chapel, which incorporated some genuine medieval fragments from the churches of St Lawrence and St George, went up on what was now open land, replacing an obelisk, and the Zig-Zags, steep winding paths at the edge of the cliffs, were installed. They were quite vertiginous and became known as The Horrors, causing young ladies to faint – a truly sublime spot. The lower paths have disappeared through cliff falls into the sea, thus proving the point.

The views out to sea, to the west and south-west, together with the balmy winds blowing in from that direction, gave the sense of a tropical or Mediterranean paradise, enhanced by the growing of palm trees and other exotic plants. John Swete commented that 'the arbutus, the myrtle and the orange tree appear indigenous'.[6] The stone or umbrella pine, associated with Italy, grew on the open hillside, and there were extensive plantations of more native species such as beech, based on the formal blocks of earlier days. Visitors were

3.4 The sea, looking south from Mount Edgcumbe, Cornwall, drawn and engraved by William Daniell, 1825

lyrical about the views and the location, David Garrick declaring it variously a Parnassus, 'this Paradise of the West' and 'the Iliad of Situations'.[7]

Although the sea and Plymouth Sound gave it its uniqueness, the views from Mount Edgcumbe encompassed other types of scenery from the vantage points in the park. There were landscape views stretching across to Exmoor, the busy town of Plymouth and the dockyard. With the movement of shipping on the water, the panorama therefore included a great deal of activity. By means of a 'hide and reveal' strategy, the drive would lead from views of the animated Sound to a calmer, open sea. The traffic on the water was seen as adding to the attractions of the place: in a revealing letter of 1778 Lady Edgcumbe wrote 'You have no idea what an amazing sight it is, 30 sail of line now lying under a terrace of shrubs as if only to ornament our Park!'[8] Eleven years later she wrote to Lady Harcourt to describe the occasion of a royal visit when 200 boats had turned out in support, oars raised in salute, 'looking like a wood'.[9] It was the height and distance away that converted close engagement with the activity into a remote objectivity, seeing the shipping as decoration rather than for its serious purpose. The

3.5   Italian Garden at Mount Edgcumbe, Cornwall, print after sketch by W Hake, c1820

height bestowed superiority, as J C Loudon implied when he wrote up his visit of 13 September 1842: 'We never before looked down on the sea, on shipping, and on a large town, all at our feet, from such a stupendous height. The effect on the mind is sublime in the highest degree, but yet blended with the beautiful. There was something to us quite unearthly in the feeling it created.'[10]

The outward views did not preclude interest within the gardens and park. Quite apart from the excitement of the Zig-Zags, there were two long drives to display the best of the internal scenery while at the same time presenting serial views of the sea. For variety there were a number of 'incidents' such as the Ruined Chapel, a stone arch and several seats. The planted amphitheatre was deformalised and made to appear like Milton's tree-clad walls of Eden in *Paradise Lost*, a point underlined by the creation of Milton's Temple at one side (1755). The Edgcumbes were a highly cultured family, and poets other than Milton made their presence felt: there are Thomson's Seat and a bust of the Italian Renaissance epic poet Ariosto, originally placed near the Orangery but later moved to the stairway in what became the Italian Garden. This was a development, along with the French Garden (also early nineteenth century) and the English Garden (late eighteenth), as an exercise in garden history or garden education, the earliest display of separate national styles together. The Italian Garden is particularly interesting (Fig.3.5), since it demonstrates an evolution from the Orangery garden of the late 1780s, when the architect, Lord Camelford, chose a quotation from Ariosto to go with the bust, to the Italian Garden proper thirty years later, when the 'Belvedere' with its stairway, niche for Ariosto, balustrade and statuary on top came into being. There may be a simple iconography of

3.6 John Nash's castellated house and adjacent garden at Luscombe, Devon, engraved by Le Petit after T Allom, c1830

the sculptures – Apollo, Venus and Bacchus being linked by association with the countryside, with Ariosto representing an epic poet who included three high-profile gardens in *Orlando Furioso* (Milton was also referred to as the English Ariosto). Other sculpture in the plots round the fountain continued the countryside theme (Ceres, Flora), while the Discobolus and Antinous provided a more athletic counterpoint. Not only is it the earliest Italian Garden by name in the country, setting a trend that would become enormously popular during the century, but it is the only one where iconography may be present: later examples were just ornamental.

Luscombe

The outward view from Luscombe, set back from the rocky Dawlish coast in Devon, almost constitutes a segment of Mount Edgcumbe, matching the vista of the sea from the amphitheatre there. Luscombe, the property of Charles Hoare of the banking family, sits in a narrow combe leading down from grassy heights and hanging woods towards the sea. Apart from the sea, the views upwards within the garden are of planted slopes at the top of the combe. In 1799 Repton was called in to embellish the grounds of this summer residence (also a home for Hoare's invalid wife) but it is not clear how much he achieved. The immediate environs of the castellated house, by John Nash, were adorned with lush planting of trees and shrubs (Fig.3.6), but although Repton had proposed in his Red Book 'a foreground of highly dressed Lawn and Pleasure Garden on which trees or shrubs may be planted to vary the surface',[11] credit is given by J C Loudon in 1842 to John Veitch, the late father of the nurseryman of that name.[12]

Encombe

This Dorset property, the seat of John Pitt, cousin of the great garden designer William Pitt the Elder, makes skilful use of the sea and incorporates it in the scenic experience of the park. It is a hilly estate, and lifted some height above the sea, which cannot be seen from most parts. However, it is an ever-present backdrop, never far from mind, and is brought closer to the house by means of the home lake (Fig.3.7), which, viewed from the house, appears to run into and become part of the sea by an illusion created by the levels – the sea is actually at some distance.

A consciously picturesque effect is created by the seventy-foot fall of a stream over a cliff down to the shore. Most waterfalls are, of course, inland, but this one is given a special character by being directly by the sea. Internally the garden has a rustic grotto with compartments including a Druidic altar, and a number of stones are deliberately positioned in the grass as seats.

There are many other coastal gardens of different periods where the sea plays a prominent role. One such in the picturesque era is Culzean, which is covered in the Scottish chapter (see p.132).

3.7　House and setting at Encombe, Dorset, anonymous print c1780

Piercefield

In the eighteenth century and into the nineteenth this estate, near the mouth of the Wye, was regarded as one of the greatest of picturesque sites – and that due principally to its external views, though there was plenty of excitement and interest within the grounds as well.[13] But it was the way in which those views were managed that is the key to the success of Piercefield (or Persfield as it was generally spelled at the time). The paths and the plantings, together with strategically placed seats, ensured optimum views of a varied and inspirational landscape: a lesser designer would not have known how to achieve such an arrangement even if he had had the eye to see where the best vantage points might lie.

The owner was Valentine Morris, who owed his income to the slave trade in Antigua, where his
father had plantations. With the advice of Richard Owen Cambridge, author and wit, he devised
a series of walks on his hillside and hilltop demesne which revealed the 'noble' situation. In
Gilpin's words, the 'ingenious proprietor'

> …hath shewn his rocks, his woods, and his precipices, under various forms; and to great advantage.
> Sometimes a broad face of rock is presented, stretching across a vast space, like the walls of a citadel.
> Sometimes it is broken by intervening trees. In other parts, the rocks rise above the woods; a little
> farther, they sink below them: sometimes, they are seen through them; and sometimes one series of
> rocks appears rising above another: and tho many of these objects are repeatedly seen, yet seen from
> different stations, and with new accompaniments, they appear new. The winding of the precipice is the
> magical secret, by which all these inchanting scenes are produced.[14]

The outward views were principally in two directions. One looked out across the flat base of
the Wye valley, where the river snaked round the farmland peninsula of Lancaut in a huge
horseshoe, to the great rock face of Wyndcliffe, part exposed and part clad with trees (Fig.3.8).
The other was to the ruined Chepstow Castle and the mouth of the river where it met the
Severn. Both could be seen from the Double View, a seat facing both ways. The only discordant
note was the dirty, muddy colour of the river. But, apart from the walks providing a series of
stunning views, there were a grotto, a Chinese seat, a cold bath, a Druids' temple, the Giant's
Cave and Lover's Leap, poised on a ledge above a 180' drop to occupy the attention within the
grounds. The Giant's Cave comprised a tunnel bored through the solid rock: over the entrance
the stone guardian crouched with a massive rock in his arms. Nearby guns were positioned
which went off creating an alarming echo.

3.8 The Wyndcliffe, as seen from Piercefield, Monmouthshire, print by J Newman, 1842

3.9 View of cliff estate at Winterdyne, Worcestershire, by TB Freeman (Bodleian Library, Oxford, Gough Maps 33, fol 70v)

The views from Piercefield pinpoint the central weakness or problem in the 'picturesque = suitable for painting' debate, namely that what was deemed suitable for a picture was, in the end, entirely subjective. Gilpin, revealingly, loved Piercefield yet pronounced it unpicturesque: 'We cannot however call these views picturesque. They are either presented from too high a point; or they have little to mark them as characteristic; or they do not fall into such compositioning as would appear to advantage on canvas.'[15] Those views were, however, in his opinion 'extremely romantic' because they let loose the imagination.

How different from Arthur Young, who has left the richest contemporary description of the place. He declared that one point in particular 'the united talents of a *Claud*, a *Poussin*, a *Vernet,* and a *Smith*, would scarcely be able to sketch,'[16] thus refuting Gilpin's claim that it was not suitable for sketching. The word romantic is used unsparingly, together with a vast downward view, that is characterised as full of the terrible Sublime. The finest views are described at great length, but there is one that exceeds all others because of the illusion created, that the distant Severn is actually at a higher level than, and closer to, the scenery in the middle ground:

> …imagination cannot form an idea of any thing more beautiful than what appears full to your ravished sight from this amazing point of view. You look down upon all the woody precipices, as if in another region, terminated by a wall of rocks; just above them appears the river *Severn* in so peculiar a manner, that you would swear it washed them, and that nothing parted you from it but those rocks, which are in reality four or five miles distant. This *deceptio visis* is the most exquisite I ever beheld.[17]

Young's conclusion was that Piercefield was the best of its kind that he had seen: 'In point of striking picturesque views, in the romantic stile, *Persfield* is exquisite.'[18] Unlike Gilpin, Young conflates picturesque and romantic, and, further, after discussing Painshill, compares the two estates with the judgment that Piercefield is 'superiorly *sublime*'.[19] For Young it encompassed the whole range of picturesque experience.

Thomas Whately also expatiates at some length on the views, especially of the Wyndcliffe, where he says the rocks piled up on each other resemble a ruined city. To him the juxtaposition of wood and rock was irresistible: 'The woods concur with the rocks to render the scenes of Persfield romantic.'[20] Gilpin, Whately and Young agree at least on the romantic feeling of Piercefield, unleashing fancies and associations.

Winterdyne

This Worcestershire garden, south of Bewdley, sits on the top and side of a steep escarpment above the Severn. It could well have found a place in the chapter on the Sublime, but is included here as a garden that is distinctly sublime within but has outward picturesque views. The paths, laid out by Sir Edward Winnington, are dangerous, and several are impassable today, cut out from the rock and clinging to the cliff face and edge. Along the way were various 'incidents' such as a Tea House, a sandstone tower (The Fort) and a summerhouse, which afforded special views across the river to the Blackstone Rock and Hermitage (see p.62). A contemporary view by T B Freeman (Fig. 3.9) shows rich planting cladding the cliff, so there was doubtless a good deal of the 'hide and reveal' experience as one edged nervously along the paths. Little is known about Winterdyne, but it is clearly a site that stands in need of recognition in any study of the picturesque garden.[21]

The last word may be left to Horace Walpole, who concluded that of all the elements of which a garden was composed, 'Prospect, animated prospect, is the theatre that will always be the most frequented…how rich, how gay, how picturesque the face of the country!…every journey is made through a succession of pictures.'[22]

1 Horace Walpole, *The History of the Modern Taste in Gardening* [1770] (New York: Ursus Press, 1995), pp.42-3.

2 Humphry Repton, *Fragments on the Theory and Practice of Landscape Gardening* (London: J Taylor, 1816), p.195.

3 *Ibid.*, p.197.

4 See Malcolm Andrews, *The Search for the Picturesque* (London: Scolar Press, 1989), pp.68-71.

5 Humphry Repton, *Observations on the Theory and Practice of Landscape Gardening* (London: J Taylor, 1803), pp.28-9.

6 Quoted in Peter Hunt, 'John Swete and the Picturesque', *Devon Gardens: An Historical Survey*, ed. Steven Pugsley (Stroud: Alan Sutton/Devon Gardens Trust, 1994), p.65.

7 *The Letters of David Garrick*, ed. D M Little and G M Kahrl (London: Oxford University Press, 1963), Vol.II, p.749.

8 Quoted in *Mount Edgcumbe Country Park* [illustrated guide book], n.d., p.10.

9 *Ibid.*, p.5.

10 John Claudius Loudon, *In Search of English Gardens: The Travels of John Claudius Loudon and his Wife Jane* (London: Century Books, 1990, pbk. ed.), p.243.

11 Quoted in Steven Pugsley, 'The Garden and Park in Devon', *Devon Gardens*, p.14.

12 Loudon, *In Search of English Gardens*, visit to Luscombe 8 September 1842, p.237.

13 For modern accounts of Piercefield, see Ivor Waters, *Piercefield on the Banks of the Wye* (Chepstow: FG Comber, 1975) and Elisabeth Whittle, '"All these Inchanting Scenes": Piercefield in the Wye Valley', *Garden History* 24:1, 1996, pp.148-61.

14 William Gilpin, *Observations on the River Wye* (London: R Blamire, 1789, second ed.), p.56.

15 *Ibid.*, p.57.

16 Arthur Young, *A Six Weeks Tour through the Southern Counties of England and Wales* (London: W Nicoll, 1768), p.136.

17 *Ibid.*, pp.132-3.

18 *Ibid.*, p.140.

19 *Ibid.*, p.192.

20 Thomas Whately, *Observations on Modern Gardening* (London: T Payne, 1793, fifth ed.), p.245.

21 See Timothy Mowl, *Historic Gardens of Worcestershire* (Stroud: Tempus, 2006), pp.79-80.

22 Walpole, *Modern Taste in Gardening*, pp.53-4, 56.

CHAPTER FOUR

Rustic Architecture

One of the principal features that appeared to distinguish the Picturesque from the Sublime in the eyes of many at the time was the sign of human intervention, usually architectural. The vastness and bareness of a mountain might well render it sublime, but judicious introduction of buildings or bridges could create or point up a picturesque scene. But the style of architecture would have to fit in with a naturalistic or rural setting, so that many buildings beloved of the mid-century pictorial garden, in which they would form decorative focal points, would be seen as incongruous in the later part of the century. The number of garden buildings tended anyway to fall away after about 1770.

It might be thought that a range of architectural styles (including classical, Gothic and *chinoiserie*) would be welcomed in the picturesque era because they provided variety, but the taste was much more for rustic artefacts, to bring them closer to the nature that surrounded them. Hence most of such structures were built from materials that could (or could supposedly) be found naturally in the grounds – tree trunks, roots, branches, thatch, moss, bark, pebbles, rocks. Simplicity was the keynote (and also the reason that most were so ephemeral that they have not survived).

The development of rustic architecture from rococo to picturesque can be traced in the publications of the period, particularly the pattern-books. It is in 1750 that we find the term 'rural' entering the coverage of these books – William and John Halfpenny's *Rural Architecture in the Chinese Taste*, balanced two years later by *Rural Architecture in the Gothick Taste*. Thomas Wright's suites of designs for rustic arbours and grottoes quickly followed in 1755 and 1758. William Wrighte's *Grotesque Architecture* (1767) bore the sub-title *Rural Amusement*. These designs were predominantly for novelty and to vary the decoration: picturesque architecture proper had to wait till the 1790s, with George Parkyns' *Six Designs for improving and embellishing Grounds* (1793) and John Plaw's *Rural Architecture* (1796). On a larger scale, a little later, came J B Papworth's *Rural Residences* of 1818, though these last two are more concerned with the house or villa.

Of all rustic structures the hermitage was the most prominent, and often the most memorable. This was in large part due to the supposed function, and in some cases to the occupant. The history of hermits, and indeed the story of contemplation in the garden, has been covered in John Dixon Hunt's *The Figure in the Landscape* (1976) and David Coffin's *The English Garden: Meditation and Memorial* (1994) and will not be discussed in detail here. But it is necessary to recognise that the idea of meditating in a garden or in a broader natural setting is venerable, going back to antiquity and the Bible, and was well established in poetry and painting. It was bound up with the concept of the garden as a retreat from the life of the world and of business, from the retirement of Roman emperors, commanders and writers onwards. Parallel was the notion of retreat for philosophical, or, more often, religious purposes: a hermit forswore the world in order to concentrate on contemplation of the divine and of moral questions. All this meant that by the time of the Picturesque hermits and contemplation were deeply embedded in cultural consciousness, though even in the seventeenth century some cynicism was expressed about the motives for solitary retreat.[1]

Melancholy, too, merged with contemplation from an early date. The 'humours' or temperaments were well in place by Elizabethan times, as seen in Ben Jonson's *Every Man in his Humour*, where a character asks for a stool to be melancholy on, and the two came together famously in Milton's poem *Il Penseroso*, where the hermit, in 'hairy gown and mossy cell', experiences the 'pleasures' that melancholy can provide via contemplation.

From early in the eighteenth century not only were hermitages constructed in gardens but working quasi-hermits were to be found. Pope, writing and dreaming in his grotto, was the most celebrated, and Stephen Duck, a minor poet, was installed as curator (and effectively hermit) in Richmond Gardens, where there were two structures, a hermitage by name and the thatched Merlin's Cave. The heyday for hermits, though, was after 1750, when their introduction was patently a gimmick, with the unfortunate participants merely hired servants not writers, philosophers or anchorites. Sometimes a permanent hermit was sought, such as Charles Hamilton advertised for at Painshill, with strict conditions and no payment until seven years had elapsed (the impecunious Hamilton's purse was safe). The traditional story is that the successful applicant, having been provided with nothing but a camlet robe, a Bible, an hourglass, a hassock and a rush mat, plus food and drink from the house, was discovered at a nearby inn after only three weeks. More often, however, someone would dress up as a hermit for ad hoc occasions when there were particular visitors to impress, such as Gilbert White's younger brother Harry, who donned a robe and a false beard at Selborne to entertain at the very hermitage he himself had constructed. If real hermits were hard to come by, wax or mechanical figures would be installed, to be operated by the guide, as at Hawkstone, where several generations of the Jones family, acted as animators, slipping behind the scenes to work the levers and speak through a tube. This was to replace the original ancient live hermit, who seems to have been permanently ninety-four. Several hermits, including the one at Hawkstone, were known as Father Francis after a poem by Gilbert West which was known by 1743.[2]

The notion of a hermit in a garden always trembled on the edge of the absurd, and ridicule was not slow in coming. Dr Johnson descended into bathos after a seemingly serious opening:

> Hermit hoar, in solemn cell,
>   Wearing out life's evening gray;
> Smite thy bosom, sage, and tell,
>   Where the bliss? and which the way?
> Thus I spoke; and speaking sigh'd;
>   – Scarce repress'd the starting tear;-
> When the smiling sage reply'd –
>   – Come, my lad, and drink some beer.[3]

Richard Graves sent up the idea of hermits in his novel *Columella* and the poem *Euphrosyne*, and Horace Walpole equated melancholy with contemplation when he wrote in 1770, 'But the ornament whose merit soonest fades, is the hermitage, or scene adapted to contemplation. It is almost comic to set aside a quarter of one's garden to be melancholy in.'[4]

Hermitages developed stylistically during the century. Early examples such as William Kent's at Richmond Gardens and Stowe, or his simple pedimented portico at Esher Place, were recognisably formal architecture, even if rough stonework was applied. At both Richmond and Stowe one turret was missing, as if to suggest a ruin and antiquity, but they were large structures and prominent buildings (Fig.4.1). A similar example was at Kensington Gardens, possibly attributable to Kent. Yet there were one or two signs that a

4.1   William Kent's hermitage at Stowe, Buckinghamshire

more primitive, rustic approach was possible and appropriate. The antiquarian William Stukeley built a jumbled structure of stonework in his garden at Barnhill, Stamford, Lincolnshire, c1730 which included a cascade, a seat, an arch crowned with a ball and pedestal, and a covered seat or alcove. A Gothic window had been taken from a medieval church.[5] And in 1724 Pope wrote about a 'Hermit's Seat' at Sherborne, Dorset, which combined rusticity in the form of rough stones with urns and pedestals in the same style.[6]

Mid-century hermitages tended to be fanciful and much less solid. In the rococo period decoration was all – Thomas Wright's designs for arbours and grottoes that might serve as hermitages are self-consciously quaint. Charles Hamilton's hermitage at Painshill, dating from about 1752, was composed of tree trunks and branches, and indeed looks like a tree-house from the front. It had a remnant of formality – a lantern above the thatched roof – but fir trunks with bark still on formed the rear of the building, and the Gothic windows were shaped by branches.

Thomas Wright's best-known (and surviving) essay in this form was the hermitage at Badminton (1747). It was originally deep within a dense grove but is now on open land, which alters the effect considerably, losing the earlier seclusion. Large knobbly tree trunks provide the framework, and the walls are of tree roots, branches and sticks. The whole is thatched (Fig.4.2). Interestingly, the interior resembles classical forms but in rough wood.[7] It was supposedly the cell of

4.2   Hermitage at Badminton, Gloucestershire

the enchantress Urganda from a sixteenth-century Spanish romance. Wright built a similar cell commemorating Bladud, the legendary founder of Bath, at Stoke Park, near Bristol, but that has long since gone.

The West Midlands trio of Enville, Hagley and The Leasowes each had buildings described at some point as hermitages. At Enville, a thatched cottage with Gothic windows of coloured glass and constructed from roughly laid stones and bricks was first mentioned in 1756 as a pheasantry and hermitage for the keeper of the fowl.[8] Much earlier, possibly c1739, was the hermitage at Hagley, one of a quartet of rustic structures in Hermitage Wood, and related to the others by style and function: one for instance was the Seat of Contemplation.[9] While the latter was just a curving seat set in an alcove, the hermitage was set in a grove of horse chestnuts and had a fountain in front. It was a square structure with two rooms, one with a couch and the familiar lines from *Il Penseroso*, slightly adapted. The materials were tree stumps, trunks and roots, the interstices being filled with earth and moss.[10] The hermitage at The Leasowes, c1740, a simple cave in the corner of a field, was criticised by Lord Lyttelton of Hagley and was subsequently demolished. William Shenstone had had the idea of creating a 'Hermit's Seat' on higher ground above it, a structure that later became known as the Gothic Alcove.[11]

At Marston, Somerset, a hermitage was put up in 1754 for the owner's youngest son, presumably as a plaything, though the furniture indicated it was habitable. A deep path cut in the surrounding wood led to a sort of small courtyard fenced with horses' heads and bones. Pococke described it as a poorly thatched cabin, with a couple of seats – one hollowed out from a tree trunk – a bed covered with straw, a chimney, and some as yet incomplete crude furniture.[12]

The hermitage at Selborne was erected in 1758 by Harry White on a wooded hill known as the Hanger. Once more there was an inscription from *Il Penseroso*. The hermitage took the form of a thatched hut and, as we have seen, Harry played the part of the hermit, but this was strictly for entertaining family visitors.[13] In general, the growing rusticity of the hermitage was accompanied by a downplaying of the seriousness with which the occupant was to be taken.

In a secluded corner at the Barrells, Ullenhall, Warwickshire, a grassy hollow surrounded by wood was surmounted by a hermitage of chestnut palings with a thatched roof. Henrietta, Lady Luxborough, who had been exiled to Barrells by her husband, had the roof decorated with clematis. She herself acted as an enforced hermit, often reading there in clement weather: the wooden seats were well cushioned for the purpose.[14]

Prior to 1765 a hermitage found its way into the remarkable collection of follies within a very small space at the eight-acre woodland garden of Sir Samuel Hellier at The Woodhouse, Wombourne, near Wolverhampton. Clearly indebted to the nearby estates of Hagley and The Leasowes, The Woodhouse (developed up till at least 1773) was a cultural garden, containing inscriptions, a Music Room, Handel's Temple, a grotto and an ornate Gothic Seat among others. Hellier's hermitage was elaborate and the result of much care and attention (including subsequent maintenance). The building was approached through a gate set in an uneven chestnut paling in which a cross was placed. The exterior opened like the mouth of a cave, with separate stone seats inside and a pebble floor. This, however, was only the entrance: the interior contained several small chambers, with trunks, roots and moss as the visible materials. The mechanical hermit, yet another Saint Francis, was positioned by an altar and was activated by springs and levers. Correspondence between Hellier and his steward, John Rogers, from 1767 to 1782 shows that the hermitage was a constant preoccupation and he was for ever seeking to expand it and elaborate the contents as well as keeping everything in good repair (a constant worry, with damp and woodworm).[15] The amount of time that Hellier spent on the hermitage invests it with almost the same significance as Pope's grotto held for the poet, yet the purpose seems to have been largely to entertain.

Robert Adam, known primarily for other architectural forms, essayed a hermitage at Kedleston, where (for once) he had charge of the design of the grounds as well as of the house. In 1761-2 a formal temple-like structure was built with a colonnade of eleven columns.[16] Only the thatched dome conveyed rusticity, so in some ways Adam was behind his time.

Advanced rusticity came in 1771 with the hermitage at Stourhead. Charles Hamilton of Painshill advised on its location (twenty years after his own) on a zig-zag path up towards the Temple of Apollo. It was constructed from wood, old knobbly oaks with their bark still on furnishing both the exterior decoration and interior lining. Henry Hoare jokingly wrote to his granddaughter that he himself would be the hermit. It had stone seats and an inner chamber: all that remains is a stone recess at one side of the path.[17]

Sometimes genuine caves, either natural or with the hollow extended, would be pressed into service to provide ready-made eighteenth-century hermitages. Such was the case in north Worcestershire, where the sandstone cliffs proffered a multitude of caves. A few had been utilised from medieval times. That at Blackstone Rock, opposite Ribbesford, was an elaborate affair with a chapel and five chambers including a study and a belfry, already in place by 1721. From the cliff the hermit had a magnificent view of the Severn and of the woods overhanging its banks, truly anticipating the Picturesque. The Redstone Rock hermitage at Stourport, down river from Blackstone, consists of multiple caves and cells which could have formed both sites for contemplation and hiding places. At Radston's Ferry, Astley, a genuinely medieval collection of cells included a chapel and altars, with space for 500 men.[18]

4.3 The hermitage at Warkworth, Northumberland, from the river, anonymous print c1780

A famous hermitage carved from the rock was at Warkworth, Northumberland (Fig.4.3). As can be seen, it is beside a river, and the rockwork was supplemented by stone wings or walls. This became a considerable tourist attraction in the later eighteenth century and was engraved by Woollett among others. The hermitage may date back as far as the late fourteenth century:

the inner part, possibly based on an existing cave, consisted of a chapel and a smaller chamber, both with altars, which was used as a chantry till the dissolution of the monasteries. It has not been appreciably altered since. But it was romanticised in the later eighteenth century by Bishop Percy's popular ballad *The Hermit of Warkworth* (1771), which told a totally different story, a lurid legend of the Bertram family that is almost certainly fiction. Where the natural rock was lacking *in situ* it might be replaced by the introduction of stones to construct the hermitage, as at Stukeley's Stamford Garden.

4.4 Hermitage at Brocklesby, Lincolnshire

By 1787 the thatched hermitage at Hawkstone showed the Picturesque in full swing. Another late century version appeared at Brocklesby, Lincolnshire, where the rear is distinctly solid, of brick, but the entrance presents a kind of arch of branches, with dressing of rough stone (Fig.4.4). Hermitages continued to be popular, though more as ornaments, into the nineteenth century: that at Bicton, Devon, with its knucklebone floor, is dated 1839.

One of the architectural tragedies of recent times was the burning down of the elaborate hermitage at Burley-on-the-Hill, Leicestershire, in 1965. Tree trunk columns supported a thatched roof, and the pebble and knucklebone floor carried the date 1807, though the hermitage boasted a resident and may have been earlier. The windows were open gratings, unglazed, and the interior had furniture of crude and uncouth shapes and forms. The ceiling was fan-vaulted and was filled in with bark: in the words of Barbara Jones, who saw it in good condition: 'The ribs were slats of wood like thin bones nailed thickly together and the pendants ended in elm bosses. To embellish this rich effect still further the junction of ceiling and wall was heavily fringed with twigs.'[19] Outside, bones were strewn around.

There has been a tendency to conflate hermitages and root-houses, as David Coffin did. While they might be similar in construction and materials, they were usually differentiated at the time, as we can see from those owners who had both in their gardens and designated them accordingly. Shenstone had a hermitage and two if not three root-houses, Lyttelton had a root-house just below his hermitage, and Hellier at The Woodhouse also had both and wrote about them under the two distinct names. One distinguishing feature was the cross that frequently surmounted a hermitage (e.g. at The Leasowes or Selborne), but the main difference was that a hermitage was usually more substantial, being fancifully or actually habitable. A root-house was generally for temporary seclusion or shelter. It could be composed of branches and trunks of trees as well as roots.

In Thomas Wright's first suite of designs, the term 'arbour' is used to cover a range of rustic structures, though at this stage (1755) they are noticeably more architectural than some later models. Quite apart from the design interest, Wright gives us the purpose of each of his 'arbours'. One is a 'cabin' mainly for shade in the summer; another is a hut or hovel, for solitude;

another is of the 'Parasol Kind', open and commanding an extensive view; one is an aviary; one is for entertainment *al fresco*; and his 'Druid's Cell, or Arbour of the Hermitage Kind' is expressly for study or 'philosophical Retirement'. The Druids had long been perceived to be, or to include, philosophers and priests: Wright was as fascinated with them as was Stukeley. The designs for grottoes are cognate: some are for ornament by shells, corals or fossils, one is 'suppos'd to be the Habitation of a Bramin or Druid' and the last is for 'a Grotto of the Antique Ruin Kind, supposed to have been the Abode of an Anchorite'. They are all of stone where the arbours were of timber, even apparently cut from the solid rock in one case – but still architectural.

4.5 Root house at Spetchley, Worcestershire

4.6 Reconstructed Witch's House at Hestercombe, Somerset

The best example of a root-house that survives is at Spetchley, Worcestershire (Fig.4.5), though that is difficult to date, and may be from a later period. The re-created Witch's House at Hestercombe might be so described (Fig.4.6), comprising a thatched hut of branches and roots, with niches inside containing the figure of a witch and paintings of an owl and cat. Most, however, have disappeared, such as the root-house at Hagley, made of stumps of wood and turfed over, with moss applied on the top and on the inside. A seat was put together from sticks. Likewise the root-house dedicated to Lord Stamford at The Leasowes was a simple structure, a curving wall with a seat, and soil on the top. An intriguing root-house (perhaps identifiable with the 'hermitage' mentioned in sale particulars) was at Blaise some time before Repton, composed of roots and branches of trees. It took the form of a domed shelter with three arched openings and knobbly columns and finial. Close by stood a Gothic window framed in a screen.[20]

Closely related to hermitages and root-houses was the Seat of Contemplation at Hagley, linked with the hermitage, pebble alcove and root-house in Hermitage Wood. This seat was a curving bench within an alcove decorated with sheep bones and a ceiling featuring a star made of coloured shells. The inscription, All is Vanity, was written in split snail shells. Other germane buildings would be temples with columns covered with bark, such as Thomas Wright designed, and Druids' Cells, again as Wright loved to create. These are to be distinguished from Druids' Temples, which are or were the upright stone circles mentioned on p.97. From the 1770s Mrs Coade's factory produced a Coade stone Druid which graced many a garden – The Vyne, Hampshire; Croome Court; Priory Park, Chichester, West Sussex (moved from the town). Not only did Druids suggest, romantically, a long distant native past but they were said to have venerated trees, particularly the oak, and the mistletoe, and fitted very easily into the Picturesque.

Bridges, too, changed with the evolution of taste into the Picturesque. For a good deal of the century the classical (or neo-classical Palladian) style held sway, but primitive and rustic bridges came into fashion particularly in the later years. To start with, 'rustic bridges' were often of rough stone, and occasionally turfed, as at West Wycombe in the 1750s, but gradually wood became the material of choice and some seemingly flimsy and perilous structures came into being. They might well bear titles such as 'Alpine Bridge', as at Hafod, where it crossed foaming and rushing waterfalls. Richard Payne Knight's bridges at Downton were certainly skimpy and close to nature. The Alpine Bridge at Hawkstone crossed a chasm in an area designated as 'Switzerland', and its shakiness produced the correct *frisson*.

4.7 Circular temple from Humphry Repton, *Observations on the Theory and Practice of Landscape Gardening*, 1803, p.53

A separate development was the use of cast-iron. Often following the model of the Iron Bridge in Coalbrookdale, cast-iron bridges proliferated at home and on the continent, though the results were regular and geometrical rather than rustic (see chapter eight). But although a primitive bridge of timber would be most apt and fitting for a picturesque scene, any sort of bridge would indicate human presence and enliven what might otherwise be a bleak landscape – see Gilpin's aquatint in Scotland (Fig.9.2).

Thomas Whately considered that, where a scene was grand/sublime or 'elegant', the plainer the bridge the better, so it could be perceived as just a crossing, not an ornament: a 'foot bridge, of planks only, guarded on one hand by a common rail, and supported by a few ordinary piles, is often more proper…it is the utmost simplicity of cultivated nature'.[21] A stone bridge was, however, preferable for a 'grand' or polished scene. It might have special impact if ruinous:

> In wild and romantic scenes may be introduced a ruined stone bridge, of which some arches may be still standing, and the loss of those which are fallen may be supplied by a few planks, with a rail thrown over the vacancy. It is a picturesque object; it suits the situation; and the antiquity of the passage, the care taken to keep it still open, though the original building is decayed, the apparent necessity which thence results for a communication, give it an imposing air of reality.[22]

Repton considered the questions of rustic architecture and appropriateness in various places in his Red Books and other writings. He did not actually object to an ornamental building or folly, provided the style fitted in with the scenery. He illustrated a circular temple (a composite of the second and fifth designs in Thomas Wright's suite of arbours nearly fifty years before) (Fig.4.7) with the comment 'in rude scenery, as on a knoll or promontory in a forest, the same idea [of a domed circular temple] may be preserved in a thatched hovel supported by rude trunks of trees; yet as the beauty of such an object will greatly depend on the vegetation, it should be planted with ivy, or vines, and other creeping plants should be encouraged to spread their foliage over the thatch'.[23] But when it came to cottages in the landscape, the whole point was habitation, as Repton proclaimed in reference to Blaise:

> Some object was wanting to enliven the scenery; a temple, or a pavilion, in this situation, would have reflected light, and formed a contrast with the dark woods; but such a building would not have appeared to be inhabited, this cottage therefore derives its chief beauty from that which cannot easily be expressed by painting; the ideas of motion, animation, and inhabitancy, contrasted with those of stillness and solitude. Its form is meant to be humble, without meanness; it is, and appears the habitation of a labourer who has the care of the neighbouring woods; its simplicity is the effect of art, not of neglect or accident.[24]

4.8 Norwegian Hut at Fonthill, Wiltshire, from John Rutter, *Delineations of Fonthill Abbey*, 1823, p.91

4.9 Log hut at Gatchina, Russia

Rustic huts and the like could take various forms, such as Beckford's primitive Norwegian Hut at Fonthill (Fig.4.8). Log cabins were popular particularly on the continent, and one extraordinary example has survived at Gatchina, Russia (Fig.4.9), where, like some of Marie-Antoinette's rustic buildings in her Hameau at the Petit Trianon, Versailles, a simple exterior concealed a sumptuous, richly decorated interior. Variations on rustic huts proliferated in the nineteenth century – moss huts (of wood, with moss pressed into the wall interstices), heath houses (heath used instead of moss and also for the thatch) and bark houses, such as the recently-collapsed Bark Temple at Exton, Rutland. Sometimes they would be in quasi-national styles, such as the Bengal cottage, the Scots cottage, the Polish hut with fir roof, and Russian, Swedish and Danish huts. A South Seas hut composed of sticks and reeds formed the focal point of 'A Scene in Otaheite' at Hawkstone in the later eighteenth century.

Whately believed in decorum, i.e. that which was apposite. A garden, he maintained, could admit any kind of architecture, however exotic and varied, if it were for adornment only. However, if it was intended to reflect the scenery and even enhance it, then the situation had to be taken into account. Large, wide extents of heath, moor or plain could be broken in uniformity by a simple cottage, while a hermitage (for instance) was best placed out of public sight as opposed to a castle, which should stand prominent on a hill. Agricultural areas, such as a large field or sheep-walk, 'will not be disgraced by a cottage, a Dutch barn, or a hay-stack'. However, buildings are limited in their power: they can nudge a scene in a certain direction but not alter it radically: 'they may abate horrors, but they will never convert them into graces; they may make a tame scene agreeable, and even interesting, not romantic; or turn solemnity into cheerfulness, but not into gaiety'.[25]

Rustic architecture, then, was particularly suited to wilder picturesque scenes (Hafod, Downton), though in those cases the less overtly architectural the better. Emotional and romantic associations might add a further dimension, and inhabited structures would add human warmth to a prospect.

1 John Dixon Hunt, *The Figure in the Landscape: Poetry, Painting and Gardening during the Eighteenth Century* (Baltimore: Johns Hopkins University Press, 1976, 1989), p.9.
2 Mike Cousins, 'Mereworth Castle, Kent', *Follies* 76, 2010, p.10.
3 Samuel Johnson, *Poems* (New Haven and London: Yale University Press, 1964), pp.294-5.
4 Horace Walpole, *The History of the Modern Taste in Gardening* [1770] (New York: Ursus Press, 1995), p.53.
5 Todd Longstaffe-Gowan, *The London Town Garden 1700-1840* (New Haven and London: Yale University Press, 2001), p.116.
6 David R Coffin, *The English Garden: Meditation and Memorial* (Princeton, NJ: Princeton University Press, 1994), p.91.
7 *Ibid.*, p.97.
8 Michael Symes and Sandy Haynes, *Enville, Hagley, The Leasowes: Three Great Eighteenth-Century Gardens* (Bristol: Redcliffe Press, 2010), p.98.
9 Michael Cousins, 'Hagley Park, Worcestershire', *Garden History* 35: Supplement 1, 2007, pp.16-18.
10 *Ibid.*, p.126.
11 *Ibid.*, pp.169, 181.
12 Coffin, *The English Garden*, p.99.
13 *Ibid.*, pp.105-6.
14 Jane Brown, *My Darling Heriott: Henrietta Luxborough, Poetic Gardener and Irrepressible Exile* (London: Harper Press, 2006), p.198.
15 Dianne Barre, 'Sir Samuel Hellier (1736-84) and his garden buildings: part of the Midlands "garden circuit" in the 1760s-70s?', *Garden History* 36:2, 2008, pp.314-16, 323-5.
16 Leslie Harris, *Robert Adam and Kedleston* (London: The National Trust, 1987), p.86.
17 Kenneth Woodbridge, *The Stourhead Landscape* (London: The National Trust, 1982), pp.27, 55.
18 Timothy Mowl, *Historic Gardens of Worcestershire* (Stroud: Tempus, 2006), pp.77-9.
19 Barbara Jones, *Follies & Grottoes* (London: Constable, 1974), p.182.
20 Nigel Temple, *John Nash & the Village Picturesque* (Gloucester: Alan Sutton, 1979), pp.48-50.
21 Thomas Whately, *Observations on Modern Gardening* (London: T Payne, 1793, fifth ed.), p.76.
22 *Ibid.*, p.77.
23 Humphry Repton, *Observations on the Theory and Practice of Landscape Gardening* (London: J Taylor, 1803), p.153.
24 *Ibid.*, p.155n.
25 Whately, *Observations*, pp.119-133.

CHAPTER FIVE

Ruins

Ruins were one of the most compelling ways in which to render a scene picturesque. They fulfilled three criteria highly valued by Gilpin and his contemporaries – visually they were irregular and broken; intellectually they would carry historical or other associations; and emotionally they would create nostalgia or perhaps sadness at the destructive power of time. They might also appeal to the imagination, in forming mental pictures of how they might have looked and been used in their prime.

A great many medieval relics were to be found in the eighteenth century. An owner might be lucky enough to have one within his property, or, if beyond, he might devise a view to it. But in the majority of cases, of course, there were no such relics, and purpose-built ruins sprang up in the most unlikely places. Reaction to such fake ruins was on the whole sympathetic, in some cases indicating a willing suspension of disbelief. It depended partly on how authentic the ruin looked: Horace Walpole commented that Sanderson Miller's fine sham castle at Hagley (Fig.1.7) had 'the true rust of the barons' wars' only five years after its construction.[1]

The taste for ruins pre-dated the Picturesque by some time. Their powerful visual and emotional appeal was experienced particularly on the Grand Tour, where not only could the remains of antiquity be seen in profusion, especially in Rome, but artists such as Clérisseau and Piranesi, both based in Rome, depicted classical ruins in a heightened, romanticised manner. Since their prints were often among the souvenirs the Grand Tourists brought back with them, memories and impressions would be coloured by these images. At the same time there was a growing feeling that Britain itself possessed old monuments and remnants that were worthy of study and of consideration by the tourist. While the ruins in Rome were classical, though some Italian Renaissance gardens were by then neglected and falling into decay as well, those in Britain were generally Gothic and medieval, whether religious (abbeys) or secular (castles).

As early as the first decade of the century, Vanbrugh as we have seen anticipated the taste for ruins in a landscape in his plea for the retention of the remains of Woodstock Manor at Blenheim. Artists and designers gradually began to promote ruins, some clearly fantasies rather than realistic proposals. In 1728 Batty Langley suggested, in his *New Principles of Gardening,* the erection of classical ruins to terminate a walk or *allée*; failing this, a painting on canvas would suffice. This was carried out subsequently at Vauxhall Gardens by means of a painting of the Ruins of Palmyra at the end of a long walk and of a ruined Roman bridge to shut off one of the cross-walks. Clérisseau taught, and influenced, William Chambers and Robert Adam, who both drew sections of ruins which may or may not have had some connection with actual proposals for, respectively, Kew and Kedleston.

The impact of ruins was taken up by several theorists and writers of the day. Shenstone considered that they derived their power of pleasing from irregularity of surface, which produced variety, together with

…the latitude they afford the imagination, to conceive an enlargement of their dimensions, or to recollect any events or circumstances appertaining to their pristine grandeur and solemnity. The breaks in them should be as bold and abrupt as possible…Events relating to them may be stimulated by numberless little artifices; but it is ever to be remembered, that high hills and sudden descents are most suitable to castles; and fertile vales, near wood and water, most imitative of the usual situation for abbeys and religious houses; large oaks, in particular, are essential to these latter.[2]

The reference to imitation suggests that what Shenstone has in mind are sham ruins (such as he put up himself at The Leasowes) rather than conservation of genuine relics. Gilpin, on the other hand, preferred ruins to be real, although that did not stop him admiring false ones more than once. But the emotional impact was all important: in Shenstone's words, 'A ruin, for instance, may be neither new to us, nor majestick, nor beautiful, yet afford that pleasing melancholy which proceeds from a reflexion on decayed magnificence.'[3] Lord Kames, while agreeing that ruins afforded 'a sort of melancholy pleasure', distinguished between responses to Gothic and to classical ruins. In his opinion Gothic ruins represented the triumph of time over strength, which Kames found a melancholy but not unpleasant thought, but classical ruins indicated the triumph of barbarity over taste, a gloomy and discouraging thought.[4]

William Chambers introduced a further dimension in *A Dissertation on Oriental Gardening* (1772), his fanciful account of Chinese gardens. He maintained that the Chinese cultivated particular areas for autumnal effect, and that ruins are best displayed in such spots to bring out their emotional appeal: '…to indicate the debility, the disappointments, and the dissolution of humanity; which, by co-operating with the dreary aspect of autumnal nature, and the inclement temperature of the air, fill the mind with melancholy, and incline it to serious reflections.'[5] This would be equally applicable to English gardens.

Thomas Whately considered issues relating to buildings in gardens, such as placing or appropriateness, as well as form, before concluding with a discussion of ruins and how they should appear in terms of positioning and their relation to plantings:

…they are a class by themselves, beautiful as objects, expressive as character, and peculiarly calculated to connect, with their appendages, into elegant groupes; they may be accommodated with ease to irregularity of ground, and their disorder is improved by it; they may be intimately blended with trees and thickets, and the interruption is an advantage; for imperfection and obscurity are their properties; and to carry the imagination to something greater than is seen, their effect.[6]

Whately believed that all ruins 'excite an enquiry into the former state of the edifice, and fix the mind in a contemplation of the use it was applied to', recollecting a past that 'is preserved only in history' and which occasions 'certain sensations of regret, of veneration, or compassion.' An old mansion might cause reflections on the domestic life and the hospitality previously enjoyed there, and any building in decay is contrasted with its former pristine state.[7] Whately admits that all this applies to genuine remains, but sham ruins can raise similar impressions though not so strongly. If a ruin is false, its design and purpose should at least be clear, in order to aid the imagination, and the appearance of age should be as plausible as possible.[8] Whately's chosen example of a real ruin is Tintern Abbey – though it illustrates his points well it is not actually a garden building, nor is it to be seen from a garden. It was often thought (e.g. by Arthur Young) that ruins generally looked best from a distance.

Gilpin thought that no entire standing house could be picturesque because it would be regular, whereas ruins were picturesque on account of their irregularity. He claimed that Britain was pre-eminent for ruined abbeys, and blessed the name of Henry VIII for bequeathing such picturesque dilapidations. Among many ruins he described, Tintern Abbey again stood out, as it did for many a tourist. He considered the site too tidy and cleaned-up, but 'the outside of the ruin, which is the chief object of *picturesque curiosity*, is still left in all it's wild, and native rudeness.'[9] This comment resembles his reaction to Fountains Abbey, which he also found too neat and kempt.

Gothic ruins, whether secular or religious, could be regarded positively, even complacently. A ruined castle would indicate the collapse of feudalism, while a derelict abbey would demonstrate the overthrow of popery and superstition.[10]

Derelict abbeys provided the perfect focus of a picturesque scene, visually and by association. Gilpin claimed that no country could compete with Britain for ruins of this kind.[11] In addition to Tintern and a number in Scotland and Wales, the most well-known to visitors were the Cistercian cluster in North Yorkshire, some of which were either in parks or could be seen from gardens. Bolton Abbey complements the adjacent water effects (see pp.148-9) in a park cultivated by successive Dukes of Devonshire, though Jervaulx Abbey in the Ure Valley, and Byland in Ryedale district were in more natural landscapes. Easby Abbey, on a bank of the Swale, Richmond, North Yorkshire, was not actually Cistercian but run by the 'White Canons' of the similar Premonstraterian order. Roche Abbey, depicted on various occasions by Paul Sandby, was a focal feature of Sandbeck Park, seat of Lord Scarbrough, and formed 'a picture inexpressibly charming' with trees around the high transept walls and light falling on the abbey from the western sun. In September 1774 'Capability' Brown was brought in to embellish the abbey and its grounds 'with Poet's feeling and with Painter's eye' (for which he charged extra), the result being to raise the ground to cover up the foundations.[12] This predictably incurred the displeasure of Gilpin, who liked his ruins wild and neglected, though other visitors approved.

Fountains Abbey, near Ripon, presents a particularly interesting case study. It was in the time of John Aislabie early in the century that the possibilities of incorporating the abbey into the grounds of Studley Royal were envisaged – the motivation may have been partly acquisitional but the visual effect was undoubtedly important, indicating a prescient taste for the Picturesque while the abbey remained in other hands. Aislabie was unable to fulfil his dream, although a sale had almost been agreed in 1720. It would have presented a complete contrast to the cool, elegant geometry of the Moon Ponds at the heart of Studley Royal. But his son William was more determined, and from 1742 set out both to commemorate John and his work and to strike out in a new, picturesque direction himself. This took the form of developing the Mackershaw Valley on the opposite side to the abbey (see p.85) and then to creating Hackfall.

Persistence over Fountains Abbey eventually triumphed, and William Aislabie purchased the abbey and its ground in 1768. John had built an artificial mount, later known as Tent Hill, to block the view of Studley Royal from the abbey, though the latter could still be seen from the gardens, particularly from the top of the mount. But from 1768 the river was shaped and the approach fashioned to provide vistas of the abbey, and from a height above the Skell valley a 'surprise' view between the trees was created from what became known as Anne Boleyn's Seat (Fig.3.1). Studley Royal finally became a superlative formal garden in the centre with picturesque wings, each of different character, to either side.

5.1 One of the thirteen glimpses of Rievaulx Abbey, North Yorkshire, from the terrace

Rievaulx Abbey constitutes a focal point on which a series of 'pictures' is directed. Situated on the flat valley below the great curving Rievaulx Terrace, half a mile in length, the abbey is glimpsed through thirteen separate gaps in the planting on the slope above it. These gaps, spread out along the length of the terrace, display the abbey in a sequence of snapshots showing it from a panorama of different angles. The terrace was the work of Thomas Duncombe II, complementing his father's curving terrace at Duncombe Park, and mirroring it with a temple at each end. The date of Rievaulx Terrace was probably 1757, a full forty years after Duncombe Terrace and exhibiting a far more picturesque taste in the treatment of how the abbey was to be viewed. Arthur Young described it in 1770 as a 'most bewitching spot', while his first glimpse of the abbey revealed 'scattered trees appearing amongst the ruins in a stile too elegantly picturesque to admit description'.[13] Young's description brings out the range of, and changes in, the scenery as a whole as seen from the terrace, though the abbey is clearly the highlight. Michael Charlesworth points out, however, that Thomas Gray and William Mason, closely following Young in date, identified the valley floor view of the abbey as the truly picturesque one. A later generation (T D Whitaker, 1820), indeed, even found the hilly landscape visible from the terrace disagreeable. The interpretation of these differing opinions and the significance of 'distancing' the abbey are discussed in Charlesworth's insightful essay.[14] Visitors, though, generally admired the view from the terrace but sometimes objected to the view of the terrace from the abbey, the temples appearing too modern and incongruous.

The Yorkshire abbeys, magnificent though they are, were not the only ones, and (for example) Paul Sandby also painted watercolours of Wenlock Abbey, Shropshire, sited on land belonging to the Welsh antiquarian Sir Watkin Williams Wynn, who is credited with saving the abbey from steady depredation of its stone. A farmhouse was attached to part of the ruin, which stood in detached fragments. The rural activity plus the vegetation growing up round the pieces of the abbey heightened its picturesque appeal.[15] Sir Watkin also owned Valle Crucis Abbey,

North Wales, but the plantings round
it were criticised.[16] Other abbeys in
Wales admired for their picturesqueness
included Neath, West Glamorgan,
Llandaff Cathedral, South Glamorgan,
and Llanthony Abbey or Priory,
Monmouthshire, where 'dreariness and
fertility' unite in a deep vale.[17] There
were several more abbeys sought out
at the time, such as Buildwas, Leiston
(Suffolk), Malmesbury and Glastonbury,
but with no garden associations (except
for straight rows of low-growing plants
at Glastonbury), likewise the monastery
at Kelso, St Botolph's Priory, Colchester,
and Castle Acre Priory, Norfolk, which,
like Wenlock Abbey, had been converted
into a farmhouse.

5.2 Ruins at Stanton Harcourt, Oxfordshire, engraved by William
Watts after Paul Sandby, 1778

On a smaller scale, and fewer in number, were ruined chapels which formed part of an old manor
house or mansion. One such was the chapel at Stanton Harcourt, Oxfordshire, which survived
along with the kitchen (Fig.5.2). Sandby acted as painting tutor to the Harcourt family, which
resulted in George Simon, Viscount Nuneham, producing a number of prints himself, with
Sandby's aid. The tower (chapel), which still exists, was used as a writing study by Alexander
Pope, and later in the century became a landmark for picturesque tourists for its history and
associations.[18]

Evidence of the perceived picturesqueness of ruins resides not only in written descriptions but
in the large number of sketches, watercolours and prints that were made of them. Sandby and
Hearne were among the most prolific
in this respect, but it was also a subject
Michael Angelo Rooker kept returning
to. Although he was not attracted
to sublime scenery, he delighted in
the detail of ruins, which was often
accompanied by staffage to bring a
human presence into the picture.[19]

There were numerous castles that
survived as well. The particular
romantic flavour of Scottish castles
is covered in that chapter (pp.131-2),
but the castles in England and Wales
carried historical associations as well
as the general ambience of ruins. Like
abbeys and priories, they were often

5.3 The 'Petrifying or Dropping Well', together with the ruins of
Knaresborough Castle, North Yorkshire, engraving from *The Complete
English Traveller*, 1771

depicted – Gilpin sketched scores of them, Sandby published a set in his views of features in South Wales (1775) and Hearne produced watercolours of several castles in various states of ruin (some being still habitable), including Beverstone, Gloucestershire; Barnard Castle, Durham; Newark, Nottinghamshire; Ludlow, Shropshire; Raglan, Monmouthshire; Caister, Norfolk; Kenilworth, Warwickshire (a favourite subject for many artists); Pleshey, Essex (only an earthwork remaining); Allington, Kent; and Chepstow, familiar feature of the view from Piercefield. And although Rooker preferred to concentrate on abbeys, nonetheless he painted Usk Castle, Caerphilly, Pevensey, Sussex, and Saltwood, Kent, as well as the more usually depicted Kenilworth and Warwick. The more famous the monument the more often it was illustrated.

If a ruined castle could be combined with another object of special picturesque quality, so much the better for the artist. The print of Knaresborough Castle, Yorkshire, places equal if not more emphasis on the natural phenomenon of the 'Dropping Well' (Fig.5.3). Mostly a castle would be depicted at a distance, on a summit, where they were intended to stand in a commanding position. The tendency, accordingly, was to place it in the middle or background of a picture, whereas abbeys could feature much more in close-up, as Rooker showed. Real ruined castles would be more likely to be outside a garden or estate, but if within they could function as a garden folly in the way that sham ones usually did. Distant castles might well be part of a picturesque view from a garden, as at Piercefield.

One of the most picturesque exploitations of a castle was at Dinefwr Park, Dyfed, in the vale of Towy, seat of the *nouveau riche* George Rice. Gilpin visited in 1770 and devoted several pages of his Wye Tour to it and no fewer than three aquatints. To him it was the essence of the picturesque:

> The scenery around Dinevawr-castle is very beautiful; consisting of a rich profusion of wood, and lawn. But what particularly recommends it, is the great variety of the ground. I know few places, where a painter might study the inequalities of a surface with more advantage…The woods, which adorn these beautiful scenes about Dinevawr-castle, and which are clumped with great beauty, consist chiefly of the finest oak; some of them of large Spanish chesnuts… The picturesque scenes, which this place affords, are numerous. Wherever the castle appears, and it appears almost every where, a landscape purely picturesque is generally presented.[20]

5.4 Goodrich Castle, Herefordshire, aquatint by Jukes from William Gilpin, *Observations on the River Wye*, second ed., 1789, opp. p.31

Five years later Brown was invited, unusually, to embellish an already manifestly picturesque site. He did not, as Price and Payne Knight would no doubt have expected, attempt to de-picturesque the park, recognising that 'Nature has been truly beautiful and Art has done no harm'. He followed the clumping of oak and chestnut with his own groups of beech, broke up an avenue into clumps and made a walk to the castle (a mile from the house).[21]

An old castle might serve a new purpose as a building in a landscape that evolved during the eighteenth century, as at Sherborne, Dorset. Or, as at Wardour, the old ruin, clad in ivy, was the dominant central feature in a lawn that extended to the Gothic banqueting house on one side and the later primitive rock grotto on the other.

On his tour up the Wye, Gilpin paused to consider the combination of castle, river, planting and natural location in an exceptional view. This was of Goodrich Castle (Fig.5.4):

> A reach of the river, forming a noble bay, is spread before the eye. The bank, on the right, is steep and covered with wood; beyond which a bold promontory shoots out, crowned with a castle, rising among trees.

> This view, which is one of the grandest on the river, I should not scruple to call *correctly picturesque*; which is seldom the character of a purely natural scene.[22]

Gilpin goes on to ruminate how nature untouched rarely creates a harmonious whole but needs a helping hand.

Sham ruins, on the other hand, were a common way to bestow on a garden a picturesque dimension. They had a long ancestry: the earliest appears to be that of c1530 in the Duke of Urbino's park at Pesaro, Italy.[23] The Ruined Priory at The Leasowes not only enhanced the medieval feeling of a group of features – Priory Gate, Priory Walk, Priory Pool – but since it was the most prominent of them it concentrated attention and elicited a picturesque response in its setting next to Virgil's Grove (Fig.2.8). The Priory is said to have incorporated some genuine medieval fragments from the old Halesowen Abbey. It was used as a dwelling. The *ferme ornée* at Woburn Farm was not particularly picturesque, but it had ornamental plantings along the circuit walk and a ruined chapel. As the owner, Philip Southcote, was a Catholic, there may have been some personal feeling behind his choice of a chapel, suggesting the suppression of Catholicism.

5.5 Ruined chapel at Mount Edgcumbe, Cornwall   5.6 Ruined abbey at Painshill

Equally, a sham ruin might be added to a scene that already contained a number of picturesque elements. The Ruined Chapel at Mount Edgcumbe (Fig.5.5), in place by 1747, stood out on a hillside overlooking the mouth of the Tamar and the sea (see pp.50-2). It too bears evidence of medieval pieces recycled. But although it gave interest to an otherwise bare slope it was only a contributor to a wide-ranging picturesque landscape. Similarly (although a very different landscape) the Ruined Abbey at Painshill (Fig.5.6), dating from 1772, was but one of a number of elements furnishing picturesque appeal – buildings, landform, plantings. It was not even the only ruin (see p.37). Hamilton may have had the Ruined Chapel at Mount Edgcumbe in mind (which he had seen in 1749) or Southcote's at Woburn Farm (which was close by), but his abbey had its own form, originally with wings. The motivation for erecting it was not, however, principally aesthetic: it was a hurried, late work, designed to cover up the site of his financially disastrous tileworks and to add to the sale value of the property.

5.7 Shobdon Arches, Herefordshire

A mixture of original medieval and eighteenth-century 'Gothick' can be seen at Shobdon Arches, Leominster, Herefordshire (Fig.5.7). The interior arches of a twelfth-century church were moved to the top of a hill when the church was demolished in 1751, to be replaced by what is called the only rococo church in England. The Arches consist of a central chancel arch with a Norman doorway on each side: these are original, but the gables and pinnacles are 1750s work. The 'ruin' is certainly an eye-catcher but it stands at the top of a formal avenue of trees.

Another, more 'authentic', sham ruin was erected at Cranbury Park, Hampshire, in 1765 by Thomas Dummer. He had recently acquired the ruins of Netley Abbey at Southampton, and took parts of the north transept to Cranbury to compose an arch in the park. This was supplemented by a cottage next to it in the form of a Gothic tower. Fifteen years later George Dance incorporated a groin-vaulted ballroom in the new house to pick up the medieval idiom.[24] But even the parts of the abbey that were left at Netley were allowed to become picturesquely overgrown.

Crowcombe Court, in the Quantock Hills, Somerset, provides a cross-over from ruined chapel to castle. The folly is in the form of a castle of sandstone and ironstone, but is constructed in part from old fragments taken not from a medieval castle but from the chapel of Halsway Manor nearby. The castle was in fact a more popular form than the abbey, priory or chapel, when it came to putting up mock ruins, and at the forefront of the movement (if it can be dignified as such) was the gentleman-architect Sanderson Miller. He was to become famous for his sham castles, starting with his own at Edge Hill, on the Radway estate, and then subsequently at Hagley and Wimpole, though that was a late execution of Miller's much earlier design. It is likely that the impetus came from two sources, the first being the history of the site (the first battlefield of the Civil War in 1642) and the acquisition of an old house, Edge or Ratley Grange. The second was the inspiration of Stowe Castle (c1738), which comprised a castellated wall with mock towers that concealed cottages for the estate workers at Stowe. Some distance from the gardens, Stowe Castle formed the perfect eye-catcher from them. It was not, however, a ruin. Miller laid the foundations for his Gothic tower in 1745, at the same time laying the foundations for his future reputation. The octagonal tower was based on Guy's Tower at Warwick Castle, though with modifications in the Gothic style such as arched windows. A smaller square tower adjacent to the main one served as a fore-building or barbican, with a solid 'drawbridge' connecting it to the castle. This fore-building itself consisted of two turrets, one entire, the other lacking its top quarter, giving the effect of a ruin.[25] The castle and turrets were supplemented by sham ruins put up on the opposite side of the road c1750 so that the overall effect of the complex was ruinate even if the castle was intact. These sham ruins included an arch and an oriel window in a wall range and a separate circular battlemented turret.[26]

Miller's principal concern was antiquarian at this point, and he added old painted glass windows and the heraldic emblems of eight local families to the main Gothic room in the tower. A sculpture of Caractacus was even ordered, though in the event it proved too large for its intended niche. However, it is clear that the appearance and the positioning in the garden or landscape became more important with future commissions, such as the attributed dovecote at Wroxton, Oxfordshire, built as a crenellated Gothic tower in miniature. This is sometimes thought to have been modelled, again, on Guy's Tower but it more resembles a strange octagon tower at Idlicote House, south-east of Stratford-on-Avon. This latter tower appears to be medieval in origin but there are signs of rococo remodelling, and it may have been used as a dovecote.[27]

The most famed of Miller's castles is the ruin at Hagley (1747-8), which followed fairly closely on the heels of the Edge Hill tower. The positioning was based on an earlier castellate building on or near the same site, both for its prominence in the park and for the superb views it afforded in several directions. The castle was, and still is, used as a dwelling, and comprised a square walled keep with four corner turrets, one of which was the inhabited tower. The others were used as a coal store, a hen house and a cow shed, so the courtyard acted as a farmyard. Initially large stones were scattered around, giving the impression they had fallen from the ruin. Some serious attempt was made to fabricate authenticity – ivy grew on the walls, and the windows may have come from the demolished Halesowen Abbey. Henry Keene made Gothic furniture from Miller's designs, and Miller is presumed to have provided the model for the chairs that were to be found in the top room.[28]

5.8 Sanderson Miller's ruined castle at Wimpole, Cambridgeshire

His other well-known ruined castle is that at Wimpole (Fig.5.8), though its genesis was protracted. Miller designed it in 1749 for Philip Yorke, 1st Earl of Hardwicke, following an invitation to do so by George Lyttelton of Hagley. Lyttelton explained to Miller that the castle was not to be a copy of that at Hagley but that it should be 'differing in many respects, particularly in this, that he [Yorke] wants no house or even room in it, but mearly the walls and semblance of an old castle to make an object from his house'.[29] It would stand on an eminence, with a backing of firs, as was usual. Further, the materials of which it was to be constructed were stipulated: 'he has freestone, or a mixture of flint pebbles and other stone, of which an old church in the parish is built, and also bricks in his neighbourhood'.[30] The project lapsed, however, and Yorke died in 1764. Some time later, twenty years after Miller's design, it was resurrected by the 2nd Earl, who asked Brown to build the castle, probably because Miller's health had deteriorated. Brown had his own ideas and altered Miller's plan, in the process making it flatter and the details less authentic (Miller for instance had proposed cracks in the walls). Jemima, the 2nd Earl's wife, thought that Brown had reduced its picturesque appeal: 'he has 'Unpicturesqued' it by making it a mere continuous solid object, instead of a Broken one.'[31] Time, however, made it more credible, as James Plumptre noted in 1800: 'The tint of this building is very much mellowed by time, and the ruin has a very good and natural effect. I have nowhere seen so good an imitation.'[32]

Miller may well have inspired others to include a sham castle in their domain. William Aislabie built a large one at Hackfall, intended to be seen from a distance (Fig.5.9), and the fake Dunstall Castle is one of the ring of perimeter buildings in the park at Croome Court (Fig.2.9), to be seen from the house. Dating from 1765-70, it is now accepted to have been by Robert Adam, though Miller was once suggested as the designer. Originally it was just a façade and may not have been particularly ruinous.[33] This must have encouraged Lord Coventry, who created another ruin, Pirton Castle, to balance Dunstall, in 1797. Adam (see pp.131-2) was eager to indulge his fantasies about (particularly ruined) castles, but did not often have the opportunity to do so in England: he designed a splendid fort for Osterley, Middlesex, where it would have been totally out of place, and on flat land, but nothing came of it. A particularly appealing castle went up at Hardwick Park with the intention that one could view the whole park from the turret. There was also a ruined castle, by an unknown hand, in a distant field at Adlington, Cheshire to complement an eclectic mix of rococo follies in the pleasure grounds.

5.9 Mowbray Castle, Hackfall, North Yorkshire

5.10 Alfred's Hall, Cirencester Park, Gloucestershire

The earliest of all folly ruins was Alfred's Hall at Cirencester, a castellate construction built between 1727 and 1732 (Fig.5.10). While located in woodland within a baroque framework of rides, it later assumed a more picturesque appearance, as shown in two engravings of 1763 after Thomas Robins. It was erected on the site of the former Wood House, which collapsed in 1727, and it contained genuine medieval pieces from the demolished Sapperton Manor (bought by Lord Bathurst in 1730). Fragments of ruin may earlier have surrounded the Wood House.[34]

A fair number of ruins were classical. Obviously, with very few exceptions (such as Hadrian's Wall), genuine classical ruins were not to be encountered, so sham examples were self-evidently spurious. But the taste for them was there, indicating either a larger than usual suspension of disbelief or a response which was partly emotional, as with other ruins, and partly intellectual, i.e. that an educated visitor might appreciate the classical associations. Intact temples in classical or neo-classical style flourished in vast numbers, and few thought them incongruous in gardens, though that was more to do with the elegance of the architecture.

In the case of Virginia Water, the array of classical columns was actually genuine, though their display was picturesque. The columns came from Leptis Magna, near Tripoli in north Africa, a far-flung part of the Roman Empire. The best, and the bulk, of the columns had gone to Louis XIV, but in 1818, at the Prince Regent's instigation, some of the survivors were shipped to Britain, where they languished for a time in the courtyard of the British Museum. In 1826 the architect in charge, Sir Jeffry Wyatville, was responsible for repairing the arched bridge that carried the public road to Ascot over the Crown land at the south of Windsor Great Park. On the north side of the bridge (which acted as part of the scene) Wyatville planned a kind of Roman forum (Fig.5.11). In addition to the twelve consignments of thirty-seven pillars from London, there were some temporary features in the form of classical-style statuary, but after vandalism they were later removed. A wall was built on each side of the columns to form an enclosure. To the south of the bridge the columns were arranged to form a temple (Fig.5.12): Wyatville referred to the ruins as a whole as the Temple of Augustus.[35]

5.11 The 'forum' at Virginia Water, Surrey, stone lithograph by W Gauci after WA Delamotte, 1828

There were two separate sets of classical ruins at Shugborough, Staffordshire. A colonnade, based on the Temple of Saturn in Rome, quickly disappeared, but the more complex pile nearby survives, though depleted. The appearance was described as classical, but all sorts of pieces were incorporated, including a Venetian window and remnants from the old medieval house, in addition to a tall slender classical column. Later on an artificial stone Druid was added, increasing the stylistic confusion.[36]

The so-called Mausoleum at Painshill was in fact built in the form of a ruined Roman triumphal arch, inspired perhaps by the Arch of Constantine although it bears some resemblance to the Roman arch illustrated by Batty Langley in his *New Principles of Gardening* (1728), where it is recommended as the termination of an *allée* or avenue. Hamilton, however, does not appear to have had a copy of the book in his

5.12 View of ruins at Virginia Water through other side of bridge, stone lithograph by W Gauci after WA Delamotte, 1828

library. The Mausoleum was constructed as two uprights with niches and a connecting span with a richly decorated panelled soffit. The span disappeared long ago. The sense of the classical was enhanced by the genuine artefacts brought back by Hamilton from Rome – funerary urns, a Roman altar, a sarcophagus – which were laid round about or displayed in the niches. The predominant nature of these artefacts was funerary, which presumably attracted the appellation of Mausoleum.

Cousin to the Mausoleum is the probably slightly later Ruined Arch at Kew (Fig.5.13), dating from 1759. The basis was brick, on which stone was grafted. There were two side rooms in the uprights, and stone was strewn around, giving the impression it had fallen from the arch, in the manner of the fragments of the castle at Hagley. The print shows how effectively vegetation, including ivy, added to the authenticity of its appearance. It served not only as an arch but as a bridge for a cattle track. The classical effect is confirmed by the view through the arch in a northerly direction to the (now gone) Temple of Victory, erected in the same year to constitute a pair with the arch.

The building known as Mowbray Point at Hackfall appeared to be a ruined Roman bath from below, though as we have seen it presented a Gothic face on the other side. Painshill had a cold bath in the manner of a Roman bath c1790, and not far away at Oatlands there was a ruined Temple of Vesta built in 1788, though there was some opinion that it was unfinished rather than a ruin.

A particularly romanticised mock ruin was that built by Sir John Soane in his garden at Pitshanger Manor, Ealing, in 1802. Constructed as a hoax calculated to appeal to a picturesque imagination, the columns protruded up from the ground. Soane carried the joke on by sketching what he imagined an archaeological excavation would show of his ruins. The half-buried ruin was not a new idea: there were particularly fine examples at Schönbrunn, Vienna (1778) and at Tsarskoye Selo, near St Petersburg (1784-6).

5.13 William Chambers' Ruined Arch at Kew, Surrey, engraved by William Woollett after Joshua Kirby, 1763

Ruins could be for satirical purposes. At Stowe a broken wall and a heap of rubble represented the Temple of Modern Virtue. This was contrasted with the Temple of Ancient Virtue, intact and modelled on one of the great archetypes of classical building, the Temple of Vesta at Tivoli. To drive the point home, a headless statue standing in the detritus of the Temple of Modern Virtue was identifiable by his garter as the current first minister, Sir Robert Walpole. His son, Horace, was not best pleased, complaining that satire had no place in a garden, but Gilpin pronounced it 'A very elegant Piece of Satyr, upon my Word!'[37] Party political gardening was, however, dead by 1750.

From this it will be seen that a ruin was a powerful tool to employ in a garden or a view from it and could make up in picturesque value what the natural landform might possibly have lacked. It also says much for the taste and sensibility of the period.

1 *Horace Walpole's Correspondence*, ed W S Lewis et al (New Haven: Yale University Press, 1937-83), Vol.XXXV, p.147.

2 *The Works in Verse and Prose of William Shenstone, Esq*, (London: R & J Dodsley, 1764), Vol.II, pp.131-2.

3 *Ibid.*, p.126.

4 Lord Kames (Henry Home), *Elements of Criticism* (Edinburgh, 1774, fifth ed), p.437.

5 William Chambers, *A Dissertation on Oriental Gardening* (London, 1772), pp.34-5.

6 Thomas Whately, *Observations on Modern Gardening* (London: T Payne, 1793, fifth ed), p.134.

7 *Ibid.*, pp.134-5.

8 *Ibid.*, pp.135-8.

9 William Gilpin, *Observations on the River Wye* (1770) (London: R Blamire, 1789, second ed.), p.50.

10 See Malcolm Andrews, *The Search for the Picturesque* (London: Scolar Press, 1990), p.46.

11 William Gilpin, *Observations, Relative Chiefly to Picturesque Beauty, Made in the Year 1772, on Several Parts of England; particularly the Mountains, and Lakes, of Cumberland and Westmoreland* (London: R Blamire, 1786), Vol.I, p.13.

12 *Paul Sandby (1731-1809): Picturing Britain, A Bicentenary Exhibition*, ed John Bonehill and Stephen Daniels (London: Royal Academy of Arts, 2009), p.184.

13 Arthur Young, *A Six Months Tour Through the North of England* (Dublin: various publishers, 1770), Vol I, pp.286 and 288.

14 Michael Charlesworth, 'The ruined abbey: Picturesque and Gothic values', *The Politics of the Picturesque*, ed Stephen Copley and Peter Garside (Cambridge: Cambridge University Press, 1994), pp.62-80.

15 *Sandby*, p.182. His watercolour of Wenlock Abbey is reproduced on p.183.

16 Andrews, *Search for the Picturesque*, pp.118-19.

17 *Thomas Hearne 1744-1817* (Bolton: Bolton Museum and Art Gallery, 1985), p.91.

18 *Sandby*, pp.174-5.

19 Patrick Conner, *Michael Angelo Rooker (1746-1801)* (London: Batsford, 1984), p.19.

20 Gilpin, *Wye*, pp.102-6.

21 Elisabeth Whittle, *The Historic Gardens of Wales* (London: HMSO/Cadw, 1992), p.45.

22 Gilpin, *Wye*, pp.30-1.

23 David Watkin, 'Built Ruins: The Hermitage as Retreat', *Visions of Ruin: Architectural fantasies & designs for garden follies* (London: Sir John Soane's Museum, 1999), p.5.

24 David Watkin, *The English Vision: The Picturesque in Architecture, Landscape and Garden Design* (London: John Murray, 1982), p.48.

25 Antony Wood and William Hawkes, 'Radway, Warwickshire: the making of a landscape', *Journal of Garden History* 7:2, 1987, p.110.

26 *Ibid.*, pp.112-13.

27 Margaret Caine and Alan Gorton, *Cotswold Follies and Fancies* (Seaford: SB Publications, 1998), p.17.

28 See Michael Cousins, 'Hagley Park, Worcestershire', *Garden History* 35: Supplement 1, 2007, pp.80-1.

29 *An Eighteenth-Century Correspondence*, ed. Lilian Dickins and Mary Stanton (London: John Murray, 1910), p.271.

30 *Ibid.*, p.272.

31 Quoted in David Adshead, 'The design and building of the Gothic Folly at Wimpole, Cambridgeshire', *Burlington Magazine* 40:11, 1998, p.81.

32 *Ibid.*, p.83.

33 See Mike Cousins, 'Dunstall Castle, Croome, Worcester', *Follies* 66, 2007, pp.10-13.

34 For an account of the evolution of Alfred's Hall, see Mike Cousins, 'Alfred's Hall, Cirencester', *Follies* 48, 2001, pp.7-15.

35 Jane Roberts, *Royal Landscape: The Gardens and Parks of Windsor* (New Haven and London: Yale University Press, 1997), pp.458-9.

36 The Druid is usually described as Coade stone, though it predates Mrs Coade's versions and in fact comprises an earlier artificial stone Druid. Information from Mike Cousins.

37 (William Gilpin), *A Dialogue upon the Gardens...at Stow* (London: B Seely, 1748), p.21.

CHAPTER SIX

Rockwork

Rockwork is often the crucial element in a picturesque view, a transforming factor. Many a garden owes its impact to some use of stonework, from a spectacular waterfall to an alpine rockery. In its largest manifestation, the mountain, the effect is likely to be sublime rather than picturesque, and consideration of mountain scenery will be found elsewhere, in the sections on Scotland, Wales, Ireland and the Lake District. In addition there are a number of gardens where the outward view is of rocks and cliffs, and those have been discussed in that chapter. The following pages are concerned with rockwork within the garden or estate.

Rockwork in gardens can be divided into three principal categories. The first is where it is completely natural, but the viewing of it is carefully contrived. The approach and the viewing point(s) may be manipulated so as to enhance the experience, which can be a matter of both sight and sound (in the case of water). The second is where the feature is basically natural but has been added to or arranged by human hand, to strengthen the effect or emphasise an aspect. The third is the completely artificial introduction of rocks, which may be from a local quarry, often within the estate, or imported from some distance.

It may take a number of forms, again under three main heads. The first comprises natural formations – free-standing rocks, crevices and caves. The next important category would be cascades, whether natural or artificial, where the picturesque consists in the combination of stone and water. The third covers artificial compilations – principally grottoes, but also deliberate assembly or scattering of rocks. This category gave rise to the specialist garden stonemason, men such as Joseph Pickford or the Lanes.

At the time the presence and appearance of stone were significant factors in a picturesque view. William Shenstone considered that 'A rural scene to me is never perfect without the addition of some kind of building. Indeed, I have known a scar of rock-work, in great measure, supply the deficiency.'[1] To aid understanding of what rocks meant in a landscape, it will come as no surprise that Gilpin is a useful source. In his tour of the Wye he examines the effect of rockwork, and although what he discusses is generally part of the landscape the points he makes are equally applicable to such ornaments in gardens:

> The rock, as all other objects, tho more than all, receives it's chief beauty from contrast. Some
> objects are beautiful in themselves. The eye is pleased with the tuftings of a tree: it is amused
> with pursuing the eddying stream, or it rests with delight on the shattered arches of a Gothic
> ruin. Such objects, independent of composition, are beautiful in themselves. But the rock, bleak,
> naked, and unadorned, seems scarcely to deserve a place among them. Tint it with mosses, and
> lychens of various hues, and you give it a degree of beauty. Adorn it with shrubs and hanging
> herbage, and you still make it more picturesque. Connect it with wood, and water, and broken

ground; and you make it in the highest degree interesting. It's *colour*, and it's *form* are so accommodating, that it generally blends into one of the most beautiful appendages of landscape.

Different kinds of rocks have different kinds of beauty. Those on the Wye, which are of a greyish colour, are in general, simple and grand; rarely formal, or fantastic. Sometimes they project in those beautiful square masses, yet broken and shattered in every line, which is characteristic of the most majestic species of rock. Sometimes they slant obliquely from the eye in shelving diagonal strata: and sometimes they appear in large masses of smooth stone, detached from each other, and half buried in the soil. Rocks of this last kind are the most lumpish, and the least picturesque.[2]

The character of the Wye valley rocks is, of course, much less fantastical and dramatic than some rockwork to be encountered elsewhere. As a general point, Gilpin thought that rocks, though irregular in shape, were better broken so as to alleviate smoothness of surface.[3]

Whately concurred with Gilpin that bare rocks were not attractive and generally needed to be accompanied by vegetation, water and perhaps signs of habitation:

they [rocks] may surprise, but can hardly please; they are too far moved from common life, too barren and inhospitable; rather desolate than solitary, and more horrid than terrible; so austere a character cannot be long engaging, if its rigour be not softened by circumstances, which may belong either to these or more cultivated spots; and when the dreariness is extreme, little streams and waterfalls are of themselves insufficient for the purpose; an intermixture of vegetation is also necessary; and on some occasions even marks of inhabitants are proper.[4]

He explains that the 'character' of rocks can be chiefly divided into dignity, terror and fancy (imagination). Rocks may change from one to the other by means of planting to conceal or reveal their entirety. Planting can also create illusion of size and cover blemishes in appearance. Water can also play a part, though it should never be still.[5] Terror can be created by such features as a rock apparently about to fall, or a violent cataract, and can be heightened by the human dimension – a footbridge over a chasm, or a steep, dangerous-looking path.[6] Whately acknowledges that rocky scenes can vary in those three categories within the same location, and gives Dovedale, Derbyshire, as an example.

As a striking instance of cliffs seen from a garden, Piercefield has already been considered under the outward view (pp.54-6). But there were others within the estate, such as the cliff face at Moccas Court or that at Downton, with a special view of the 'The Rock' on the Teme from upstream of Hay Mill Weir – this was one of the series depicted by Thomas Hearne and is reminiscent of the view from Moccas. In the case of Bolton Abbey, Yorkshire, there was a prodigious amount of rockwork of varied appearance within the park, some of which was hewn into seats or other shapes, and there were cascades both natural and artificial. For a fuller account of this memorable site, see pp.149-51.

In the case of Brimham Rocks, also Yorkshire, a moor was developed as a sort of theme park in rock intended as a tourist attraction from the eighteenth century: until the dissolution of the monasteries it had been grazed by sheep belonging to Fountains Abbey. The fantastical shapes of the millstone grit stones, blasted by wind and sand over millions of years, have caused them to be given names such as the Druid's Writing Desk (there is no actual Druidic association although there was once thought to be). In 1792 Lord Grantly built an inn and reception house for visitors among the rocks. One structure was called Lovers' Leap, in common with several other hazardous points in gardens, e.g. at Bolton Abbey, Piercefield and Plumpton Rocks. Brandrith Crags, on the way to Bolton Abbey, was another set of rocks, though not so extensive, and more part of the landscape though still a visitor attraction. As at Brimham, there is a rocking-stone perfectly poised on its base so that it cannot fall, and, again as at Brimham, fanciful Druidic connections were made in the early nineteenth century. Yet another rock grouping is at Almscliff Crag (once known as Altar Cliff), to the south-west of Harrogate, a gritstone tor with, once more, a rocking-stone and several cavities. A huge fissure was known as the Fairy Parlour, a natural tunnel that penetrated deep into the hill.

Plumpton Rocks

Sometimes the natural rock formations in a garden would be presented in a picturesque dressing. Plumpton Rocks, near Harrogate, Yorkshire, is the epitome of the picturesque garden, based on rock but with an artificial lake added, together with winding paths and what were originally wide-ranging plantings from trees to flowers. This property, once the seat of the old family of Plumpton, was sold to Daniel Lascelles in 1755, the brother of the owner of Harewood House. The site burgeoned with millstone grit rocks of weird shapes and stupendous size, and could have been just a tourist spectacle, as Brimham Rocks was, but Lascelles created the perfect picturesque garden out of it by the masterstroke of joining ponds and flooding the hollows to create the lake (Fig.6.1) and by substantial planting. The result was 'the nearest place on earth to heaven', as Queen Mary is supposed to have said.

6.1 Plumpton Rocks, near Harrogate, North Yorkshire

Plumpton Rocks has not been over-described nor had much critical attention paid to it, but the accounts by Karen Lynch and the late Helen Lazenby provide historical background and a commentary.[7] The grounds covered some thirty acres, including the lake of about six, so it was not a landscape on a massive scale – but the effect was intensified by being limited in area. Lascelles started work on the grounds more or less at once, employing as gardener John Banks, who had been working at the site since the 1740s, probably operating it as a tree nursery for Harewood. Banks provided 1800 trees from his own stock in 1756, and also bought large quantities from the two great Yorkshire nursery firms of the time, Perfect's of Pontefract and Telford's of York. 'Plumps', in other words, clumps of trees were planted, a band of firs sheltering the young, less hardy species. Trees grown included pines, sycamore, elm, larch, beech, horse chestnut, rowan (mountain ash), Spanish chestnut, poplar, walnut, lime and hornbeam.[8] The following year shrubs made their appearance, both flowering and evergreen, among the rocks. Even flowers were grown – this might not have pleased Gilpin, but visitors were charmed by the contrasts with the huge, bizarre rocks.

There was plenty of interest and variety at Plumpton. The lake was held back by a dam at its southern end, designed by John Carr as quite an ornamental structure with arches, piers and finials, and there was also a boathouse, seemingly cut out from the rock but actually joined as an arch and covered with turf. The opening of the boathouse is architectural, with a keystone. Of course it was the rocks that provided the central focus, and there were startling outcrops mainly on the east side of the lake, with paths winding around them, while to the west there were woodland walks with superb views of the rocks across the lake. On the east side there was a lawn with shrubberies surrounded by rocks. The plantings continued among the rocks, which themselves were given names such as the Lion's Den, Echo Rock and Needle's Eye. On top of one was a 'Chinese seat', furnishing a fine view. Even within the estate there were objects to view apart from the rocks, such as the crenellated barns, reminiscent of those at Badminton.

Several of the rocks were grassed and planted on top, leaving the sides bare. On top of the most prominent, the 'Chinese rock' in the lake, what was actually described as a small garden was grown. This rock almost joined the rocks on the mainland – the crevice was known as Lovers' Leap, after a supposed contest between two suitors who had to jump the gap. The survivor won the young lady's hand. This probably apocryphal tale serves to justify the name that links it with the other Lovers' Leaps mentioned above. Turner painted two evocative paintings of the rock in the lake in 1798 that hang in Harewood House: one is reproduced on the front cover.

Plumpton was referred to as a Chinese rock garden, and a similar appellation was applied to the Mackershaw Valley adjacent to the Studley Royal water gardens. Where the latter are formal, the valley is contrastingly naturalistic, though it had some decoration in the form of a Roman monument (called by some the 'Devil's Chimney') and an open Chinese pavilion both high on the far steeps of the valley. The stream in the valley was crossed by several small bridges, some of which were in Chinese fretwork style, and the term 'Chinese landscape' seems to have been used in consequence of the *chinoiserie* artefacts in combination with the bare scars of rock exhibited by the cliffs and part terracing of the slope into shelves of rock. Both Plumpton and the Mackershaw Valley appear to have been labelled Chinese on the strength of the natural rock being combined with landscape decoration and additions.

Several commentators have associated rocks with China, and it is true that some images of Chinese landscapes or gardens available in the West via prints or painted objects contained rockwork, usually of an artificial kind, i.e. rocks piled up in bizarre shapes, or even to create small false mountains with cavities and recesses. A number of the illustrations in Maggie Keswick's magnificent book *The Chinese Garden: History, Art and Architecture* (1978, revised 2003) indicate formations of 'tufa' and other stone which bear a strong resemblance to formations found in British gardens, but detailed knowledge of the Chinese compilations would have been impossible at the time. Lord Macartney, on a failed trade mission to China in 1792-3, discussed similarities between English and Chinese gardens more generally, but admitted that there could have been no connection.[9]

The Mackershaw Valley can be seen as a trial run for the wilder landscape at Hackfall (pp.135-8). In this respect it was not so much the 'Chineseness' of the scene that transferred to Hackfall, where there is no *chinoiserie*, but the bringing of the rock scars into view to optimum advantage.

Rokeby

Rokeby (pronounced Rookby), near Barnard Castle, is now in County Durham but at the time was part of the North Riding. The seat of J S Morritt from 1769, it contained a park bounded by two rivers, the Greta and the Tees, whose confluence created a stirring sight. Although Rokeby offers a number of features, such as the old Mortham Tower (in the background in Fig.6.2), a view along the Tees to the ruined Egglestone Abbey and bridges of various design, including the oft-painted Greta Bridge, it is for its rockwork that it most merits attention. Arthur Young, visiting in 1769, found Rokeby greatly to his taste:

6.2 FitzHugh's Tomb and Mortham Tower at Rokeby, County Durham, stone lithograph by WR Robinson, c1820

> The tea-room is very romantically situated on the rocky banks of the *Greta*, raging like a torrent over the rocks, and tumbling in a romantic manner under the window. A little below it joins the *Tees*, under noble rocks of freestone over-hung by wood. – Above the room, the other way, are some very romantic rocks on the side of a terrass by the water.[10]

The Tees also is walled by rock, and at the mouth of the Greta joining it are some enormous rocks in the river bed.

The whole park was given a romantic overlay, in the more historical sense of the word, by Walter Scott in *Rokeby* (1813), supposedly inspired by contemplation in what has become known as Scott's Cave overlooking the river. The poem is concerned with an imaginary episode in the Civil War following Marston Moor in 1644. Illustrations such as the tomb in the foreground of Fig.6.2 spread the reputation and mystique of Rokeby. The editor of the poem describes the river at Rokeby as it actually was in the early nineteenth century, together with some local lore. The river ran in a deep trench of limestone and marble, creating considerable noise as it passed over solid rock with shelving slopes:

> The banks partake of the same wild and romantic character, being chiefly lofty cliffs of limestone rock, whose grey colour contrasts admirably with the various trees and shrubs which find root among their crevices, as well as with the hue of the ivy…At other points the rocks give place to precipitous banks of earth, bearing large trees intermixed with copse-wood.[11]

On the other side the tall white cliffs were fringed with shrubs: the editor informs us the spot was known locally as Blockula, the haunt of Swedish witches.

Caves

There are numerous examples of caves cut into rock escarpments within the purview of a garden. For instance, Timothy Mowl has drawn attention to a couple of Cheshire landscapes with caves that attracted romantic associations and may well have had a previously unsuspected influence on other gardens. The two gardens are Carden and Broxton Old Hall, where walks were cut across the range of rocks in the Peckforton Hills and various caves and hollows were excavated. At Carden Park the largest cave was occupied by the 'English Hermit' John Harris for more than twenty years till 1765, after which he lodged in several other caves in the hills for at least another forty-five years, by which time he had attained his century. Other of the caves had grilles, and ledges and seats were also cut into the rock.[12] A similar arrangement of cut walk, ledges and caverns is to be found at Broxton Old Hall, which offers a Bear Cave and a hermitage complete with Gothic window.[13] The trio of Worcestershire caves used as hermitages has been mentioned in the chapter on rustic architecture (p.62).

At Quarry Bank (p.119) and Badger Dingle (p.46) there were caves in the natural rock, while at Hawkstone the grotto hill (p.144) was honeycombed with extensive tunnels and caverns, possibly (according to legend) mined by the Romans, though modified and ornamented in the eighteenth century. Sometimes it is difficult to tell whether a grotto/cave is entirely natural, man-made or a mixture of the two. The Hermitage at Warkworth has been mentioned before (pp.62-3), but in this context it is relevant to note that it was carved out of the rock as well as having stone wall extensions. Fig.6.3 shows the rock more clearly, from the rear side, away from the river (see Fig.4.3 for the river view).

In the case of Belsay, Northumberland, an entire quarry was given over to form a garden within its walls early in the nineteenth century. In a garden which already boasted an old castle, deliberately

6.3 Hermitage at Warkworth, Northumberland, engraved by J Greig after L Clennell, 1815

made more ruinous, and a castellate farm building, Bantam's Folly, Sir Charles Monck made use of the quarry from which stone had been used to build the new Hall from 1807. It was filled with a superb collection of ferns but also included a variety of plantings that would thrive in this sheltered space, including (later) Himalayan rhododendrons. The sheer rock face was high and imposing, with two tall arches, one known as the 'rock arch' (Fig.6.4), and was softened in many places by plants climbing and covering it. To accentuate the height of the rock walls a yew hedge marched along the top.

Cascades

Some cascades have been considered already, and more will be found in the chapters on Scotland and the Sublime, but those within an estate were often artificial or given a substantial helping hand in the cause of the Picturesque.

6.4 Quarry garden at Belsay, Northumberland

The three cynosures of the West Midlands each had cascades based on springs in the hills but designed specially for their effect. Enville had a cascade in Essex Wood (1750s) but the pride was the series of cascades issuing from the Cold Bath, created in the 1750s and modified in 1770. They ran for quarter of a mile through pools, dams and drops into Temple Pool, where they could, until 1769, be viewed from the Chinese Temple in the pond. The drops were arranged asymmetrically; one had a rock arch over it; and stones and bricks were laid in the bed to stir the water and make it sparkle. The effect was described by William Marshall in 1785 in terms of sublimity:

> …the most brilliant scene we had ever beheld presented itself. A SHENSTONIAN CASCADE, in full flow and fury; foaming and bellowing, as if the mountain were enraged: pouring down a river of water, white as snow, and apparently so copious, as to make our situation alarming.[14]

Alas, the scene is very placid today. At Hagley, the cascades were not so violent, but formed an 'opera scene' between trees that acted like theatrical wings, creating a tableau to be viewed from the Palladian Bridge. And at the third of the gardens, The Leasowes, there were cascades in

6.5 Virgil's Grove at The Leasowes, West Midlands, engraved by James Mason after Thomas Smith, c1752

6.6 Cascade at The Leasowes, West Midlands, print by Willmore c1800

Virgil's Grove, surrounded in dark woodland (Fig.6.5), contrasting with the open fall near the Stamford root-house, where the water poured over rock, large stones and cinders, all carefully contrived though based on a natural flow (Fig.6.6). Dodsley commented excitedly:

> …a fairy vision, consisting of an irregular and romantic fall of water, very unusual, one hundred and fifty yards in continuity, and a very striking scene it affords. Other cascades may possibly have the advantage of a greater descent, and a larger torrent, but a more wild and romantic appearance of water, and at the same time strictly natural, is what I never saw in any place whatever.[15]

6.7 Cascade at Hestercombe, Somerset

The cascade(s) at The Leasowes may have been the inspiration for Bampfylde's unexpected steep fall at Hestercombe (Fig. 6.7). Here a rill in a brick channel feeds a totally artificial cascade though it looks natural. In turn it probably inspired Henry Hoare at Stourhead, who certainly engaged Bampfylde's help in adding a cascade to liven up a hillside.

Both the last two are narrow waterfalls down a steep descent. More common, however, were broad falls which might not necessarily have great height. One such was Capability Brown's at Blenheim, an artificial construct forming part of his damming of the River Glyme and the expansion of the water that constitutes the lake. Another, influential example was the cascade at Virginia Water, Surrey, subsequently replaced and built anew in a fresh position (Fig.6.8). Originally the rockwork was continued behind by the grotto, which in the second version was actually incorporated next to the cascade.

6.8 The replacement cascade at Virginia Water, Surrey, print by MJ Starling after T Allom, c1830

6.9 Cascade at Stowe, Buckinghamshire

A pre-picturesque cascade could be found at Stowe (Fig.6.9). This was a combination of cascade and ruin, and it looked not only forward but back, to the Italian Renaissance. Gilpin, in his *A Dialogue upon the Gardens...at Stow* (1748), voices the sort of opinion that he would continue to hold, though at this early date he was perhaps framing it for the first time: '... indeed, I think the Ruin a great Addition to the Beauty of the Lake. There is something so vastly picturesque, and pleasing to the Imagination in such Objects, that they are a great Addition to every Landskip'.[16] George Bickham produced a guide to Stowe in 1750 (with later editions) in which the cascade is now described as an 'Artificial Piece of Rock-Work'. Not only is it a ruin but it is adorned with figures of fauns, satyrs and river gods, thus harking back to old Italian gardens. The cascade would run for nine hours at a time in three separate strips of water.[17] It was, however, distinctly architectural as opposed to natural, but made picturesque by its ruinous form and plantings above it.

Formal architectural cascades were something of a speciality of William Kent, who favoured a triple arch form, as at Chiswick or Claremont, albeit with some rustication and rockwork. It is not really until the mid-century that the naturalistic approach, as at Virginia Water, takes off. In the late 1750s Charles Hamilton constructed a cascade at Painshill which some visitors found too orderly, but which incorporated rocks and tree roots.[18] To augment the feeling of a wild, mountainous area, similar boulders were scattered around nearby. And at West Wycombe a relatively formal cascade was given a rococo superstructure c1750 in the form of a rock arch, which unfortunately has not survived.

One cascade where the rocks were brought in (from Creswell Crags not far away) was at Thoresby, Nottinghamshire, where one of the rocks already had a large tree growing in its fissures. As with the Painshill cascade, it was fed through lead pipes so that water appeared through gaps and ledges of the rocks. But the most spectacular of all artificial picturesque cascades was at Belton, Lincolnshire, where the water poured down in different directions, giving contrasting viewing angles, and crowned by a ruin. The cascade survives, though in much reduced form, having suffered 'restorations' in the nineteenth and twentieth centuries. It was the work of Sir John Brownlow III, created Viscount Tyrconnell in 1718, who set up the complex of Gothic ruin, cascade and footbridge probably in the 1740s, making it a very early manifestation of the Picturesque. It was painted by Thomas Smith of Derby and subsequently engraved by Vivares (Fig.6.10). The picturesque quality of the waterfall and its embellishments comes across with a romantic impact.

6.10 Cascade at Belton, Lincolnshire, engraved by François Vivares after Thomas Smith, 1749

At two of the sublime estates, Hafod and Hackfall, there was no shortage of waterfalls already there, but Thomas Johnes and William Aislabie were determined to improve on nature. We shall see how they arranged and added to the natural rock to increase the excitement occasioned by the fall (see pp.137-8).

The combination of rock and water did not always mean a cascade. Humphry Repton, in considering the lake at West Wycombe in the 1790s, thought the water should be agitated by rock to make it more appealing: 'The glassy surface of a still calm lake, however delightful, is not more interesting than the lively brook rippling over a rocky bed.'[19] At Harewood, Repton recommended placing rocks slanting at an angle in the river bed, and illustrated what he had in mind, complemented by a suitable bridge and a distant cascade.

Grottoes

The most common use of rockwork in gardens was, of course, the grotto. If there were rocks naturally in the garden, a cave would generally be exploited and adapted, but human intervention was obvious, certainly in the first half of the century. Gay's Cave at Amesbury, Wiltshire (between 1734 and 1738), has a rustic but noticeably architectural front, while Pope's grotto, the most famed of all, was carefully fashioned into tunnel and side chambers. The legend above the grotto, 'Approach – Great Nature studiously behold', referred to the geological fragments stuck on the walls, not to the structure. William Kent's grotto at Esher Place, Surrey, even had a classical portico. The grottoes at Stowe and Stourhead (1748) were also architectural in having a central chamber and side chambers or wings.

The first truly naturalistic (though artificial) cave grotto was Stephen Wright's at Claremont (1750). Replacing Kent's rather formal triple-arch cascade (a spring fed the lake at this point), Wright, who had been assistant to Kent, moved in a new direction. Using a number of different types of rock, all brought in, he had a cave built, with boulders forming wings on each side. The cave was decorated with gems and painted pebbles, though most has been lost now. In charge of construction was the mason Joseph Pickford, who subsequently worked at Oatlands and at Painshill, probably on the cascade there.

The Claremont model ushered in an era of natural-seeming grottoes. Dating from the early 1750s was Thomas Sandby's at Virginia Water, and during the decade Joseph Lane, of Tisbury, Wiltshire, was learning his craft in the rebuilding of the house at Fonthill, where he subsequently went on to construct a number of grottoes for Alderman Beckford. From this time onwards grottoes developed in various directions, some heavily decorative, some with extensive shellwork, some primitive – while some even retained a formal architectural framework or frontage, despite naturalistic appearance within.

Shell houses or rooms were one thing (and popular), shell grottoes were another. Goldney, in Bristol, was the most lavish, Thomas Goldney III bringing his ships home laden with shells from the West Indies alongside commercial goods. The exotic shells mingled with local minerals ('Bristol diamonds') on the walls of the grotto, which was developed from 1737 but was formal rather than picturesque, with encrusted columns emphasising the architecture. The change of taste and style in the 1750s can be seen in Thomas Wright's grotto at Hampton Court House, Middlesex, where a rockwork exterior clad with burnt clinker concealed an astonishing shellwork chamber and a ceiling decorated like the heavens (Fig.6.11).

Some grottoes burrowed deep into the hill, such as Sir Francis Dashwood's Hell-Fire Caves at West Wycombe (from 1750) or the poet Scott's grotto at Amwell, Hertfordshire, where in both cases long tunnels gave on to chambers, some of which were ornamented. The entrances to both were formal, however. In similar vein, cut into the rock below Hagley Hall, Rugeley, Staffordshire (not the well-known Hagley), is an unsung late eighteenth-century grotto, a network of passages and chambers. The visitor passed (the caves are now sealed off) through an entrance arch into a

6.11 Ceiling of Thomas Wright's grotto at Hampton Court House, Middlesex

warren of vaulted tunnels and rooms, a colonnaded rotunda, arcades, dome and altar.[20] It seems like a mixture of West Wycombe and Amwell, with something of their quality, and a serious attempt at underground architecture.

The grotto at Painshill, started c1762, broke new ground in being both naturalistic and full of sparkling crystals. The main chamber, dripping with stalactites covered with satin spar, was a scene of fantasy and wonder, and owed

6.12 Grotto at Croome Court, Worcestershire

6.13 Grotto at Belcombe Court, Wiltshire

little even to Italian precedents, where the stalactites to be found in some Renaissance grottoes were of the more solid spugne, lacking lightness and sparkle. Stonework was used subtly and for different effect – most of the exterior was dressed with 'tufa', spongestone, while the rear exit was of primitive boulders. The new dimension of decoration spread to other grottoes, notably Oatlands nearby, where a distinctly formal two-storey structure built in the 1760s was transformed inside in the 1770s by the Lanes, one chamber in particular (actually called 'grotto' at the time) being given the stalactite treatment much as Painshill had. A late example, the tea-room grotto at St Anne's Hill, Chertsey (1790), had similar stalactite work in the lower storey. It is attributed on stylistic grounds to Josiah Lane.

A grotto not ascribed to the Lanes is at Croome Court, Worcestershire (Fig.6.12), which may possibly have owed something to Painshill in its use of 'tufa' as decoration augmenting the rockwork. The landscape was largely the work of Capability Brown, not normally known for championing grottoes, though others such as James Wyatt had later input. The grotto initially arose in the 1760s under the mason Robert Newman, and further decoration was added in the form of a coade stone statue of the River Goddess of the Severn, Sabrina (date stamped 1802), and 'Derbyshire petrifactions', probably spar or 'bluejohn', were ordered by the Countess of Coventry in 1783.[21] It has been much altered and 'repaired' over the years.

A curious grotto forms part of the rococo assembly at Belcombe Court, Wiltshire. There is no evidence that it was by the Lanes, but it was in their home county and one or other might have been involved. It is a two-storey structure (Fig.6.13) with small chambers below and an upper deck which serves as an open balcony with rock parapet. The grotto opens directly on to the pond.

The most sumptuous grotto of all, certainly rivalling Painshill, was that at Ascot Place, Berkshire. It has proved mysterious and elusive with regard to its date and designer, though provisionally it can be allocated to the 1780s and tentatively attributed to Josiah Lane, although an alternative possibility is that it might partly represent the dismantled and relocated first grotto at Virginia Water under the direction of a mason called Turnbull.[22] It is a lakeside grotto, completely artificial though natural in appearance, and has an accompanying cascade adjacent. The grotto contains a number of passages and individual niches and chambers, but it is the decoration that is stunning. Like Painshill, it has stalactites, but they are larger and longer. The other particularly striking feature is the patterning of coloured stones or minerals – some in zig-zags, some in bands. The size and intricacy of the grotto make it a fitting challenger to Painshill. There is evidence of planting on top, which would have enhanced its picturesqueness – a not uncommon practice, as witness the much earlier hermitages at Richmond and Carshalton House.

Josiah Lane seems, in the later years of the century, to have moved towards a more primitive, unadorned look with his grottoes. That at Wardour Castle (1792) presents a somewhat incongruous appearance. Crude and disorderly in construction, it sits on a formal level platform or terrace (Fig.6.14). There are niches and corners inside the grotto, but no large roofed chambers. There is also evidence of water, which was presumably raised to flow down the side of the grotto as a rough waterfall. Another essay in the primitive style, with some burnt slag added, was at Duntish Court, Dorset. This could possibly be by the Lanes, though there is no evidence.

Josiah Lane's masterpieces were the rockwork at Bowood and the series of grottoes at Fonthill. The latter have proved as difficult to date as the grotto at Ascot, and it is equally problematic to divide the credit between Josiah and his father. Joseph Lane certainly built at least two grottoes for Alderman Beckford: but Josiah, in addition to creating more, may well have modified his father's earlier work during his own employment by William Beckford. The boathouse grotto (Fig.6.15), with its architectural exterior and structure, must date to Joseph's time, before the romantic taste of William Beckford took over. The boathouse, now suffering the depredations of time, has lost some of its portico, but the combination of boathouse, cold plunge bath and columns along the side, with a studded stone feature in the ceiling, survives, along with the remnants of rustic rockwork in the interior at the back.

The other grottoes at Fonthill are all of primitive style: if there was shell or mineral decoration it has not lasted. This gives the impression that all bear the trademark of Josiah, but although one is actually inscribed 'J.L. 1794' it is impossible to be certain. But they are each very different in size and construction, making the circuit round the lake in Fonthill Old Park, where they are all stationed, a sequence of wonders. South from the boathouse is the largest and most extensive of the structures, an angled tunnel under the road which incorporates two large chambers into which it opens out before finally issuing into an area near the lake marked by two more constructions. This grotto is mostly of rock (from Beckford's own quarries) with some stalactitish bumps of rock and various apertures to the sky and to the light.

Adjacent to this subterranean grotto is the Hermit's Cell, an above-ground structure in a dell. There are signs of habitation – a fireplace, an incised image of a magus, a carving of a god, and ammonites set into the exterior walls (Fig.6.16). Nearby, on more open ground, is the strange edifice called by Rutter an imitation of a cromlech. Now heavily overgrown, it appears to be a two-storey feature with a stairway leading to the

6.14 Josiah Lane's grotto at Wardour Castle, Wiltshire

THE BOAT HOUSE.

6.15 Boathouse at Fonthill, Wiltshire, from John Rutter, *Delineations of Fonthill and its Abbey*, 1823, p.96

6.16 Hermit's cave at Fonthill, Wiltshire

upper deck. Perhaps significantly, Beckford's garden at Monserrate contained a cromlech-like structure which may have served as inspiration (or vice versa, depending on dates).

If the Alderman and Joseph Lane were responsible for grotto-making, it would have been on this western side of the lake nearer the house. The grottoes on the eastern side are much more likely to have been the work solely of Josiah, though there is too little evidence to be sure. The main grotto here, really three grottoes in one, is a waterside chamber with stone stalactites (not plaster and lath, as at Painshill or Oatlands) and passages leading down from the bank on each side into it. There is a path that cuts this grotto off from the one behind it, slightly inland, which is characterised by passages around a cold bath. Finally, and supplying the bath, is a structure above and behind it, reminiscent of the grotto at Wardour, which is basically a conglomeration of rocks over which a stream known as the 'petrifying spring' ran.

The final two grottoes on the east side are caves cut into the quarries where Beckford made his Alpine garden (p.111). Although they are obviously based on the cavities resulting from excavation, there are some remnants of cut columns and arches inside, plus a statue or two. One of the caves contains the supposed Josiah Lane initials. The naturalistic effect is shown in Fig.6.17.

In addition to grottoes and cascades, some gardens displayed a range of scattered rockwork. Charles Hamilton was perhaps the first to see the possibilities and the romantic effect of extending rockwork beyond the grotto, in his outcrops on Grotto Island at Painshill. These clumps and cells by Joseph Lane, including an elaborate 'tufa' arch (Fig.6.18), were built of brick and then faced with spongestone. It was Hamilton who designed the cascade and rococo valley at Bowood, where Josiah Lane (with assistance) executed a complex of rockwork to rival Fonthill. The cascade masked a grotto behind the falling water, a network of passages, where openings gave a view through a gauze of spray (Fig.6.19). Some way behind the cascade was the Hermit's Cell, decorated with ammonites probably from a little later. But it was in front of the cascade that the imaginative use of rockwork burst out. On each side of the small valley were passages, arbours, niches and clusters of stone in all sorts of forms and sizes (Fig.6.20).

6.17 The quarry caves at Fonthill, Wiltshire, engraved by W Hughes, from John Rutter,
Delineations of Fonthill and its Abbey, 1823, p.92

It is related to the stonework at Painshill, but the impact is rather different: at Painshill the 'tufa' gives an eerie feeling of strangeness and fantasy while at Bowood it is more wild, primitive and 'natural'. John Britton, writing in 1801, said that the scene was truly picturesque and grand, and that it would appeal particularly to the painter and admirer of the Picturesque, 'for here he may indulge himself in the reveries of fancy and by a small effort of imagination, may think himself among the wild waterfalls of North Wales, or the thundering cataracts of Switzerland'.[23] Yet the cascade is not to be taken by itself, imposing though it is, and (as with the grotto at Painshill) should be seen in the context of the surrounding rockwork.

6.18 'Tufa' arch at Painshill, Surrey

6.19 Charles Hamilton's cascade at Bowood, Wiltshire

6.20 Rockwork at Bowood, Wiltshire

6.21 'Druids' Temple' at Ilton, Swinton, North Yorkshire

The grotto at Wardour was also supplemented by rockwork in the trees behind it and (though possibly later) a circle of stones to one side, forming a sort of henge domesticated by seats. Henges, or Druids' Temples, as they were often called, almost constitute a genre in their own right: they were quite common, starting with the circle of four upright stones at Hagley c1750. Among several examples may be singled out General Conway's at Park Place, Henley, and the early nineteenth-century 'cromlech' at Parc Glynliffon, Gwynedd. John Nash designed three upright stones and a capstone for Blaise, but this configuration was not executed. At The Woodhouse, Wombourne, Sir Samuel Hellier constructed a Druids' Temple in the 1770s, inspired perhaps by that at Hagley, not far away. It comprised a circle of upright stones, capped, with a free-standing stone to one side. Fragments of stone, urns, pitchers and bones lay strewn around. On a stone block was inscribed 'Procul este Profani' (Begone, you who are uninitiated) as if to suggest the closed nature of Druidic lore.[24]

Undernoticed has been the vast estate of Swinton, North Yorkshire, where Adam Mickle in the early years of the nineteenth century laid out a garden with lakes and profuse rockwork around the water, studded like almonds round a trifle, in addition to a set piece grotto. As part of the wider estate there is a Druids' Temple at Ilton, an elaborate henge still used at midsummer for neo-Druidic rituals (Fig.6.21). The formations of stones make it the artificial equivalent of the natural rocks at Brimham, being piled up fancifully.

One final use of rockwork may be mentioned, and that is the *souterrain*, an underground passage that might go beneath a road or path. A good example is at Stourhead, where the underpass (1760s) led back towards the lake. At Studley Royal, the Serpentine Tunnel, lined with stone, cuts and curves through the hill below the Octagon Tower, delaying the view at the upper end: the date of the early 1730s makes it an anticipatory picturesque conceit. Humphry Repton designed a *souterrain* to run through a mount at Ashridge, Hertfordshire, but that was not executed till well into the nineteenth century.

1 *The Works in Verse and Prose of William Shenstone, Esq.* (London: R & J Dodsley, 1764), Vol.II, p.144.

2 William Gilpin, *Observations on the River Wye* [1770] (London: R Blamire, 1789, 2nd ed.), pp.23-5.

3 William Gilpin, *Observations, Relative Chiefly to Picturesque Beauty, Made in the Year 1772, on Several Parts of England; particularly the Mountains, and Lakes, of Cumberland, and Westmoreland* (London: R Blamire, 1786), Vol.I, p.107.

4 Thomas Whately, *Observations on Modern Gardening* (London: T Payne, 1793, 5th ed.), p.96.

5 *Ibid.*, pp.102-5.

6 *Ibid.*, pp.109-11.

7 See Karen Lynch, '"Extraordinary convulsions of nature": The Romantic Landscape of Plumpton Rocks', *With abundance and variety: Yorkshire Gardens and Gardeners across Five Centuries* (Yorkshire Gardens Trust, 2009), pp.123-42, and Helen Lazenby, *Plumpton Rocks, Knaresborough* (Yorkshire Gardens Trust, 1997).

8 Lynch, *ibid.*, pp.125-6.

9 Lord Macartney, *An Embassy to China*, intro. Jonathan Spence, ed. H Cranmer-Byng (London: Folio Society, 2004), p.73.

10 Arthur Young, *A Six Months Tour Through the North of England* (Dublin, 1770), Vol.I, p.345.

11 Walter Scott, *Rokeby: A Poem* (Edinburgh, 1813, fifth ed.), pp.323, 327.

12 Timothy Mowl and Marion Mako, *The Historic Gardens of Cheshire* (Bristol: Redcliffe Press, 2008), pp.62-4.

13 *Ibid.*, p.73.

14 William Marshall, *On Planting and Rural Ornament* (London: G and W Nicol, G and J Robinson, T Cadell and W Davies, 1803, 3rd ed.), Vol.I, p.328.

15 *Works of Shenstone*, II, p.341.

16 William Gilpin, *A Dialogue upon the Gardens…at Stow* (London: B Seely, 1748), p.5.

17 George Bickham, *The Beauties of Stow* (London: G Bickham, 1750), p.3.

18 Michael Symes, *Mr. Hamilton's Elysium: The Gardens of Painshill* (London: Frances Lincoln, 2010), pp.74-5.

19 Humphry Repton, *Observations on the Theory and Practice of Landscape Gardening* (London: J Taylor, 1803), p.35.

20 Timothy Mowl and Dianne Barre, *The Historic Gardens of Staffordshire* (Bristol: Redcliffe Press, 2009), pp.138-40.

21 Timothy Mowl, *Historic Gardens of Worcestershire* (Stroud: Tempus, 2006), p.54.

22 Mike Cousins, 'The Grotto, Ascot Place, Berkshire:- another Lane grotto?', *Follies* 67, 2007, pp.12-13.

23 John Britton, *The Beauties of Wiltshire* (London, 1801), pp.221-2.

24 See Dianne Barre, 'Sir Samuel Hellier (1736-84) and his garden buildings: part of the Midlands "garden circuit" in the 1750s-70s?', *Garden History* 36:2, 2008, pp.321-2.

CHAPTER SEVEN

Picturesque Plantings

There is no question that trees, and to some extent shrubs and bushes, could contribute enormously to picturesque effect. In some instances there would be natural afforestation or ancient woodland, but in the majority of cases affecting gardens and estates the woodland would be deliberately planted, whether for commercial or aesthetic purposes, or both. Many mountainous areas, such as in Scotland or Wales, might be largely devoid of trees (as Dr Johnson remarked on his Scottish tour), and would require planting to make them properly picturesque.

Having credited the introduction of so many exotics, particularly from North America, with producing 'the richness of colouring so peculiar to our modern landscape…new tints in the composition of our gardens',[1] Horace Walpole goes on to define a category of garden that fits in aptly with the Picturesque. This he calls the forest or savage garden: 'I mean that kind of alpine scene, composed almost wholly of pines and firs, a few birch, and such trees as assimilate with a savage and mountainous country.' As exemplar of this category he cites the wood in the western part of Painshill. The firs and pines were, however, mostly of North American origin rather than Alpine, though the appearance was similar. But the point was that conifers had been brought in specifically to create an effect and to confer a character on that part of the gardens.

In an age that set considerable store by the effects of colour and shape of plantings, Thomas Whately devoted a section of his *Observations on Modern Gardening* to wood and its appearance in the landscape. The propriety of mixing different tints or forms is discussed in language that owes much to picturesque thinking. He distinguishes between the possible types of planting: wood (trees plus understorey); grove (no underplanting); clumps which can be close (a thicket) or open (a group); and single trees.[2]

Whately considers that a picturesque landscape – what he calls 'a romantic situation' – demands variety of planting that reflects the unequal surfaces of the ground:

> *Rudeness*, not greatness, is the prevailing idea; and a choice, directly the reverse of that which is productive of unity, will produce it; strong contrasts, even oppositions, may be eligible; the aim is rather to disjoint than to connect; a deep hollow may sink into dark greens; an abrupt bank may be shewn by a rising stage of aspiring trees; a sharp ridge by a narrow line of conical shapes: firs are of great use upon such occasions; their tint, their form, their singularity, recommend them.[3]

Repton, in his *Observations on the Theory and Practice of Landscape Gardening* (1803), explored the analogy between a painter's landscape which balances light and shade and the landscape gardener's corresponding approach: 'The light and shade of natural landscape requires no less to be studied than that of painting. The shade of a landscape-gardener is wood, and his lights proceed either from a lawn, from water, or from buildings.'[4] In devising an effective balance, the reader is enjoined to observe the principle of intricacy, in order to steer a course between uniformity and confusion.

From the comments made by various writers at the time, it emerges that plantings *en masse* are acceptable if balanced against other elements such as lawn and water, but that, where trees dominate a scene, they should be varied in species, form, colour and density of planting. But there can be no doubt that a picturesque landscape is dependent on plantings.

Whately considered that wood could strongly affect natural lines and contours of terrain, remedying deficiencies and enhancing heights. Disagreeable hollows could be filled in by trees; and rising ground could be made to appear even higher by covering it 'with wood of humble growth towards the bottom, and gradually taller as it ascends'. If a downward incline needs to be emphasised, trees planted in a downwards line will do that, but if they are planted across the slope the angle will be reduced. If a line of trees runs along the edge of a steep slope they 'give it depth and importance'.[5] By such means an owner could manipulate the landform to produce a picturesque appearance.

Trees not only enliven a landscape but can determine its character by expressing their own. Thus, William Shenstone declared that all trees had a character analogous to that of people and that oaks were the perfect image of the 'manly character' – particularly the British:

> As a brave man is not suddenly either elated by prosperity, or depressed by adversity, so the oak displays not it's verdure on the sun's first approach; nor drops it, on his first departure. Add to this it's majestic appearance, the rough grandeur of it's bark, and the wide protection of it's branches…A large, branching, aged oak, is perhaps the most venerable of all inanimate objects.[6]

The oak was, indeed, singled out by Gilpin for contributing more than any other tree to the characteristic English landscape.[7]

In the case of yew, there are obvious associations with churchyards and death, but in landscape they were frequently grouped around some feature such as a building, with the result that today the building may have disappeared but the yew trees indicate where it was, or that there was something of interest there. In particular instances the mournful associations of the tree might be evoked, such as those which surround the Mausoleum at Painshill.

Cypress, too, had associations of death, and thus might contribute to a romantic garden. At Betz, in France, the painter/designer Hubert Robert and the Duc d'Harcourt created a garden from 1780 that included a 'Vallée des Tombeaux', where cypress was joined by cedars, firs, sycamores, thujas and poplars to enhance an overall mood of sadness. Poplars will always have a special association with Rousseau's tomb at Ermenonville, France, where the idea of poplars on a small island containing a tomb was copied in several countries. The Scottish version is a tiny islet at Little Sparta, designed by Ian Hamilton Finlay.

In general, trees with dark foliage (usually evergreens) would engender a sombre feeling and light ones (e.g. lime or robinia) a more cheerful one. Mood in a garden could therefore be manipulated by choice of species. In mass planting the principal consideration would be

7.1 Tree with withered top, from *Gilpin's Forest Scenery*,
1883 ed., p.19

decorum, i.e. the appropriateness of the plantings to the situation. A steep hillside would therefore best be planted with such trees as would tend to grow there anyway, as Walpole recommended.

In his *Forest Scenery,* Gilpin examined the forms of individual trees in relation to their picturesque effect. As a lover of irregularity and asymmetry he admired the shapes produced by trees that had suffered disease, injury or the ravages of age:

> What is more beautiful, for instance, on a rugged foreground, than an old tree with a *hollow trunk*? or with a *dead arm*, a *drooping bough*, or a *dying branch*?...From the *withered top*, also, great use and beauty may result in the composition of landscape, when we wish to break the regularity of some continued line which we would not entirely hide.[8]

By beautiful, Gilpin means attractive in a picturesque sense. He illustrated the 'withered top' breaking the line of an eminence in Fig.7.1. He went on to bring in the paintings of Salvator Rosa as a comparison, and declared that the sight of a ruined tree could raise associations and stir feelings:

> These splendid remnants of decaying grandeur speak to the imagination in a style of eloquence which the stripling cannot reach; they record the history of some storm, some blast of lightning, or other great event, which transfers its grand ideas to the landscape, and, in the representation of elevated subjects, assists the sublime.[9]

This is tantamount to raising trees to the status of buildings for purposes of evoking historical associations or affecting mood. Gilpin then concentrates the bulk of his text on examining the aesthetic qualities of individual trees, along with some of their component parts such as branches and spray.

7.2 Imaginary landscape with trees, from Humphry Repton, *Fragments on the Theory and Practice of Landscape Gardening*, 1816, p.67

Repton cautioned against planting single trees in case they grew to impede the view. While the beech and the ash would permit a view under their branches, conifers would not, and might have to be cut down. To illustrate the point he composed a landscape (Fig.7.2), describing it as tame and beautiful rather than romantic or picturesque (though we might not agree), but pointing out that the small trees on the right would only grow upwards and not obscure the view. However, the two small fir trees would grow so tall and broad as to block out most of the landscape.[10]

'GILPIN'S FOREST SCENERY.'   239

Three ill-shaped trees, formed into a good group.
[*Page* 241.

7.3   Three ill-shaped trees, formed into a good group, from *Gilpin's Forest Scenery*, 1883 ed., p.239

Thomas Whately considered the proper location of single trees, particularly in relation to clumps.[11] The considerations were proportion between the tree and the lawn or other ground in which it was to grow; to provide variety of species and the distinctiveness of a specimen tree; to form a loose group or grove if planted near each other; to provide irregularity if not planted in a pattern; to relate by species to further woods; and to make use of existing mature trees where possible, which will have an impact the young tree will take a long time to emulate.

Having considered trees as individual features, Gilpin goes on to discuss them in combination, starting with clumps, which can vary from three or four trees together in a foreground to a detached wood in the distance.[12] The clump together must produce the right effect, depending on the closeness of planting, the pattern of planting, and the choice of species. Some kinds of tree will sort best with their own kind; others may effect a pleasing contrast juxtaposed with different trees. To illustrate placing, Gilpin shows how what he considers to be three ill-shaped trees can be combined into a pleasing group (Fig.7.3). Even though Gilpin often regarded an odd number as essential to picturesque grouping, he is prepared to allow for an even number if they are well matched (Fig.7.4). By contrast he uses an odd number to illustrate a badly-composed group (Fig.7.5).

Whately paid special attention to clumps, distinguishing them from groves and woods, though he admitted they could be considered as small forms of either. Clumps are either independent or relative: if independent, their beauty as single objects is the chief consideration, but if relating to other plantings the effect of the entire mass of woodland is the prime requirement. Trees of different kinds do not produce a unified 'head', and separate pinnacles of different heights do not combine well, but the overall pattern should be irregular. Clumps may admit understorey planting of shrubs and bushes.[13]

The criteria of planting clumps are considered next. Whately disapproves of any planting that suggests the hand of art, so a hill or swell should not be crowned with a clump (as Brown often did) but the trees should continue down the slopes. A large number of clumps will look unnatural, but a smaller number may relate to each other as long as they diversify the line of woodland, with gaps and glades. Clumps are best seen from below, or on the level. At best they can form distinct objects of interest or, in the distance, unite into a mass.[14]

For both Whately and Gilpin (and for others) the main considerations are aesthetic rather than botanical, though Gilpin adds the element of possible associationism. But for both of them the appearance of plantings must be natural even though the viewer may be well aware that they have been grown deliberately.

7.4 A well-balanced group of an even number of trees, from *Gilpin's Forest Scenery*, 1883 ed., p.243

7.5 An ill-balanced group of trees, from *Gilpin's Forest Scenery*, 1883 ed., p.245

In practice the principal players of the Picturesque were keenly aware of the contribution plantings could make and acted accordingly. The most extravagant was Thomas Johnes of Hafod who planted profusely to cover his hills and even in the lower valley areas. The site was originally far from woodless, however, and old and well-established timber gave Johnes a good start. Though records have mostly been destroyed, it is estimated that he planted up to four million trees, though quite a number failed. The plantings were mostly on meagre hill pasture and consisted predominantly of larch, though he also grew oak, beech, alder, elm, birch, ash, rowan and Norway spruce.[15] The aquatint of 1810 reproduced as Fig.10.5 gives an idea of the combination of the sublimity of the waterfall and the complementary plantings, which colour the whole tableau.

Uvedale Price continued the woodland planting of his forebears at Foxley. There was already a substantial extent of old wood, and plantings proceeded steadily over more than a century. Some was specifically for coppicing, so there is evidence of timber management for commercial purposes.[16] 500 acres were wooded, more than half the total estate, when Price was still in his twenties. By exchange of land and purchase of additional woodland, Price, with the help of his land agent Nathaniel Kent, had extended his sylvan holdings to about 700 acres by 1774.[17] It is clear that Price was deeply concerned with management of what was a composite of different types of timber – ancient woodland, coppices, groves and his own plantations encircling the Yarsop valley – and that he was attempting to play the benevolent squire. However, there are equally certainly picturesque considerations to the planning and placing of the plantations .

At Downton, Richard Payne Knight put into practice his belief that trees that naturally grew in the region or had been long established should be chosen. He did not like conifers, other than yew, and the set of watercolours by Thomas Hearne indicates such traditional species as oak, lime or beech. In his younger days he seems to have ordered 20,000 Scots pines, which would have been totally out of character with his later self, but there is no trace of them now and they may well not have been delivered.[18]

William Marshall's *On Planting and Rural Ornament* came out in 1796, though published in its original form in 1785, and is therefore highly relevant to this discussion. After considering the practicalities of propagating, growing and managing timber, the author goes on to consider the ornamental effect of planting. He takes the view that nature can always be improved on, but that planting must be appropriate to its situation. Accordingly he objects to the presence, in the foreground of a polished scene at The Leasowes, of a group of old ragged Scots pines as 'a pimple on this fine face'. Yet the same trees would have their place elsewhere: 'Every part of a view, and each article of the same dress, should be in character: these ragged ill favoured Firs, staring on a rugged point, in a rocky, ragged, picturesque scene, would be in place.'[19]

Marshall also stresses the importance of suiting the type of planting to the building(s) which it surrounds. The planting might therefore be gendered: for the 'Hunting Box', the style of planting should be 'masculine', with hardier sorts of shrubs (box, holly, laurustinus) and oak and beech as the most appropriate trees.[20]

Planting (according to Marshall) can sustain a beautiful or picturesque scene in combination just with lawn and water. In his description of Piercefield, which was famed for its rocks and the views of the Wyndcliffe, he observes that the prospect from the house actually excludes rocks and cliffs but is nonetheless worthy of being painted:

> The view from the house is soft, rich, and beautifully picturable: - the lawn and woods of Persfield, and the opposite banks of the river: - the Wye, near its mouth, winding through 'meadows green as emerald', in a manner peculiarly graceful: - the Severn, here very broad, backed by the wooded and highly cultivated hills of Gloucestershire, Wiltshire, and Somersetshire. Not one *rock* enters into the composition: - The whole view consists of an elegant arrangement of lawn, wood and water.[21]

Marshall then goes on to suggest what he thinks would be improvements, particularly by way of separating the Sublime from the Beautiful in the views.

'Capability' Brown was not often applauded for range of planting, but at Fisherwick, Staffordshire, he supplemented a colossal plantation (hundreds of thousands of trees), mostly of oak with some firs, by some mixed groups. The site was predominantly flat, with some modest rising ground behind the house, and planting was the only way to make something of it and disguise the flatness. Marshall detested the plentiful firs in the park and wished them replaced by deciduous trees, but he was highly complimentary about smaller, concentrated ornamental grouping. Even the conifers (if American) are admissible in such groups:

> The planting, too, is done in a masterly manner; the trees are well chosen, well arranged, and well planted; and are every where luxuriant, and flourishing. The Planes and American Firs, which are scattered in groups and single trees, over the lawns, and especially over a slope shelving to the banks of the Tame, are superiorly elegant…[Brown's] great aim has obviously been to throw

the whole place, as seen from the approach, into one grand composition; and he has succeeded. For in this point of view, the general assemblage is not only striking, as a passage in ornamental nature; but puts on an air of magnificence, which Fisherwick, taken in detail, cannot claim.[22]

Marshall sums up the effect of the park, the grounds, the surrounds of the house and, in all, the variety produced, giving entire credit to Brown.

Picturesque planting would often relate to the age of the trees – mature, well-grown specimens would both by form and character augment picturesque quality. So, from the point of view of design, the arrangement of such trees would be beholden to an earlier generation. Most owners, of course, would retain majestic old trees in their new plans for planting, so more often than not the plantings on an estate would be a mixture of old and new. But where plantations were totally new (as in some Scottish cases) the desired picturesque effect might take some time to arrive.

Nor was the idea of extensive woodland as ornament new, harking back to Roman times, and manifest in some Italian Renaissance gardens or the forests out of which some French baroque gardens were cut, such as Marly or Versailles itself. Forests were well established on estates in this country, e.g. at Cassiobury, Hertfordshire, by the seventeenth century, though sometimes that would be for commercial purposes. For a mixture of visual and commercial forestry still practised today, the huge estate of Cirencester Park, Gloucestershire, where a number of woods were joined together, would be hard to equal.

The effects of picturesque planting can still be seen at a number of sites, though after two centuries or more there is generally little original timber remaining. At Painshill, already cited by Walpole as the exemplar of the forest or savage garden, the western woodland was not only composed of the species appropriate to a hilly or mountainous country but it looked as if it was completely natural although mostly newly planted:

> it is a wood, which overspreads a large tract of very uneven ground; the glades through it are just cleared of the bushes and plants, which are natural to the soil; sometimes they are closed on both sides with thickets; at other times they are only cut through the fern in the openings; and even the larches and firs, which are mixed with beech on the side of the principal glade, are left in such a state of apparent neglect, that they seem to be the product of the wild, not decorative of the walk.[23]

Uvedale Price commented along similar lines when he described what pleased him most in the woodland walks was not what had been done but what had *not* been done, the result looking entirely natural though the result of the work of a supreme and sensitive artist.[24] By a semi-fortuitous set of circumstances this woodland retains its character today even though it has been virtually totally replanted.

Just as at Hafod and Painshill relatively recent plantings have served to retain the feeling of the original, so at Hackfall an abundantly wooded landscape remains as such, though much is self-seeded from initial plantings. It had, however, become overgrown, and recent clearance work has uncovered rockside paths and views through the wood that were until now unimaginable. The woodland originally showed to especially good effect from two viewpoints, Fisher's Hall,

7.6   General view of park at Hagley, West Midlands, with plantings, engraved by François Vivares after Thomas Smith, 1749

down near the river, and Mowbray Point, high up on the rim of the great bowl. From Fisher's Hall one could see the whole of two deep dingles leading down to the river, where hanging woods, scars of rock and water in various forms could be admired. From Mowbray Point one looked down on the same 'woody Dells' but also across to 'a vast extent of country, enriched with corn, meadows, and groves, a tract of unequalled beauty and exuberant vegetation'.[25] In an appendix to this account of 1822 the rarer native plants at Hackfall are listed, giving thirty-four plants and shrubs (not trees), which demonstrates the understorey that would accompany extensive woodland. As they were natives, some no doubt grew of their own accord though the classification of 'rarer' suggests several planted introductions.

Studley Royal was almost as famed for its woodland, though the water gardens came from an earlier, more formal date. Nonetheless there is an amphitheatre slope above them with substantial planting, and trees shaded the principal walks – ilex, oak, sycamore, cypress and luxuriant bay. In the naturalistic Mackershaw valley the 'Chinese landscape' was a mixture of rock and plantings, while from the Octagon Tower one could see not only this landscape but, specifically, Mackershaw wood. As with Hackfall, there are long lists of the rarer native plants at Studley and Mackershaw given in the 1822 account.

Richness of planting marked out some of the proto-picturesque landscapes mentioned in

Chapter Two. Fig.7.6 shows the extent and density of planting at Hagley, though the massing appears artificial juxtaposed with the clearings in front of two Seats (Pope's Seat the nearer, left of centre). But George Lyttelton was a plantsman who recognised the need for variety, and many exotics were introduced, principally from North America. The plantings were very varied, in size, scope and species and contrasted vividly with stretches of open lawn of differing sizes. Thomas Whately used the word elegance to describe the majority of the plantings, but there was a wilder area, more conformable to the 'savage' wood at Painshill:

> The grove behind the rotunda separates this from a large, airy, forest glade, thinly skirted with wood, careless of dress, and much overgrown with fern. The wildness is an acceptable relief in the midst of so much elegance and improvement as reign in the neighbouring lawns; and the place is itself pleasant; in no part confined; and from a Gothic seat at the end is a perspective view of that wood and tower, which were seen before in front, together with the Witchberry hills, and a wide range of country.[26]

Although the wood itself is thin, the character of the glade is that of a space within a forest, and is overgrown rather than open lawn. The light and shade of woods and glades was very much part of the picturesque effect.

At The Leasowes, planting was a determining factor in the construction of the landscape, both from a design point of view and from the species chosen. The trees were all natives – oak and beech predominantly, plus willow, larch, chestnut and Scots pines – with Shenstone choosing not to avail himself of the exotics that were by then flooding into the country. The effects were, accordingly, overwhelmingly 'natural' and traditional. The most intensive planting was in Virgil's Grove, a dense wood darkened by yew and with an understorey of hazel and other smaller trees (Fig. 6.5). Wild flowers were encouraged – primrose, violet, hyacinth, wood anemone – with fern, liverwort and aquatic weed in the watery parts. And although Shenstone was worried lest the Grove should too much resemble a garden, he planted some flowers to add colour and cheerfulness: 'I have two or three Peonies in my grove, y^t I have planted amongst Fern and bramble in a gloomy Place by ye water's side. You will not easily conceive how good an Effect they produce.'[27] But the shrubbery near the house was quite a different matter: as a discrete secluded spot it had no bearing on the overall appearance of the landscape, and Shenstone could let himself go with trees, shrubs and flowers producing a riot of colour that owed a great deal to plants from foreign climes.

At Hestercombe (c1750-80) Bampfylde decorated his landscape (small by most standards at thirty-five acres) with a mixture of plantings, but very much in an irregular taste. Arthur Young paid a visit in 1770 and described it as 'a rural sequestered vale with wood; much of the ground wild and romantic', adding that 'The grounds are finely thickened with wood, which is so artfully managed, as to make the extent appear vastly larger than it really is.'[28] This is akin to what Charles Hamilton achieved at Painshill, making his 'forest' appear much larger than it actually was.

At Halswell, also in Somerset, Sir Charles Kemeys Tynte, possibly aided by Thomas Wright, laid out a garden full of varied and often curious buildings. Timothy Mowl detects an iconography in the scheme, particularly with regard to Freemasonic symbolism concentrated in Mill Wood.[29] The wood, in this interpretation, becomes something of a *sacro bosco*, a sacred grove, with references to Moses and to Druids. The effect of the wood, dense with oak and bushes, was to stir feelings in the best picturesque tradition:

> the awful shade – the solemn stillness of the scene, broken by nothing but the fall of distant waters; have altogether a great effect, and impress on the mind a melancholy scarcely afforded by the cheerful view of a rich vale with the water winding through it, which is seen on crossing the park towards the house.[30]

Young added that the wood was fit for contemplation, and concluded that '*Halswell*, upon the whole, has received rich gifts from nature, and very pleasing ones from art.'[31]

Stoke Park (Stoke Gifford), near Bristol, presented the owner, Norborne Berkeley, and the designer, Thomas Wright, with ready-made woodland. Two mature woods already existed, kept apart by a long sweeping clearing. Wright developed the pair of woods, together with a third behind the house in novel ways: he sculpted them in order to produce a series of garden rooms or glades, which he called 'saloons', accessed by paths winding through the woods. The saloons were of different sizes and for different purposes – one, for example, was for the display of Bladud's Temple, dedicated to one of the legendary founders of Bath and reputedly the father of King Lear. Some contained flower beds, urns or seating, and a 'Saloon of Oaks' surrounded a rotunda. Two tunnels connected the woods or carried water. Also in one of the woods is the (restored) sarcophagus in memory of the 4th Duke of Beaufort. Further monuments, all of a solemn and serious nature, were/are found out on the open lawns and slopes beyond the woods.[32]

7.7 A venerable oak at Moccas Court, Herefordshire, engraved by Benjamin Pouncy after Thomas Hearne, 1798

Thomas Wright was keenly interested in making woodland more colourful and floriferous, and at Stoke Park roses were grown in profusion in the spinneys. The planting lists indicate many exotics, shrubs and flowers.[33] In his suites of designs for arbours and grottoes (1755 and 1758) he often suggested close planting to back these buildings. For an arbour of rough wood he suggests a backdrop of forest trees, but for a more elaborate domed variant he recommends honeysuckle and ivy on the exterior of the building, with the wood a little way back. A rustic aviary might be placed in the centre of a grove, the structure to be of maple trunks and the decoration to be ivy, honeysuckle and moss. A further design, for a regular though rustic arbour or quasi-grotto, demands a location near the sea, or in a region of rocks and mountains. The designs for six grottoes specify mixtures of shrub and a range of trees such as cedar, cypress, yew, holly and box, with an emphasis on evergreens and flowering shrubs. In each case the planting is intended to complement or enhance the grotto (and vice versa).

Moccas Court has been considered as a Wye landscape, but from a planting point of view it
has its own interest. Thomas Hearne, limner of Downton for Payne Knight, composed eight
watercolours of Moccas in c1788-9, which can be taken as a complement or companion set to
the Downton series. Four of the eight are concerned with trees or park views, and the large oak
in Fig.7.7 clearly fascinated Hearne as well as presenting a tellingly picturesque image that would
have won Gilpin's approval.

For sheer opulence and variety of planting, Fonthill stands ahead of any other picturesque
landscape. Although some wood previously existed, planted by Alderman Beckford and
his predecessors, the estate was mostly rather barren and it was William Beckford who was
responsible for the transformation into a wonderland of vegetation that clothed the slopes,
quarries, rockwork and lakes in the grounds. Beckford (1760-1844) grew up at a time when
the landscape garden was at its peak, and full use was being made of the exotics introduced
from North America in particular. From an early age he showed an interest in gardens,
and while in Portugal in self-imposed exile he designed the gardens at Monserrate. He was
the great-nephew of Charles Hamilton of Painshill, and visited him in retirement at Bath.
Hamilton would no doubt have told him a lot about Painshill, but his ten-acre garden at
Lansdown House was also to be inspirational to Beckford because of the variety and freedom
he had managed to squeeze into such a small space: 'a thousand beauties…It is probable that
the sight strengthened the love of rural economy and gardening which was afterwards so
marked a trait in Mr. Beckford's history'.[34] Not that economy seems the right word for the
extravagant Beckford.

The estate reached nearly 6000 acres by the time Beckford had acquired considerable tracts
of the surrounding land. The landscape was constructed piecemeal: different areas were
successively planted up in keeping with the character of that particular part. From 1781, the
year he attained his majority, Beckford planted assiduously – sometimes several hundred
thousand trees in a year, occasionally not less than a million.[35] The planting was varied,
including native trees, exotics, shrubs and bushes, and was used to mask or cover what had
been rather monotonous stretches of down and heath. Unlike 'Capability' Brown, who
preferred bare banks, Beckford brought his trees right down to the water's edge: 'The lake,
which always produces the most brilliant and captivating effect in a landscape, is here a
beauty of the superior order. Free from the formality of straight outline, its banks are thickly
wooded…'[36]

The pleasure grounds fell into two main areas, surrounding the Abbey and around the old
house and lake, the former attributable largely to Beckford and the latter inherited, but
augmented, by him. Around the Abbey, 'within the Barrier', John Rutter considered the task of
describing the scenery almost impossible, but tried nonetheless:

> The great principle upon which this labyrinth of groves has been constructed, is that of
> exhibiting an union of the wildest and the most ornamented scenery, - the picturesque and the
> beautiful, in close society. The utmost profusion of expense has been bestowed, not to amaze
> the senses by some rich and magical effect of art, but to keep the mind in a perpetual enjoyment
> of the most striking beauties, and richest decorations of nature;…The walks of Fonthill are
> ever reminding us of the ordinary features of woodland landscape, but we as constantly feel the

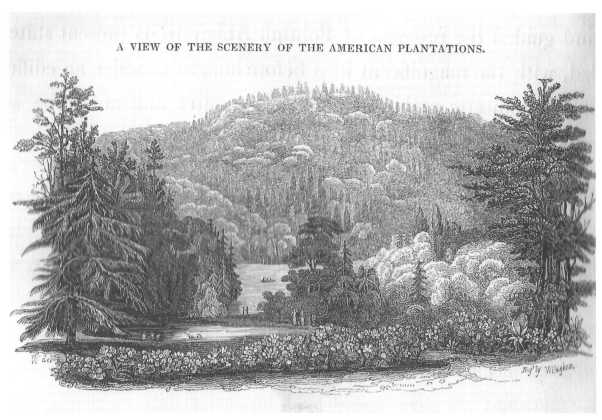

A VIEW OF THE SCENERY OF THE AMERICAN PLANTATIONS.

7.8 'American garden' at Fonthill, Wiltshire, from John Rutter, *Delineations of Fonthill and its Abbey*, 1823, p.82

presence of the creative power of unbounded means and exquisite taste, in rendering these woods what poetry might depict of the woods of Arcadia.'[37]

Rutter detects in the plantings the 'true spirit of English gardening, carried to its utmost extent of a bold and varied simplicity':

> Every tree, every shrub, and every flower, has contributed to the production of one unequalled effect of wild profusion. The woodbine and the jasmine not only interlace the thickets with their green and fragrant tendrils, but the rose and rhododendron bloom beneath the larch and the hawthorn, and the furze and the lily blossom in equal companionship…The union of the garden and the grove is almost universal.[38]

In this area there were lawns skirted by oak, fir and hawthorn; a larch walk; the Beacon Terrace, with birch, laburnum and acacia mingling with oak and fir; the Norwegian Lawn with its hut (Fig.4.8), a log house; but above all the American garden to the north of Bitham Lake (Fig.7.8), 'a labyrinth of sweets', in Rutter's phrase. It was one enormous shrubbery, cut through with paths winding past rhododendrons, magnolias, azaleas, the Carolina rose and allspice, together with the (true) robinia, wild rosemary and arbutus (strawberry tree).

The walks outside the Barrier, in the 'Old Park', provided scenes of a very different character. They were often wild and uncultivated, giving an air of neglect, and were punctuated by the sequence of grottoes around the lake (see pp.94-5). Nonetheless, shrubs were to be encountered, such as roses, syringa, lilac, laburnum, laurel and hawthorn, on the east side of the lake,

7.9 Flower garden at Nuneham Courtenay, Oxfordshire, engraved by William Watts after Paul Sandby, 1777

up towards the quarry grottoes (Fig. 6.17). This part was known as the Alpine garden, and multitudes of wild flowers surrounded the paths.

In order to appreciate the spectrum of planting, a twenty-seven mile route was planned, including a single Nine Miles Walk. In addition there were numerous small vermicular paths. Even where a straight approach drive was required – the Great Western Avenue, a mile long and a hundred feet broad – in order to display the Abbey, it was turfed, not gravelled (perhaps following the example of Beckford's great-uncle Charles Hamilton, who had turfed the Green Walk at Holland Park), and it undulated, with irregular plantings on each side blurring the borders.[39] Flowers were not forgotten, and Beckford sometimes mixed cultivated with wild species in his smaller plots, which included a Chinese garden dedicated to the cultivation of the rarest flowers.[40]

Picturesque planting could be conducted on a more intimate basis as well. Mark Laird has charted the rise of the varied eighteenth-century shrubbery, and the use of colour, in his book *The Flowering of the Landscape Garden* (1999), and trees might well form part of such smaller-scale creations. A good example would be the flower garden at Nuneham Courtenay, Oxfordshire (Fig.7.9), designed in consultation with William Mason. The garden, dating from 1773, comprised a lawn with kidney-shaped beds edged with box. Planting in the beds was 'graduated', with the tallest species in the centre. Cultivated flowers were mixed with wild, and there was a definite influence of Rousseau (who was a visitor), with a message that one should follow nature and be uplifted by it. The garden gradually became more romantic, the beds being allowed to grow and spread on to the lawn and the bowers becoming festooned.

Artists in the later years of the century painted a great many woody scenes. Those who had a particular feeling for such views include Hearne, Constable, Gainsborough, Richard Wilson and Paul Sandby. Hearne composed studies of individual trees as well as groups, and in addition to his series for Downton and Moccas Court he produced a set for Ashburnham, Sussex, in old age, with much of the Downton spirit. From as early as the 1750s, Sandby's watercolours, in his views of Windsor Great Park, bring out the irregularity and picturesque qualities of the scenes depicted, almost all by means of an emphasis on variety of planting. Later on he took particular trouble to portray individual trees, as in his series for Luton Park (Luton Hoo), Bedfordshire (c1765), *Tree Felling* and *The Rainbow* (both c1800) and *Morning* (c1794), which is dominated by an ancient beech.

1 Horace Walpole, *The History of the Modern Taste in Gardening* (1770) (New York: Ursus Press, 1995), p.46.

2 Thomas Whately, *Observations on Modern Gardening* (1770) (London: T Payne, 1793, 5th ed.), p.37.

3 *Ibid.*, p.42.

4 Humphry Repton, *Observations on the Theory and Practice of Landscape Gardening* (London: J Taylor, 1803), p.62.

5 Whately, *Observations*, pp.25-6.

6 *The Works in Verse and Prose of William Shenstone, Esq* (London: R & J Dodsley, 1764), Vol.II, p.134.

7 William Gilpin, *Observations, Relative chiefly to Picturesque Beauty, Made in the Year 1772, on Several Parts of England; particularly the Mountains and Lakes of Cumberland, and Westmoreland* (London: R Blamire, 1786), p.9.

8 *Gilpin's Forest Scenery*, ed. F G Heath (London: Sampson Low, Marston, Searle & Rivington, 1883), p.18.

9 *Ibid.*, pp.23-4.

10 Humphry Repton, *Fragments on the Theory and Practice of Landscape Gardening* (London: J Taylor, 1816), p.66.

11 Whately, *Observations*, pp.60-2.

12 *Gilpin's Forest Scenery*, pp.235-49.

13 Whately, *Observations*, pp.55-7.

14 *Ibid.*, pp.57-60.

15 Jennifer Macve, *The Hafod Landscape* (Pontrhydygroes: The Hafod Trust, 2004), p.23.

16 Stephen Daniels and David Watkins, 'A Well-connected Landscape: Uvedale Price at Foxley', *The Picturesque Landscape: Views of Georgian Herefordshire*, ed. Stephen Daniels and Charles Watkins (Nottingham: University of Nottingham, 1994), p.42.

17 *Ibid.*, pp.42-3.

18 Tom Wall, 'The Verdant Landscape: The Practice and Theory of Richard Payne Knight at Downton Vale', *ibid.*, pp.53-4.

19 William Marshall, *On Planting and Rural Ornament* (1796) (London: G & W Nicol, 1803, 3rd ed.), Vol.I, p.316.

20 *Ibid.*, p.278.

21 *Ibid.*, p.289.

22 *Ibid.*, pp.311-12.

23 Whately, *Observations*, pp.193-4.

24 Uvedale Price, *An Essay on the Picturesque* (London: J Robson, 1794), p.277.

25 *The Tourist's Companion* [to Ripon and its environs] (Ripon: T Longdale, 1822), p.73.

26 Whately, *Observations*, p.203.

27 *Letters of William Shenstone*, ed. Duncan Mallam (Minneapolis: University of Minnesota Press, 1939), 4 June 1750, p.206.

28 Arthur Young, *The Farmer's Tour Through the East of England* (London: W Strahan, W Nicoll, 1771), Vol.IV, p.2.

29 Timothy Mowl and Marion Mako, *Historic Gardens of Somerset* (Bristol: Redcliffe Press, 2010), pp.61-76.

30 Young, *Tour*, p.14.

31 *Ibid.*, pp.20-21.

32 See Timothy Mowl, *Historic Gardens of Gloucestershire* (Stroud: Tempus Publishing, 2002), pp.91-3.

33 David Lambert and Stewart Harding, 'Thomas Wright at Stoke Park', *Garden History* 17:1, 1989, p.80.

34 Cyrus Redding, *Memories of William Beckford of Fonthill, Author of 'Vathek'* (London: Skeet, 1859), Vol.II, p.148.

CHAPTER EIGHT

The Industrial Picturesque

If the Picturesque was, above all, concerned with scenery, then it would respond to alterations in the landscape itself. Some alterations were agricultural, the result of enclosure and changes in methods of farming, but it was the Industrial Revolution that had considerable impact on the face of the landscape in certain areas of the country. It might take various forms: mines, quarries, forges, mills and factories. Each would make its own mark on the natural landscape or produce smoke and flame, powerful and sometimes violent expressions of the industry being carried out. As was mentioned in Chapter One, the Picturesque has been criticised in recent years for placing visual and subjective reaction above all else, at the expense of understanding or appreciating the life of those who toiled in the workplace. William Gilpin, for example, has attracted disapproval for admitting that he did not want to visit the lead mine above Seathwaite in the Lake District, nor enter the Cornish tin mines – he was content to view them at a distance and comment on their appearance in the landscape.[1] His viewpoint is thus regarded as that of the leisured, detached tourist and artist: he was, however, dependent on a product of the lead mine for one of his tools of art, the pencil.

It so happened that the Industrial Revolution had its beginnings in an eminently picturesque spot. The area of Coalbrookdale, originally more extensive than the valley known by that name today, possessed well-wooded ravine scenery centred on the Severn Gorge and a series of pools that ran down into the river at right angles to it. What happened when Abraham Darby's furnaces discharged their cast iron and the eponymous Iron Bridge rose to span the Severn was that the landscape continued to be regarded as picturesque precisely because of (not despite) the industrial activity. Coalbrookdale became a Mecca for tourists and those seeking technological know-how, and it was for commercial reasons that it was in the interests of the town (later known as Ironbridge) to encourage depiction of the foundries, furnaces and mills as prominent objects in the view. So, despite the noxious side-products of the industry – the smoke, the noise, the sulphurous stench – paintings and prints showed an attractive landscape with the evidence of industry, though focal, kept neat and constrained. Smoke would be kept to a minimum, and the cleanliness of the workers' cottages was emphasised unrealistically. A view of the upper dale looking northwards by William Williams, 1777 (Fig.8.1), shows furnaces in the centre of the painting but tourists enjoying the scene in the foreground, and a mass of thick woodland leading to the Wrekin in the background.

Industrial buildings and processes became symbols of local and national pride in technology and commerce when presented as art and, though often sanitised in the interests of selling artworks to the consumer, nonetheless the force and fury of the furnaces occasionally made for a dramatic painting, as in Philip de Loutherbourg's lurid *Coalbrookdale by Night* of 1801, with smoke and orange flame from what were known as the Bedlam furnaces lighting up the sky (Fig. 8.2).

8.1 Afternoon view of Coalbrookdale, with Wrekin in background, painting by William Williams, 1777
[Shrewsbury Museums and Art Gallery]

The engineer George Perry in 1758 described Coalbrookdale's natural scenery lyrically before adding that 'The Beauty of the scene is in the mean time greatly increas'd by a near view of the *Dale* itself, *Pillars* of Flame and smoke, rising to a vast height, large *Reservoirs* of Water, and a number of *Engines* in motion, never fail to raise the imagination of Strangers.' However, the picturesque qualities move towards the Sublime: 'tho' it must be confess'd that all these things, join'd to the murmuring of the *Waterfalls*, the noise of the *Machines*, and the roaring of the *Furnaces*, are apt to occasion a kind of Horror in those who happen to arrive in the dark Night.'[2]

The Iron Bridge (1779) spanned the river at the most spectacular point of the gorge (Fig.8.3). It rapidly became iconic and was copied extensively in gardens, both as decoration and a symbol of the new technology and use of cast-iron. Quickest off the mark was Russia, which developed its own sophisticated ironworks in the late 1770s and produced what is said to be the earliest surviving copy of the Iron Bridge, near the Concert Hall in the park at Tsarskoye Selo (c1783). This was followed almost immediately by another copy at the Tauride Palace, St Petersburg. A further copy, one-quarter scale, was constructed at Wörlitz, Germany (Fig.8.5), as one of a number of features that reflected (particularly British) advances and Enlightenment thinking. In the later nineteenth century it was copied at that wild Northumberland garden at Cragside by the industrial entrepreneur William Armstrong in the form of the first steel bridge, one innovator emulating the achievements of a predecessor.

8.2 *Coalbrookdale by night*, painting by Philip de Loutherbourg, 1801 [© Science Museum Pictorial/Science and Society Picture Library. All Rights Reserved.]

Quite apart from imitations of the Iron Bridge itself, garden bridges were commonly constructed of cast-iron from then on, challenging stone as the material of choice. Indeed, although the Iron Bridge is often credited as the first in the world, an earlier iron bridge (1769) appeared as a footbridge in the park at Kirklees Hall, Yorkshire. Gardens such as Tsarskoye Selo and Wörlitz had clusters of several bridges of differing designs, and iron marched steadily on in this country right through the nineteenth century. For picturesque purposes, however, it was usually deemed more appropriate to have a simple rustic bridge of timber – cast-iron structures would be too obviously formal architecture.

8.3 Iron Bridge near Coalbrookdale, Shropshire

It was not only in the field of bridges that cast-iron showed its possibilities. Ornaments and finishings began to be employed in gardens: the drops in the arches of the Gothic Temple at Painshill reveal a very early use of the material. Eventually vases and sculptures would be formed of cast-iron. One construction, which would have been expected to be of wood, was the elaborate Gothic gateway at Tsarskoye Selo (1780), a rococo tracery confection taken from one of Decker's English pattern-books (Fig.8.4).

8.4 Iron arch at Tsarskoye Selo, Russia, after a pattern-book design by Decker

Sometimes the factory or mill would itself form a central part of a picturesque scene. The Sawmill at West Wycombe, Buckinghamshire, was adorned with flintwork and pavilions, and the house was topped by statues of William Penn and a haymaker, symbols of honourable management and labour. The Sawmill was at once functional and one of a number of decorative flintwork buildings in the eastern part of the park. Technology would have its own appeal and interest: many visitors commented,

8.5 Bridge at Wörlitz, Germany, quarter scale of Iron Bridge

for example, on the ingenious water wheel devised by Charles Hamilton at Painshill, which was replaced by the even more impressive cast-iron wheel by the firm of Bramah in the 1830s. Today's visitors often make a point of examining the machinery which is open for inspection in the pump house.

Industrial buildings began to be illustrated in prints, as indicators of local pride and also of an awareness that they might be attractive to a contemporary viewer or purchaser. The print of a scene on the River Esk in Yorkshire purports to centre on the new bridge as the feature of interest, but care is taken to include the cotton mill as an attraction in the view.

8.6 Iron forge at Downton, Herefordshire, engraved by Benjamin Pouncy after Thomas Hearne, 1798

Mostly, though, it was a case of owners seeking to surround the workplace with attractive gardens, the factory tying the layout firmly to the here and now and serving as a constant reminder of the industrial processes being carried on. The workplace would therefore be inescapably at the heart of the design both physically and conceptually. But the success of the gardens depended, of course, on the taste of the owners. There were many who either created new gardens or took over existing estates without having any taste except for money. These were the sort of *nouveaux riches* capitalists decried by John Parnell after the poetic estate of The Leasowes ran through a number of insensitive owners: 'In the name of Order, Decency, &c., &c., what has Captain *Turnpenny* of Birmingham & Powell of Liverpool or any other traficking West Indian slave masters to do with urns Inscriptions mottoes, shady Recesses dedicated to Poets Muses, &c., &c.'[3]

Richard Payne Knight knew how to accommodate industry in the naturalistic Picturesque of his own grounds at Downton. It was the ironworks that had largely built up the family fortune, though by Payne Knight's time it was tenanted by his uncle, Edward Knight. In 1784, having renovated the forge, Payne Knight let it for thirty-one years.[4] Although it was a little way down the river from the walks in Downton Vale, its presence would have made itself felt by sight, sound and smell and thus be part of the scene and the experience. The print (Fig.8.6) shows the Bringewood Forge in a suitably rustic setting.

A particular case where the factory owner had every incentive to surround himself with gardens

8.7   Soho Manufactory and grounds, Birmingham, engraved by J Walker 'from an original drawing', possibly by John Phillp, 1798

that expressed and confirmed his taste was that of Josiah Wedgwood. At his factory he not only produced ceramics but commemorated his neo-classical style of decoration by calling his property Etruria, from the Etruscan sources for some of his designs. From 1766 Wedgwood developed the site, 250 acres of open moor just north of Stoke-on-Trent, to include a new canal and facilities for coal and clay.[5] He built the factory plus a house for himself and a village for the workers. Although Wedgwood was acquainted with 'Capability' Brown it was to William Emes that he turned for advice on the gardens. Emes was responsible for a Chinese bridge, a summerhouse, fish ponds and plantations of beech, chestnut, lime and oak, together with nurseries.[6] Kitchen and flower gardens, a bowling green and two lakes further ornamented the scene, and Wedgwood took a keen personal interest in the gardens. Decoration and work were merged in, for example, the bowling green, which was open to the workers. Apart from the house, nothing survives of the eighteenth-century layout.

Two miles north-west of Birmingham was the estate of Soho, Handsworth, the property of Matthew Boulton (1728-1809), also no longer there. Boulton is well known as one of the prime movers of the Industrial Revolution, a partner of James Watt in the field of steam engines and steam power, while his Soho Manufactory and Mint (two separate buildings) produced coins, medals, ormolu, silverware and jewellery (and, later, steam engine components). Among Boulton's many interests in science, engineering and the natural world was a love of gardens, and from the 1760s onwards he created a landscape of eventually about eighty acres. The factories were substantial, employing up to 1000 people, and visitors came in large numbers to see them (Fig.8.7). A commercial tea-house was set up next to the Mint. Water power was a problem, and although the large lake was formed partly for practical purposes, the efficacious solution, steam, was only forthcoming when Boulton joined forces with Watt in 1774.

A fascinating monograph, *A Lost Landscape: Matthew Boulton's Gardens at Soho* (2009), describes the gardens, and the process of creating them, in detail. Boulton visited many gardens, made notes on them, and had a library on the subject. As with other industrialists' estates such as Etruria and Quarry Bank (see below), the Soho landscape was seen as enhancing the appeal of the factory as a visitor attraction. Boulton himself wondered 'How shall I plant & form my Western Ground so as to be handsome to ye sight of those going to ye Manufactory?'[7] What he created was a fine garden of the mid-century pictorial type, rich in plantings and 'incident', but one that also depended on the industry being carried on there – water was pumped up the hill to irrigate the highest reaches of the gardens, courtesy of Boulton's steam engines.

From an unpromising common of heath and poor soil Boulton formed an integrated landscape of beauty and industrial productivity. He was his own designer, claiming that he had planted every flower and tree, and that he had aimed to please himself, not to emulate the fashionable picturesque theorists: 'Nor Knight nor Price nor Burk sublime/I ape, in landskip, nor in Rhime'.[8] Although maintaining that he was independent, Boulton had nonetheless to devise his landscaping according to the conventions and modes of the time, and gained a great deal of inspiration from his garden tours and reading. In particular his knowledge of local gardens and parks, such as Hagley and The Leasowes or some owned by fellow industrialists, and his tours, especially to Painshill, gave him plenty of ideas for planting and putting up garden buildings.

Boulton was not the only one to combine function and ornament in garden hydraulics. Phillida Ballard notes that he might well have been familiar with other industrialists around Birmingham such as Joseph Webster at Penns, Sutton Coldfield, and Samuel Galton at Duddeston, Aston, whose functional mill ponds also served as aesthetic features in the view.[9]

8.8 Bridges and mill at Quarry Bank, Cheshire

The 'Green Frog' dinner service sent by Wedgwood to Catherine the Great contained quite a number of picturesque images of industry. Given the rapid and intense interest of the Russians in developing their own cast-iron industry, the inclusion of such images is not surprising. Indeed, Catherine invited several iron-workers to come over to Russia. The service, accordingly, included views of mills, charcoal-burning in the Forest of Dean, canals, collieries, glassworks and half-a-dozen illustrations of Coalbrookdale. In each case the industry depicted is made to look picturesque by relating it to, and making it part of, a wider landscape.[10] Water was generally part of the processes, whether in providing power or in distribution of products via barges and canals, and is prominent in these illustrations.

The gardens at Quarry Bank, Styal, north-east Cheshire, are a perfect example of industrial Picturesque, combining a huge cotton mill with the owner's house and pleasure grounds which are themselves topographically picturesque, owing much of the effect to the quarried rock. It was built in 1784 by Samuel Greg, and took advantage of the new technology – Arkwright's water-driven spinning machines.[11] The mill was followed after 1800 by a model village for the workers. The pleasure grounds were for the benefit of the owner, and tucked away on a slope to one side, but the mill was visible from there as well as from the mill meadow which faced the range front on. The mill was at the flat base of a steep valley, beside the mill-stream that powered its machinery, and there was a zig-zag path down to it.

The gardens comprise a lawn on the opposite side of the stream and more cultivated gardens cut against the slope beside the house. They are mostly formal in nature, with beds and paths dating from the 1820s onwards. However, the sandstone rockface forms a contrast above the beds, with a grotto-ish recess and steep paths. The cave was said to have been inhabited at separate times by a hermit, a pauper family and a blacksmith.[12] Set at some way up and behind is a Viewpoint, which commands an extensive prospect in which the garden, two differing bridges and the industrial range are integrated, the latter serving as a constant reminder that it provided the wherewithal for the creation of the gardens (Fig.8.8).

In Scotland there were many sites associated with picturesque rivers and falls. There were cotton mills in New Lanark connected with the Falls of Clyde, and different types of mill (paper, gunpowder, carpet) on the River North Esk in Midlothian. The Vale of Leven in Dunbartonshire, which was on the tourist circuit, was the scene of varied industrial activity in the late eighteenth and early nineteenth century.

Thomas Whately drew attention, in a section on rocks in his *Observations on Modern Gardening* (1770), to the added *frisson* that activity or industry could create in areas of rock. Machinery might also increase the sublimity of such scenes: 'Mines are frequent in rocky places; and they are full of ideas suited to such occasions. To these may sometimes be added the operations of engines; for machinery, especially when its powers are stupendous, or its effects formidable, is an effort of art, which may be accommodated to the extravagancies of nature.'[13] Nature and industry thus combine to produce an artistic effect.

8.9 Landscape at New Weir, Herefordshire, print by G Rowe after C Radcliffe, 1840

By way of illustration Whately goes on to describe the results of industry in a spectacular scene on the Wye, the New Weir in Herefordshire (Fig.8.9). He claims that the scene, splendid enough in itself,

> becomes more interesting and important, by the business to which it is destined. It is a chasm between two high ranges of hill, which rise almost perpendicularly from the water; the rocks on the sides are almost heavy masses; and their colour is generally brown; but here and there a pale craggy shape starts up to a vast height above the rest, unconnected, broken, and bare: large trees frequently force out their way amongst them; and many of them stand far back in the covert, where their natural dusky hue is deepened by the shadow which overhangs them. The river too, as it retires, loses itself in woods which close immediately above, then rise thick and high, and darken the water. In the midst of all this gloom is an iron forge, covered with a black cloud of smoke, and surrounded with half-burned ore, with coal and with cinders; the fuel for it is brought down a path, worn into steps narrow and steep, and winding among precipices; and near it is an open space of barren moor, about which are the huts of the workmen. It stands close to the cascade of the Weir, where the agitation of the current is encreased by large fragments of rocks, which have been swept down by floods from the banks, or shivered by tempests from the brow; and the sullen sound, at stated intervals, from the strokes of the great hammers in the forge, deadens the roar of the water-fall. Just below it, while the rapidity of the stream still continues, a ferry is carried across it; and lower down the fishermen use little round boats, called truckles, the remains perhaps of the antient British navigation, which the least motion will overset, and the slightest touch may destroy. All the employment of the people seem to require either exertion or caution; and the ideas of force or of danger which attend them, give to the scene an animation unknown to a solitary, though perfectly compatible with the wildest romantic situation.[14]

Whately's reaction is emotional yet strangely detached: the dangers of nature are blended with the dangers of the workers' occupations in a manner that gains his approval because the sublimity of the effect is heightened. William Gilpin, too, considers the forge only as it enhances the appearance of the view: 'in the midst of which, volumes of thick smoke, thrown up at intervals, from an iron-forge, as it's fires receive fresh fuel, add double grandeur to the scene.'[15] He quickly goes on to describe the river and its particular effect at the point of the New Weir, where the cascade, though of no great height, was sufficiently turbulent to produce the authentic sublime thrill: 'But here, the violence of the stream, and the roaring of the waters, impressed a new character on the scene: all was agitation, and uproar; and every steep, and every rock stared with wildness and terror.'[16]

Another garden, now partly recovered by archaeology, that combined a picturesque setting with a forceful, not to say dangerous, industrial process was Basingill, near Sedgwick, Cumbria, where a Quaker, Isabella Wakefield, created an early nineteenth-century layout which included her father's gunpowder mills.[17] The site was an abandoned quarry with steep walls, where a terrace, steps, a dropping well, walks, a wooden bridge and arbours, were set out just above the noisy River Kent. A viewing platform looked on to the particularly dramatic waters of Levens Force. However, relics of an industrial past were not always regarded as picturesque: Sir George Beaumont removed the spoil of mining and the remains of engine houses in his grounds at Coleorton, Leicestershire, when creating a garden that Wordsworth had a hand in. When Isabella Wakefield married, she moved to Dingle Bank, near Liverpool, where sandstone cliffs above the Mersey were exploited for their view and for the effects of wind and spray.[18]

Picturesque scenes could be given new identity by industrial activity yet continue to serve as a more peaceful backdrop to it. Gilpin noted that only half a mile from Tintern Abbey

> are carried on great ironworks; which introduce noise and bustle into these regions of tranquillity. The ground about these works, appears from the river to consist of grand woody hills, sweeping, and intersecting each other, in elegant lines. They are a continuation of the same kind of landscape, as that about *Tintern-abbey*; and are fully equal to it.[19]

Some developments associated with the Industrial Revolution had begun earlier in the century. Following the example of collieries in the north-east, where coal was transported to the river along rail tracks, Ralph Allen, owner of Prior Park, just outside and overlooking Bath, constructed a mechanical railway in the 1730s by which stone could be carried down from his quarries on Combe Down to the wharf on the River Avon. This track occupied part of the road (now Ralph Allen Drive) which goes alongside the steeply sloping grounds of Prior Park, as shown in Fig 8.10, which is an engraving of 1750. Gillian Clarke explains how the system worked:

> Models of railways and carriages were sent south to Bath, and Allen engaged the Bristol engineer, John Padmore, to construct the railway. The trucks were worked by horses on the level; two were used for a loaded truck, or to return an empty one uphill; loaded trucks descended the long hill by gravity. With its ingenious controls, a truck could be braked and if necessary stopped on the steepest part of the hill by one man.[20]

Although the gardens were of considerable interest (more so, actually, than appears in the print), it was the railway that became more of a tourist attraction, as demonstrated by the gaze of the visitors and the fact that the artist draws such attention to it.

Early in the field of industry being twinned with garden-making was Herbert Mackworth at The Gnoll, Neath. From 1727 he dammed streams above the house into a sequence of pools, creating a body of water sufficient to power the machinery in his coal mines and copper-smelting works lower down. The grounds were landscaped in the 1740s, with a long artificial cascade leading down from the largest pond. Near the top was a made cave; the water fell over drystone steps; and an arched bridge and root-house stood at the bottom.[21]

A fully integrated garden and industrial complex, in this case a brass foundry, was to be found at Warmley, east of Bristol. William Champion, another Quaker industrialist, produced brass, copper and spelter in a manufactory set in a modest garden laid out between 1746 and 1769.[22] He was the first commercial producer of zinc. The garden was more rococo than picturesque, perhaps, but the industry lent it a topical and partly picturesque flavour. As was usual, water was necessary for powering the processes, so in this instance the Warmley Brook led into a designed lake of thirteen acres, now dry and mostly built over. On an island in the lake stood (and still stands) a hideous cement colossus of Neptune, with blank clinker or slag as adornment including a 'fig leaf'. Slag was used for several decorative purposes in the garden – a large arch

8.10 Garden and railway at Prior Park, Bath, print by Anthony Walker, 1750

which spanned the brook, the exedral walling of the Echo Pond, and the grottoes, which were at once functional and garden features. The grotto tunnels contained a pumping engine and recycled the lake water via a twenty-foot waterfall said to have been based on the falls at Tivoli. The grotto had a main chamber and pools but no shell or crystal decoration (Fig.8.11). Slag is actually found in patterns on the walls, and a sort of Hell mouth is made of a vaulted arch deep in the passages.[23]

Warmley gardens contained a number of other features – elm walk, viewing mount, summerhouse, boat house, clock tower, chequered wall. Of these, the summerhouse was originally used to control the water flow into the lake and was built from copper slag blocks.[24] The boat house may have housed an engine for pumping water, while the clock tower (later rebuilt) was used for making pins, boots and drain pipes. The chequered wall consisted of clinker, brick and slag blocks. The principal brass works probably lie under more recent buildings, but we can see that several of the processes were carried out in garden buildings that were constructed partly or wholly from waste.

Warmley was unusual in unifying garden and industry, but the by-products of industry – waste such as slag and clinker – were often put to good use in the garden. In particular, grottoes were frequently adorned by the burnt and blackened material. Individual pieces would be stuck on the walls alongside fragments of glass, pebbles that were sometimes painted, and crystals and other minerals. Use of slag would create a rather sinister, possibly even frightening, effect that might well produce a picturesque *frisson*. Cinders even found their way into the waters of the cascade near the root-house dedicated to Lord Stamford at The Leasowes and into the pools at Hagley.[25]

The grotto at Goldney, Clifton, Bristol, bears the marks of more than one industrial product. Created by Thomas Goldney III, yet another Quaker and a business partner at Coalbrookdale and Warmley, the grotto took from 1737 to 1764 to complete. The tunnels to the north and west of the grotto are of brick faced with slag, which also dresses the southern entrance to the tunnels. The extensive floor tiling is made from clay fired and glazed at Coalbrookdale. Another connection is found in the Tower (1764), which housed a beam-engine to draw water from the well beneath to service the

8.11 Remains of grotto at Warmley, Bristol

small canal in the garden and the cascade within the grotto. Engine parts (and later a new cylinder) were obtained from Coalbrookdale.[26]

1 Stephen Copley, 'William Gilpin and the black-lead mine', *The Politics of the Picturesque*, ed. Stephen Copley and Peter Garside (Cambridge: Cambridge University Press, 1994), pp.42, 47-9, 57.

2 Quoted in *The Green Frog Service*, ed Michael Raeburn, Ludmila Voronikhina, Andrew Nurnberg (London: Cacklegoose Press, 1995), p.53.

3 John Parnell, 'Journal of a tour thro' England and Wales, Anno 1769', British Library of Political and Economic Science, MS Coll. Misc.38, Vol III, p.85.

4 Tom Wall, 'The Verdant Landscape: The Practice and Theory of Richard Payne Knight at Downton Vale', *The Picturesque Landscape: Visions of Georgian Herefordshire* (Nottingham: University of Nottingham, 1994), p.55.

5 Timothy Mowl and Diane Barre, *The Historic Gardens of Staffordshire* (Bristol: Redcliffe Press, 2009), pp.186-8.

6 *Ibid.*, p.188.

7 Quoted in Phillida Ballard, Val Loggie and Shena Mason, *A Lost Landscape: Matthew Boulton's Gardens at Soho* (Chichester: Phillimore & Co, 2009), p.xiii.

8 *Ibid.*, p.3.

9 *Ibid.*, p.6.

10 See *The Green Frog Service*, pp.210-15.

11 Timothy Mowl and Marion Mako, *The Historic Gardens of Cheshire* (Bristol: Redcliffe Press, 2008), p.107.

12 Tim Longville, 'The Garden by the Mill', *Country Life*, 3 April 2008, p.90.

13 Thomas Whately, *Observations on Modern Gardening* (London: T Payne, 1793, fifth ed), p.111.

14 *Ibid.*, pp.111-13.

15 William Gilpin, *Observations on the River Wye…*(London: R Blamire, 1789, second ed), p.39.

16 *Ibid.*

17 See Abby Hunt and Paul Everson, 'Sublime Horror: Industry and Designed Landscape in Miss Wakefield's Garden at Basingill, Cumbria', *Garden History* 32:1, 2004, pp.68-86.

18 *Ibid.*, p.82.

19 Gilpin, *Observations*, p.52.

20 Gillian Clarke, *Prior Park: A Compleat Landscape* (Bath: Millstream Books, 1987), p.12.

21 Elisabeth Whittle, *The Historic Gardens of Wales* (London: HMSO/Cadw, 1992), p.40.

22 For a description, see Timothy Mowl, *Historic Gardens of Gloucestershire* (Stroud: Tempus Publishing, 2002), pp.93-6.

23 *Ibid.*, pp.94-6.

24 *Warmley Garden and Grotto*, leaflet produced by Kingswood Borough Council, 1987.

25 Michael Symes and Sandy Haynes, *Enville, Hagley, The Leasowes: Three Great Eighteenth-Century Gardens* (Bristol: Redcliffe Press, 2010), p.122.

26 See Robert J Savage, 'Natural History of the Goldney Garden Grotto, Clifton, Bristol', *Garden History* 17:1, 1989, pp.1-40.

CHAPTER NINE

The Scottish Picturesque

The image of Scotland in the eighteenth century has tended to be tarnished by Dr Johnson's scathing remarks on the scenery and the inhabitants, though there was doubtless some exaggeration intended to provoke and tease Boswell. However, in picturesque terms, it is necessary to take account of some at least of his criticisms. To a visitor today Scotland might well seem the most picturesque part of the United Kingdom, but to many eighteenth-century eyes the vast mountain ranges, the expanses of moor, the inhospitable climate and the lack of vegetation and human habitation spelled not the Picturesque but the Sublime. It was William Gilpin, as we might expect, who tried to separate the two on his tour of the Highlands (tour 1776, published 1789). He stated that 'A *Poverty of landscape* from a want of objects, particularly of wood, is another striking characteristic in the views of Scotland',[1] and that, though majestic and grand, such scenes were aesthetically monotonous. '*Simplicity*, and *variety* are the acknowledged foundations of all picturesque effect',[2] he wrote, concluding that the lack of features was the source of sublimity. Continual rain and mist contributed as well.

It was bareness that was often complained of. Vegetation – trees – would bring a scene to life, as would evidence of habitation, but in the mountains too often there were no signs of growth or animation. Dr Johnson even claimed that, from the Tweed to St Andrews, there were no trees that predated the century, condemning the paucity of wood.[3] That claim, however, contains an admission that at least there was some new planting.

Most commentators at the time (and indeed often today) treated the whole subject of the Picturesque from an English and Welsh standpoint. Indigenous Scots were much more likely to appreciate the power of the Scottish landscape. There were fewer English who toured Scotland than England and Wales and who would have discovered that for mountain scenery the country was in a league of its own, reminding those who had been on the Grand Tour of the Alps: as Thomas Gray remarked in 1765, 'Since I saw the Alps, I have seen nothing sublime till now.'[4]

But of course not all Scottish scenery was bare or sublime, and Johnson had, unfortunately, bypassed the whole of the central belt, where there was a good deal of early planting. Henry Skrine lamented:

> I wish Dr. Johnson had passed from Blair to Dunkeld, before he branded Scotland with the imputation of being bare of wood; for I never remember to have seen richer groves of oak, beech, and birch, or finer single trees, in any part of England. But he seems to have travelled only through the worst parts of the country.[5]

John Stoddart, visiting in 1799 and 1800, distanced himself from Johnson, declaring that he had misrepresented Scotland. By dint of some rather contorted reasoning he tried to reconcile the romantic, the Sublime and the Picturesque by subjugating the former two to the latter: 'the whimsical breaks and abruptness of the romantic, or the continuity and massiveness of the sublime, may all, by the powerful operation of nature, be rendered subservient to the picturesque effect'.[6] Even Gilpin conceded that, in particular, some foreground features were picturesque.

9.1 Cascade with Ossian, anonymous print c1780

Mention of the romantic raises an important factor colouring the way in which some Scottish scenery was viewed from the 1760s. Following various Jacobite defeats, most notably that at Culloden in 1746, Scottish nationalism slowly healed and reasserted itself, partly in the form of historical (or pseudo-historical) poetry. In the wake of a schoolmaster, Jerome Stone, who translated Gaelic verse said to have been written in pre-Christian times by the bard Ossian, the young James Macpherson took up the cause. His first publication was *Fragments of Ancient Poetry, collected in the Highlands of Scotland, and translated from the Galic or Erse Language* (1760), rendering into English prose a number of stories of Gaelic heroes transplanted into Scotland. The success of this work prompted the production of two epic poems, *Fingal* (1762) and *Temora* (1763), completing the Celticising of the Gaelic originals.[7] They plunged their translator, Macpherson, into a controversy straight away which still has not cleared entirely. Many (including Johnson) questioned the authenticity of the supposed source poems, but even though some of the translations are likely to be fabrications, there is no denying the poems' force and impact.[8] It is possible that Macpherson took some inspiration from Thomas Gray, whose poem *The Bard*, set against a background of Welsh mountains, was published three years before the *Fragments*.

The Ossianic poems bring to mind the parallel case of Thomas Chatterton. He was only ten when *Fingal* came out, and died, in still disputed circumstances, at seventeen in 1770, with his poems collected together in an edition of 1777. He thus postdates Macpherson and may well have absorbed something from him. Chatterton's main claim to (precocious) fame was his production of several poems allegedly composed by Thomas Rowley, a monk from the Bristol of three centuries before – but all was invention. His death was celebrated and depicted as the first flowering of romanticism, and he was commemorated by a garden monument (Fig.1.10).

The significance of Ossian/Macpherson for the way in which Scottish scenery was viewed was considerable. Malcolm Andrews has described how virtually every tourist brought a copy of these 'primitive' poems with them, which both provided an accompaniment to the landscape and induced an extra dimension of feeling for it.[9] The verse (rendered in strongly rhythmical prose) spoke not only of heroic deeds, legends and long-gone bards but of the background scenery, which was often of a sublime nature and thus identifiable with what the tourists were actually looking at. For example, Charles Cordiner exclaimed at the cascade near Curril in 1780 (Fig.9.1):

a wild and beautiful cascade in its fall: the noise of the torrent echoing in a lofty and deep cavern; the cavern shagged with shrubs and aged trees, among which the wild-fowl make their nests; the rivulet murmuring round insulated piles of rock; and the distant prospect of these halls and monuments of antient heroes, forcibly recall to mind the images of the *Ossian* song.[10]

An inevitable consequence, fuelled partly by reborn nationalism but also doubtless by a desire to increase tourism, was that particular features, whether natural or artificial, began to attract Ossian's name and those of his heroes, such as Fingal. Accordingly, Fingal's Cave became an appellation for a spot celebrated in image and music, and not just locally but throughout the western world. Glencoe, site of a notorious battle, became associated with various of the names in Ossian.[11]

9.2 Duniquaich, Inverary, aquatint by William Gilpin, from Gilpin's *Observations...the High-Lands of Scotland*, 1789

Ossian became identified with a number of locations, including gardens. The spirit of Ossian was detected at the summit of Duniquaich, Inveraray (Fig.9.2),[12] while at Glen Almond an excavated coffin became known as Ossian's Grave.[13] But it was in the grounds at Dunkeld that Ossian made his presence most felt. A seat of the Dukes of Atholl, Dunkeld had grounds laid out in the earlier eighteenth century, but it was more intensively landscaped from 1757 by the third Duke. Work continued for several decades, the picturesque qualities of the site being progressively exploited. A hermitage afforded the best view of the most spectacular of the waterfalls, and a second, more crude and rustic structure of coarse stones appeared above it – this building, something of a grotto, came to assume the title of Ossian's Cave, complete with an Ossianic inscription, among verses from English poets. A stone seat nearby, perched perilously above the foaming waters, was called Ossian's Seat, although these names seem to have been somewhat interchangeable. But it was the hermitage itself that attracted most attention. Christopher Dingwall and Don Aldridge have examined the history and cultural significance of this iconic building, reconstructed in modern times and in any case rebuilt, probably substantially, in the 1780s.[14] In this latter manifestation it was known as Ossian's Hall. A large panel bore a painting of Ossian singing his lays: a spring caused the panel to slide aside, and the waterfall was revealed. The chamber behind the panel had a bow window and was lined with mirrors that reflected and multiplied the effect of the waterfall, rather as Pope had done by the skilful placing of mirrors in his grotto at Twickenham. The mirrors replaced previous panes of red and green glass that caused the cascade to appear like fire or rolling down like molten lava, an effect that failed to impress Gilpin and some others. Gilpin also found the presence of flowers and shrubs in the adjoining garden incongruous.[15]

Despite reservations about the coloured glass, the mirrors and the flowers, the waterfall itself never failed to excite. R J Sulivan commented on the overall effect of the scene just before the Hermitage became Ossian's Hall:

The situation of this place, surrounded on all sides by hills, many of them covered to the summit with oak growing luxuriant and wild, and with a variety of other trees, and washed by branches of the Tay and of the Braun, is highly picturesque and diversified: especially at the spot called the Hermitage, where the Braun, rushing down the precipice, foams through a glen, wildly confined by a wood of the most exquisite foliage, and at length joins itself to the Tay.[16]

The cult of Ossian extended far beyond Scotland. In the grounds at Hagley, Worcestershire, a set of four upright stones erected as a sort of Druid circle in the mid-century were referred to later on as Ossian's Tomb,[17] following Lord Lyttelton's acquisition of a copy of the poems as soon as they came out. A large cavern in the 'Heights of Abraham' near Matlock, Derbyshire, acquired the name of Ossian's Hall, while in attempting to describe a panoramic view of the wild landscape at Hafod in mid-Wales George Cumberland had to evoke the spirit of Ossian and quote appropriately.[18] And at Mon Repos, Vyborg, close to the Russo-Finnish border, a pine-clad and rocky site overlooking a vast stretch of water has been seen as laid out under the influence of Ossian.

Not totally dissimilar to the configuration at Dunkeld was the hermitage placed beside a waterfall, the Linn of Corriemulzie in the Forest of Mar. This property, owned by Lord Fife, was in a wild setting but this particular scene was 'gardenised' by means of a path and steps, the hermitage and some of the plantings (Fig.9.3). Charles Cordiner provided a commentary to this print:

> An easier access and more pleasant path invites to the Hermitage, where the torrent, rushing down the cliffs, constitutes the characteristic beauty of the scene represented in the plate. That Glen penetrates deep among precipices, which lie under the brow of a most majestic rocky mountain, among whose cliffs the pines and poplars are waving high in the air.[19]

Cordiner goes on to say that this spot encourages reverie. It has not always found favour, however, and the artificiality of the man-made accoutrements has been judged to jar with the wildness of the forest.[20] Yet a third hermitage overlooking a dramatic waterfall was constructed, probably in the 1760s, at Taymouth Castle. A cascade, one of the Falls of Acharn, was concealed from sight by plantings and an artificial mound pierced by dark tunnels which led to the viewing room.[21]

9.3 Cascade and hermitage at Corriemulzie, Forest of Mar, from Charles Cordiner, *Remarkable Ruins and Romantic Prospects of North Britain*, 1788

At Cora Linn, a fall of eighty feet plunged headlong into the River Clyde, with rock ledges breaking the fall and a further example of a viewing tower or house (1708). Gilpin thought the falls were best seen from this 'lofty seat in a gentleman's garden'.[22] The scene was both grand and picturesque to him. Thomas Newte was much taken by the picturesque setting of the falls: 'woody banks, the romantic face of the country, and the form of the rocks over which they dash, so varied, as to give the mighty torrent the grandest, as well as the most diversified appearance.'[23] The tower was poised on rock above the falls, and at one time was fitted up with one or more mirrors,[24] which must have amplified the spectacle just as the hermitage at Dunkeld did.

Newte was even more overcome by the boiling turbulence of Cauldron Linn in Glen Devon (Fig.9.4). The sight would

9.4 Cascade at Cauldron Linn, River Devon, print c1820

appal every spectator. Just below this, the whole river is precipitated, in one sheet, from a height of an hundred feet, upon huge stones, torn from the faces of the rock. This fall, from the boiling appearances just mentioned, is called the *Chaldron Linn*. The immense sheet of water pouring from the rock, exhibiting in its upper parts all the colours of the rainbow, and appearing below, where it falls on the rocks, like white dust or vapour; this admirably contrasted by the dark and silent face of the abrupt rock, in most parts rugged and naked, but in some presenting a few shrubs and pendulous trees: these circumstances united, make an impression on the mind of something that is solemn and awful; arrest the giddy tumult of human hopes and fears, and invite to serious reflection, and sublime contemplation.[25]

Christopher Dingwall has argued convincingly that picturesque and sublime scenery was incorporated in gardens and wider landscaping long before the taste for such scenery emerged in England through theory and practice. This also indicates that appreciation of wild landscape came earlier to the Scots than it did to many of their southern neighbours.[26] However, it did not mean the abolition of formal garden elements, many of which survived, to co-exist with the wilder parts, as has been shown by the flower garden at Dunkeld. Chatelherault, South Lanarkshire, is a good example, with baroque formality of layout – a broad, mile-long avenue on the scale of Badminton or Cirencester Park from the house to Hamilton Palace, and a *parterre de broderie* – juxtaposed with an exceedingly picturesque gorge set to one side of and behind the house, which acted as a hunting lodge and summer pavilion. One wing was for entertaining, another for dogs. The ravine, with steep wooded slopes, is seen at particular advantage from the bridge, since the trees now mask the river from above. Opposite is the ruin of Cadzow Castle to add flavour to the natural qualities of the view.

Lady Hanway observed that one could see the castle from the gardens, and enthused: 'one of the most romantic walks you can conceive – the water gushing through breaks in the opposite rock, falls with a pleasing noise into the river that rolls beneath your feet, with a hanging wood above.'[27] Gilpin was likewise smitten, commenting that the walks encouraged ideas of solitude, and that the interwoven elements of wood, rivulets and winding paths produced an assemblage 'of soothing

9.5   Folly beside rock path at Mount Stuart, Isle of Bute

ingredients, that they have a wonderful effect on the imagination. I must add, that I do not remember ever meeting with a scene of the kind, which pleased me more than the wild river views about Chatelherault.'[28]

Mount Stuart, Isle of Bute, would be another instance of the 'artipicturesque', combining formality with its opposite. The gardens have been changed over the centuries, especially by Thomas Mawson in the early twentieth century, but the impact owes much to nature, in particular the background of the sea. A formal green avenue leads to a folly, a composite of classical and rustic, but behind it a perilous path wends its way below impending rocks (Fig.9.5). Another garden with the sea beyond the house lawn was Dunglass, East Lothian, which could also boast a (genuine) medieval chapel, a wooded glen, cliffs and a small sixteenth-century fort within which a summer-house and bowling green were installed in the eighteenth century.[29]

Sometimes artificial elements would unite well with the natural dramatic landscape. Gilpin noted that at Doniquaick (modern Duniquaich) the features – bridge, lake, hill, the plantings, a building on top – blended into a composition that pleased his picturesque eye and impelled him to sketch it (Fig.9.2). The hill was itself clad with pines and birch, which became more sparse as they ascended. From the watch-tower on top of the hill (870 feet) Gilpin reckoned it to be one of the grandest views in Scotland.[30] The panorama covered an extensive view of Loch Fyne, Inveraray Castle and the plantings in the valley.

9.6   Dalkeith Palace and park, Midlothian, engraved by William Angus after J Barrett, from Angus's *The Seats of the Nobility and Gentry*, 1788

A picturesque landscape park might be found not all that far from the house. The engraving of Dalkeith by William Angus after Barrett (Fig.9.6), taken from Angus's *The Seats of the Nobility and Gentry*, depicts woodland, some of which has clearly been planted, a bridge and water swirling round rocks. Stoddart observed that the river had a pleasing wildness in the dark wood.[31] Dalkeith was one of the seats of the Dukes of Buccleuch: their main residence was Drumlanrig, an estate ringed round by distant mountains which Gilpin and others earlier, like Daniel Defoe, found disagreeable. From the early nineteenth century, however, extensive planting was carried on at Drumlanrig, creating the vast woodland that exists today. The balance of forest and far-off mountains would have gone a long way to propitiating Gilpin.

9.7 Habbies How, Midlothian, illustrating a scene from *The Gentle Shepherd* (1725), engraved by R Scott after J Stevenson, late eighteenth century

9.8 Scene on the River Esk, near Edinburgh, after a drawing by Sir John Carr, 1809

Scenery might be 'arranged' by means of plantings and paths. So, although not a garden, Habbies Howe, Midlothian, above Peggy's Pool has something of a garden air. The two ladies in Fig.9.7 represent characters from Allan Ramsay's comedy *The Gentle Shepherd* (1725), where Peggy and her friend Jenny have been washing their laundry and are about to take a swim. Birches and shrubs ornament the scene. Other views of Habbies Howe equally portray a seemingly cultivated picturesque spot. Another area, again not a garden, but showing evidence of design, is shown in the print in Fig.9.8, taken from Sir John Carr's *Caledonian Sketches, or a Tour Through Scotland in 1807*, which displays a path and deliberate plantings that alternately cover and reveal the rock, though Carr attributed them to the hand of Nature.[32] The spot is on the River Esk, south of Edinburgh, between Roslin Castle and Hawthornden.

Among numerous estates in picturesque settings may be mentioned Dunira, Perthshire, which lay on flat land subject to flooding but had a background of woods and steep mountains. The focal point, not far from the house, was a waterfall cascading down between jagged rocks and crossed by an exiguous Alpine bridge, much in the manner of those at Hafod and Hawkstone. The surroundings of high rocky steeps were punctuated by viewing-points provided by huts, moss houses or other types of seat.[33]

The power and turbulence of waterfalls were attractions in many a Scottish landscape, a meeting of the Picturesque and the Sublime. They were often regarded as romantic as well, stirring the imagination. The 'rumbling bridge', rendered variously as grumbling brieck or rumbling-brig, a couple of miles from Dunkeld impressed both Sulivan and Gilpin. The former wrote, 'This is a romantic fall of water, which by its velocity has formed an arch in the center of a rock through which it passes,'[34] while Gilpin commented that the arch had been completed by art to form the bridge.[35] Another 'rumbling bridge', actually two in one (Fig.9.9), could be found on the River Devon. Further north lay Taymouth, a particularly potent example of the genre:

> the romantic girting of the woods, and the roaring of a cataract from the summit of one of the highest of the hills, are beauties so surpassing most things that are to be met with, that Taymouth must inevitably stand high in the estimation of all true lovers of the sublime.[36]

The gardens of Taymouth, however, were more formal and contained a large collection of buildings – numerous temples, an open seat of Aeolus, a sham fort designed for the view, and a turning-seat. The formal terracing was gradually naturalised, and a Surprise Walk curving

along the hillside afforded magnificent 'peek'
views in the woods across a stunning valley to
the mountains.[37] A Neolithic stone circle just
outside the park became known as the Druid's
Temple.

More dramatic than any were the Falls of
Bruar, to the west of Blair Castle. Here
nature provided the feast, but the spectacle
was enhanced in the late 1790s by paths, two
bridges and viewing-huts.[38]

In the case of The Dream, a winding glen in
the Aird, beyond Inverness, the scene included
a ruined abbey as we have seen in Yorkshire
and at Tintern. The name either derives from
an early Scottish word or carries the idea of
a vision, since the place seemed unreal. The
mountainous landscape

9.9 'Rumbling Bridge' at River Devon, on border between
Clackmannanshire and Perth and Kinross, print by W Banks,
c1800

is extremely magnificent, picturesque, and wild.
The deep vallies and rugged glens of the western
hills, above the Abbey of BEAULIEU, yield many of these romantic scenes, which would afford
the choicest subjects for the pencil of such Artists as delight in the wilder prospects of Nature – in
those grand combinations of precipices, woods, and torrents, which constitute the noblest stile of
Landscape.[39]

Here rocks reared up at random in the water, which churned furiously round them, while ash,
birch and fir combined with deep purple heather to contrast with the bare rock.

While most theorists of the Picturesque and the Sublime came from outside Scotland, Sir John
Clerk of Penicuick and Sir John Dalrymple have been cited in the opening chapter in regard to
their views on principles of landscaping. Dalrymple in particular addressed Scottish landowners
to show how they might improve their surroundings and make good any natural deficiencies in
the terrain.

An important feature of several landscapes and estates was the castle, which could add
considerably to the romantic appeal. In some cases it might be an old ruined castle, but more
often it was an existing house or even one built in the eighteenth century for effect not for any
military purpose. Central to the castle cult was the Adam family of architects, especially the
most well-known, Robert. It is clear that he had an obsession with castles, generally situated
on a high cliff, and sketched over a thousand capriccios or fantasies of them. Of a very large
number of commissions undertaken by Robert and his brother James, more than eighty were
in the castle style, the majority in Scotland in the 1770s and 1780s.[40] The family, starting with
their father, William, was responsible for a great many houses, but quite often there would be a
medieval castle still used as the residence which William or his sons would modify into a new

house with some elements of castellation to preserve its former character. This new house might embrace the old castle or be built immediately adjacent. William developed his own estate, calling it Blair Adam, which contained an old castle in the grounds, which William extended. Ancient castles would frequently be given special prominence in the view. He was also responsible for Inveraray Castle, while yet another son, John, designed Douglas Castle in 1757. The impulse for castle building was manifestly romantic, with historicist associations.

9.10 Approach to Robert Adam's viaduct bridge at Culzean, South Ayrshire

Perhaps Robert's greatest project in this vein was at Culzean, south of Ayr, the archetypal castle on a bluff, overlooking the Firth of Clyde and the island Ailsa Craig, leading out to the Irish Sea. The castle presented an irregular outline and included castellation on the large courtyard which embraced farm offices. A viaduct in the form of a dog-leg bridge leading from a ruined arch (Fig.9.10), inspired possibly by Hadrian's Villa at Tivoli, was composed of old and discoloured stones recycled from the demolished former house – also to give the impression of age. The property covers 600 acres of woodland, gardens and cliff walks, together with three miles of coastline. Following the reign of Thomas White as designer of the grounds from 1790, most planting and garden building construction was carried out in the early nineteenth century, but Adam was responsible for the 'Cat Gates' with Coade stone felines.

At Blair Adam, John took over from his father (d 1748) and, with the help of the great 'treemonger', the 3rd Duke of Argyll, planted 540 acres by 1784.[41] Some formality, such as avenues, lingered on for a time, but much of the hill planting, largely of larch and pine, gave a more picturesque appearance. The centrepiece was the Glen, planted 1762-3, where a path led up beside a stream and furnished a number of prospects of woodland.[42] The rocky eminence known as South Kiery Craigs was skilfully planted for effect, both in looking from it and at it. The height of the trees was carefully balanced against the height of the rocks.[43]

Dalrymple's own seat at Oxenford, Midlothian, was singularly picturesque. Three miles from the Firth of Forth, the castle, redesigned by Robert Adam, stood on a hill with an extensive view that included the ruins of two ancient castles, Crighton and Borthwick. As at Culzean, Adam designed a causeway bridge on the approach to the house, which was surrounded by parkland that gave way to naturalistic plantings.

Cullen, Banffshire (not to be confused with the close homophone Culzean) was another Adam garden though the designer Robert Robinson, who had an extensive practice in Scotland, was brought in in 1766. William Adam's bridge of 1744, which survives, was complemented by a naturalistic deep glen below it. Even prior to Robinson's arrival there had been a serious attempt at creating variety nearer the house, with special plantings of American oak, chestnuts and walnuts, together with a mount, a shrubbery and a Chinese bridge.[44] Charles Cordiner described it as a romantic situation on the verge of a rocky precipice, with the glen winding several miles into the country. The walks along the side of the stream were often 'precipitous, picturesque, and rocky',[45] while Stoddart observed that 'the high grounds are covered with plantations, chiefly of fir; and the rocks are bold, massy, and full of caverns'.[46]

As a pendant to the Scottish Picturesque, it is appropriate to mention a few examples of other related scenery, namely in Ireland. There were comparable ranges of mountains, steeps, loughs and valleys, together with numerous ruins, which

9.11 The Salmon Leap at Leixlip, County Kildare, print by GK Richardson after WH Bartlett, c1820

provided similar viewer experiences. Tourist interest was particularly centred on two areas, the Wicklow Mountains and Killarney. Some features were totally natural, such as the Giant's Causeway, County Antrim, with its unbelievable basalt columns (cf. those on the Isle of Staffa in Scotland), but in a few gardens it was art that led towards the Picturesque. Leixlip Castle, County Kildare, had a cascade called the Salmon Leap backed by dense planting (Fig.9.11), and the castle 'dominated a most romantic setting on top of a hill above the Liffey'.[47] Even a basically rather unexciting site such as Carton, County Kildare, could be rendered more picturesque by landscaping, especially the river, which at one point poured over a cascade near a shell cottage. More fully picturesque was Heywood, County Leith, which contained slopes, a river, nearly 100 cascades, diverse planting and numerous follies such as a Gothic entrance gate, a Gothic ruin, a Temple of the Winds, a bridge and a stone cross. The plantings were irregular and tending to wild.

9.12 Cascade at Powerscourt, County Wicklow, print by J Cousen after WH Bartlett, c1820

Powerscourt, County Wicklow, was at the heart of the Irish Picturesque. Arthur Young, visiting in the late 1770s, confessed that 'this horrid precipice, the pointed bleak mountains in view, with the roar of the waterfall, all conspire to raise one great emotion of the sublime.'[48] The waterfall, in particular, was a great attraction of the time and was painted by numerous artists (Fig.9.12). Nearer Dublin was Luttrellstown, seat of the first Lord Carhampton, a 400-acre estate which contained fourteen miles of woodland rides and through which the River Liffey passed, often between steep cliffs. 'The romantic, originally-ruined arch is perhaps the finest of its kind in Ireland, the tufa dripping with ivy and ferns.'[49] Young commented with similar enthusiasm on the scene below a Mr Lambert's house on the River

Boyne, 'a most romantic spot; rocks on one side, rising in perpendicular forms very boldly; the other steep wood, the river bending short between them like a land-locked bason.'[50]

1 William Gilpin, *Observations, relative chiefly to Picturesque Beauty Made in the Year 1776 On Several Parts of Great Britain; particularly the High-Lands of Scotland* (London: R Blamire, 1789), Vol.I, p.117.

2 *Ibid.*, p.121.

3 Samuel Johnson, *Journey to the Western Islands of Scotland* (London, 1775), p.9.

4 *The Correspondence of Thomas Gray*, ed. P J Toynbee and L Whibley (London: Oxford University Press, 1971), Vol.II, p.894.

5 Henry Skrine, *Three Successive Tours in the North of England, and Great Part of Scotland* (London, 1795), p.58.

6 John Stoddart, *Remarks on Local Scenery and Manners in Scotland during the Years 1799 and 1800* (London: William Miller, 1801), Vol.I, p.57.

7 Christopher Dingwall and Don Aldridge, *The Hall of Mirrors, New Arcadian Journal* 47-8, 1999, pp.36-8.

8 See *ibid.*, pp.40-1.

9 Malcolm Andrews, *The Search for the Picturesque* (London: Scolar Press, 1990), p.202.

10 Charles Cordiner, *Antiquities & Scenery of the North of Scotland in a Series of Letters, To Thomas Pennant, Esq*. (London, 1780), p.77.

11 Stoddart, *Remarks on Local Scenery*, II, p.33.

12 Christopher Dingwall, 'Gardens in the Wild', *Garden History* 22:2, 1994, p.141.

13 Andrews, *Search for the Picturesque*, p.217.

14 Dingwall and Aldridge, *Hall of Mirrors*, pp.34-48.

15 Gilpin, *Observations*, I, p.120.

16 (R J Sulivan), *Observations Made During a Tour Through Parts of England, Scotland and Wales* (London: T Becket, 1780), p.208.

17 Michael Symes and Sandy Haynes, *Enville, Hagley, The Leasowes: Three Great Eighteenth-Century Gardens* (Bristol: Redcliffe Press, 2010), p.129.

18 George Cumberland, *An Attempt to Describe Hafod* (London, 1796), p.31.

19 Charles Cordiner, *Remarkable Ruins and Romantic Prospects of North Britain* (London: Peter Mazell, 1788), no pagination.

20 A A Tait, *The Landscape Garden in Scotland* (Edinburgh: Edinburgh University Press, 1980), pp.119-20.

21 Dingwall, 'Gardens in the Wild', p.147.

22 Gilpin, *Observations*, I, p.72.

23 Thomas Newte, *Prospects and Observations on a Tour in England and Scotland* (London: G G J and J Robinson, 1791), p.56.

24 Dingwall, 'Gardens in the Wild', p.137.

25 Newte, *Prospects*, p.255.

26 Dingwall, 'Gardens in the Wild', pp.133-6.

27 (Lady Hanway), *A Journey to the Highlands of Scotland* (London: Fielding & Walker, pre-1790), p.32.

28 Gilpin, *Observations*, II, p.66.

29 Tait, *Landscape Garden in Scotland*, p.126.

30 Gilpin, *Observations*, I, pp.184, 187.

31 Stoddart, *Remarks on Local Scenery*, I, p.125.

32 Sir John Carr, *Caledonian Sketches, or a Tour through Scotland in 1807* (London: Matthews & Leigh, 1809), p.82.

33 Tait, *Landscape Garden in Scotland*, p.123.

34 Sulivan, *Observations*, p.208.

35 Gilpin, *Observations*, II, pp.124-5.

36 Sulivan, *Observations*, p.209.

37 Andrews, *Search for the Picturesque*, p.222, and Tait, *Landscape Garden in Scotland*, pp.56-62.

38 Dingwall, 'Gardens in the Wild', pp.149-53.

39 Cordiner, *Remarkable Ruins*, second volume (1795), no pagination.

40 Stephen Astley, *Robert Adam's Castles* (London: The Soane Gallery, 2000), p.5.

41 Tait, *Landscape Garden in Scotland*, p.99.

42 *Ibid.*, p.101.

43 Dingwall, 'Gardens in the Wild', p.153.

44 Tait, *Landscape Garden in Scotland*, p.84.

45 Cordiner, *Antiquities and Scenery*, p.49.

46 Stoddart, *Remarks on Local Scenery* II, p.316.

47 Edward Malins and the Knight of Glin, *Lost Demesnes: Irish Landscape Gardening, 1660-1845* (London: Barrie and Jenkins, 1976), p.60.

48 Arthur Young, *A Tour in Ireland* (1776-9) (London: T Cadell, 1780), Vol.I, p.103.

49 Malins and Glin, *Lost Demesnes*, p.74.

50 Young, *Tour in Ireland*, I, p.33.

CHAPTER TEN

The Sublime

The Sublime was seen, and felt, at its most intense at close quarters, when danger loomed forcibly. Far-off mountains might be sublime in terms of suggesting huge scale, but were not threatening. Gilpin, however, thought that distant mountains could be picturesque,[1] but not at closer range, since their bulk and dominance in the view would render them unfit for a picture. A cliff or mountain in the middle ground, however, might be sublime in provoking feelings of vastness, bleakness or eternity. Most sublime effects were natural, though possibly enhanced or pointed by man's intervention, and could be encountered as 'natural scenery' in several parts of the British Isles, especially the Lake District, the Peak District and the mountainous regions of Wales and Scotland. Other parts – Devon, Cornwall, Yorkshire and the Avon Gorge at Bristol, with its St Vincent's Rocks, for example – contain rock and water features that stand on the borders between the Picturesque and the Sublime. Fig.10.1 shows a lonely cottage with a steep garden in the shadow of the lowering 'Prating Rock' in Somerset. But this chapter concentrates on the Sublime within the curtilage of an owner's garden or estate.

Hackfall

The landscape of Hackfall, near Grewelthorpe, North Yorkshire, was for many the essence of both the Picturesque and the Sublime. It was a self-contained entity, with no large house to anchor it, and represents an attempt to create something new, a dream that could be fulfilled in isolation from the demands of an estate of prime residence. It was mainly developed between the years 1749 and 1767 by William Aislabie, whose seat was at Studley Royal, seven miles south of Hackfall. Aislabie had already, in the 1740s, cultivated the Mackershaw valley at the side of Studley Royal as a picturesque steep-sided combe, with a path in the base criss-crossing the stream seven times. The naturalism, and display of rock (pp.85-6), was something that Aislabie would take to further lengths in the topographically superb site of Hackfall.

Edward Harwood has written the fullest and most detailed account of Hackfall, drawing on visitors' descriptions and archival sources.[2] From this

10.1 Cottage and plot below the 'Prating Rock' in Somerset, engraved by S Middiman after SH Grimm, 1789

we gain a good idea of what it looked like at the time – which was very different from what we see now, though considerable and welcome restoration work has been undertaken in recent years. The changing appearance matters because it has affected the degree of our possible perception of sublimity. In the latter years of the twentieth century Hackfall was so overgrown that, ironically, the sense of the Sublime was heightened because so many paths were hazardous or impassable, and there was so much water in the hills that progress was constantly hampered by diminutive streams. What restoration has achieved is to improve the paths and carry out a great deal of clearance, with the result that internal views have come back into being and also the bare rock has been revealed, so that much of the former sublimity has been recovered. The result is that while some of the woodland walks are safer, the newly-exposed paths under the rock face produce the original *frisson*.

Hackfall is best imagined as half of a huge mixing-bowl. Around the rim at the top sit buildings – Mowbray Castle, Mowbray Point and its separate kitchen – and two massive dingles march down within the curve of the bowl to the River Ure which winds about at the foot. There are innumerable springs in the hills, and water is ubiquitous: even when it cannot be seen it is always heard. Stone creates the sound – there are many cascades; small stones interrupt the cross-streams; and the Ure swirls turbulently among its boulders. The concave interior of the bowl is heavily wooded (deliberately planted originally but mostly self-seeded now), and there are a few follies *en route*, such as Fisher's Hall, a grotto and a rustic temple. The land was originally acquired in 1731 by Aislabie's father John and used partly for sheep pasture (the fields beyond the rim) and partly for quarrying stone and commercial forestry within the bowl.[3] Ornamental gardening came only from c1750.

It is clear that the main thing that has been lost is the balance between wild and controlled gardening. While most of Hackfall was wild in respect of woods, rock and water, it was orderly in the sense that growth was kept in check and vistas carefully contrived. What has continued to exercise commentators is Fountain Plain, an apparently smooth and neat clearing with flat lawns and pool with a fountain in the middle, approached by a broad *allée* slightly embanked, as painted by an unknown artist c1767. If Hackfall as a whole is characterised as a savage picturesque/sublime garden, what are we to make of this unexpectedly formal area? For some it jars incongruously, while a few more kindly disposed might see it as a contrast the more sensibly to appreciate the surrounding wildness. It may be an echo, a reminder of, and a tribute to, Aislabie's supremely formal water gardens at Studley Royal.

From Mowbray Point, a strange construction with a Gothic rear as seen from the fields and the appearance of a Roman ruin from the front (inside the bowl), an exceptionally sublime scene met the view. Poised alarmingly on the rim, the building masked a surprise swoop both internal and external. William Gilpin described how folding doors were thrown open, whereupon 'you are struck with one of the grandest, and most beautiful bursts of country, that the imagination can form'.[4] While looking down the precipice one could see all the way down to the river, as well as across to Fisher's Hall and the castle. The outward panorama encompassed thirty or forty miles of magnificent Yorkshire countryside while the internal vistas plunged worryingly yet upliftingly as they penetrated deeper and higher across. Gilpin thought that, overall, the views of the country were what made Hackfall and that some of the artificial features were 'trivial' and spoiled it: Mowbray Castle was even dismissed as 'paltry' although it is a substantial ruin – but not a real one, hence his displeasure.

10.2 The Forty-Foot Fall at Hackfall, North Yorkshire, engraved by J Rogers after N Whittock, 1830

We have seen throughout this book how often picturesque effects were contrived or manipulated. The most remarkable of the features within Hackfall were the cascades, plentiful in number and often given a helping hand. Examination of what survives of them today shows a good deal of deliberate placing of stone, and sometimes working of it, although the results were convincing enough at the time for visitors to remark on their naturalness, particularly viewed from a slight distance, as the seats indicated they were to be. The cascades were varied, from the dramatic to the smooth ribbon of water sliding over mossy rock in the Forty-Foot Fall, where the excitement came from the height of the fall rather than its violence: the water 'seems to gush forth by enchantment'.[5] From Kent's Seat (a curious commemoration in this most unKentian place) the Alum Spring cascade was seen, the alum linking it to the petrifactions decorating Fisher's Hall. Similarly the grotto, presumed to be a covered seat, provided a view of the Forty-Foot Fall (Fig.10.2). The Weeping Rock produced a cascade near the river (Fig.10.3), aided by channels cut in the rock, and with one's back to Fisher's Hall one could gain a view inland of two separate cascades up the glens.

Some of the buildings have survived, although of those all have received, or are in need of, attention. They vary from Gothic to rustic and classical (ruin), and the use of the old local

10.3 View from Weeping Rock at Hackfall, North Yorkshire, etched by Laetitia Byrne after F Nicholson, 1809

knightly name Mowbray adds a fanciful medieval and dynastic air to two of them. The smaller huts present problems of appearance and identification: the rustic cottage in Fig.10.4, for instance, does not tally with anything in contemporary descriptions, and has even been identified with the Rustic Temple in Fountain Glade, which it is clearly not. It may, however, be the small building indicated below Mowbray Castle in Fig.10.3 (1809), which is usually said to be Fisher's Hall: though in the right alignment, it is

10.4 Cottage in wood at Hackfall, North Yorkshire, from George Cuitt, *Wanderings and Pencillings amongst Ruins of the Olden Time*, 1855, p.9 (original drawing 1830)

too high above the river to be the Hall, however, and resembles the cottage much more. Fisher's Hall is shown in its proper, lower position in a vignette of 1822. There was a kitchen for Fisher's Hall, but that was even lower.

The prints reproduced here all show how wooded Hackfall was. They are, admittedly, some years after its creation, so the trees might have grown beyond what Aislabie had intended, but the contemporary accounts, and the one sketch of the time, by Arthur Young (1769), demonstrate the preponderance of wood.

Young considered many features of Hackfall to 'partake so much of the sublime', and that the sound of water 'gives room for the imagination to play'.[6] The romantic, Picturesque and Sublime, in short, come together in this unforgettable garden.

Hafod

While equally sublime, Hafod (pronounced Havod), in mid-Wales, some sixteen miles east of Aberystwyth, is very different to Hackfall. Although recognised and appreciated at the time as a masterpiece of landscaping in a bleak and inhospitable region, it has subsequently acquired an aura of romanticism due to the tragedies surrounding Thomas Johnes and his family, piquantly chronicled by Elisabeth Inglis-Jones.[7] It is a huge estate, originally about 13,000 acres, of which 5,000 acres or so were landscaped, and much was let out to tenant farmers who persisted in old ways and did not take kindly to the agricultural improvements Johnes wished to foster. Although much of Hafod was bare and mountainous when Johnes inherited it in 1780, the slopes of the valley towards the house were already well wooded, though Johnes was to add an enormous amount of timber, as we have seen.

Fig.10.5, an aquatint of 1810, encapsulates much of Hafod: wild, rugged, seemingly natural but artfully fashioned. The depiction of the Peiran falls is revealing – the size and force of the waterfall are exaggerated, the visitors are clearly connoisseurs of the Picturesque (they even have a viewing ledge), but the hand of art and labour is apparent too, with the controlled plantings, the made path and the gardener with his wheelbarrow reminding us of the necessary toil. These

10.5 The Peiran falls at Hafod, Dyfed, aquatint by J Stadler after John 'Warwick' Smith, 1810 (By permission of Llyfrgell Genedlaethol Cymru / The National Library of Wales)

10.6 The 'Alpine Cave' at Hafod, Dyfed, aquatint by J Stadler after John 'Warwick' Smith, 1810 (By permission of Llyfrgell Genedlaethol Cymru / The National Library of Wales)

falls were one of several set-piece scenes in the sublime
manner. Others included alpine and rustic bridges
and in particular the Chain Bridge, which spanned the
abyss of the Ystwyth Gorge, connecting rock with rock.
Johnes intended the perilously positioned bridge to
frighten the visitor (even to death),[8] so was more than
alert to the sublime possibilities.

Most of the wilder scenes were to be encountered on the
Gentleman's Walk, a 3.7 mile circuit. This contrasted
with other, shorter and more comfortable and decorative
walks, notably the Lady's Walk (2.2 miles). On the
longer walk, several of the bridges could be taken in,
together with a second formidable cascade, above
the Mossy Seat; a tunnel; and, above all, the Cavern
Cascade. Having negotiated a path cut as a ledge
against the rock face, the visitor performs a detour up
the stream and clambers up rock steps to reach the cave
entrance. Proceeding along the passage (deliberately

10.7 The falls below the Devil's Bridge, near Hafod,
Dyfed, anonymous print, 1844

mined by Johnes for the effect), one hears an increasingly mighty roar of the cascade before one
sees it, a reminder of the power of sound in the landscape, especially water (cf. Hackfall). The
reverberation in the tunnel multiplies the sound of the cascade to an alarming degree, playing
on the imagination. Then it opens up into a cavern confronting the water – a shaft of rock down
which a sixty-foot fall shoots and froths below.

But Hafod is far from being a series of frightening scenes, and there is or was a great variety of
layout, including peaceful meadows, bare hills contrasted with wooded, and two flower gardens
high up, one for Mrs Johnes and one for their crippled daughter Mariamne (one can only
assume she had to be carried up). What is lacking, and what differentiates it so clearly from
Hackfall and Hawkstone, is the presence of garden buildings, so the landscape looked unspoiled:
Johnes himself was anxious to stress that 'by *beautifying it* I have *neither shorn or tormented it*'.[9]
It is important to see the Devil's Bridge, three or four miles away, as part of the overall Hafod
adventure and as an appetiser for the landscape. It was at the Bridge that Johnes established
the Hafod Arms so that visitors could stay overnight, savour the sublime spectacle of the
Mynach Falls and then spend the day at Hafod itself, approached via an arch over the road as
if to indicate entrance to a special world. An illustration of the bridge is given here (Fig.10.7),
showing visitors negotiating the steep path beside the fall. Taking a tumble was far from
unknown.

In creating his paradise in the mountains Johnes seems to have been guided by a number of
influences and impulses. Apart from being cousin to Payne Knight he was a friend of Price,
and thus had close contact with the cutting edge of the Picturesque. The influence may have
spread both ways, since Johnes was starting work on Hafod a decade before the advent of the
picturesque publications of 1794. It may seem surprising that Johnes neglected exploiting the
'capabilities' of the Fish Pool Valley when he lived at Croft, but Hafod manifestly offered far
greater scope – and a greater challenge. Johnes may have absorbed some picturesque scenery

when in Scotland in the late 1760s;[10] and a publication that he himself was said (by Gilpin) to have had in his hand and mind when laying out Hafod was William Mason's *The English Garden* (probably the second edition, 1783). While Mason did not specifically promote the more sublime aspects of a garden, he favoured flower gardens of the sort that he had helped design at Nuneham Courtenay, Oxfordshire, and which may have had some bearing on Johnes' two familial gardens. Mariamne's garden was designed in 1795 by James Anderson, a Scottish agricultural consultant.

Johnes visited Gilpin in the New Forest in 1787 and showed him a portfolio of sketches of Hafod (presumed to be those by Thomas Jones, 1786). After the visit Gilpin wrote to Mason that 'if you want to see an exact translation of your book into good Welsh, you must go to Mr Johnes' seat in Cardiganshire'.[11] Gilpin was obviously deeply impressed by Johnes and the sketches he had been shown, for he incorporated a description of Hafod in the second edition of his Wye Tour (1789) although he had never seen it (the tour long predated the development of Hafod).

The wonders of Hafod provoked rapturous responses from visitors by now schooled in a taste for the Picturesque. The main account in Johnes' own time was George Cumberland's *An Attempt to Describe Hafod* (1796), republished by the Hafod Trust in its bicentenary year. Cumberland moved in artists' and writers' circles, and his description of Hafod shows him to be thoroughly conversant with the trends of the time. He paid at least four visits to Hafod, during one of which he compiled the material for his book.[12] It opens with some comments about the picturesque qualities of Hafod, making the perhaps startling claim that it surpasses anything Cumberland ever saw in the Alps, Switzerland or Italy. For him Hafod also takes the best of Welsh or Herefordshire picturesque scenes and concentrates them in one place. With a continual tendency to quote from Milton, Cumberland describes the surrounding country and then turns to the separate walks. What he describes is presented vividly and eloquently but it is still a landscape in progress, for a number of features had yet to come into being. He sums up his thoughts at a final, remote spot which supplies the essence of Hafod:

> Here, turning about, a thousand romantic objects present themselves: the rural bridge – the rocky channel it bends across – the murky shades around – the fretful waters of the foaming flood – the wood-crowned rocks ascending high behind you – and the fine climbing forest in front, terminated above by Grogwinian's silvery fall, shooting through the trees, and leaping from shade to shade – these, altogether combining with the recent traces of the pictures you have just left, fetter a pensive mind to the spot, and force from the poet, or painter, at least a sigh at parting.[13]

Hawkstone

Again of very different character is Hawkstone, near Hodnet, north-east Shropshire. The countryside around is mainly flat, especially the Cheshire plain to the east, but by a geological convulsion Hawkstone contains sandstone cliffs that rear up three hundred feet. Unlike Hackfall and Hafod, where water was central and focal, Hawkstone was not blessed with any aqueous source, and the 'Hawk River' (a lake, artificially contrived by William Emes, with a massive embankment), was not added until 1784, possibly as a result of comments by visitors such as Philip Yorke and Dr Johnson who regretted the lack of water. The Sublime at Hawkstone accordingly showed itself in steep narrow paths, precipices and clefts in the rock. In addition there was a pre-existing romanticism in the medieval and even Arthurian legends surrounding the Red Castle. The work of developing Hawkstone fell largely to Sir Rowland Hill (1705-83) in terms of hard landscaping, though his son Sir Richard Hill (1732-1808) was responsible for the lake and a good many of the follies and other ornamentation. Guidebooks appeared from 1776, the most popular being by T Rodenhurst (1783), whose text, with updatings, was still being reissued in 1850. As at Hafod, an inn was put up for visitors (c1790) and this determined the start of the set circuit. The inn was, in fact, a good deal closer to the walks than Hawkstone Hall itself, lying back on the flat, away from and behind the hill. Tourism was thus kept well away from the residence, and the cliffs of Hawkstone provided a self-contained attraction.

Much of Hawkstone was dramatic, not to say hazardous, but the Hills added further dimensions. For a start, as we can see from Rodenhurst's comprehensive descriptions, it was more literary and even religious than is often realised. Inscriptions, some very lengthy and usually in verse, abounded: thus, at the very start of the walks the visitor is enjoined:

> Here, Friend of Taste, thy course begin,
>   And Nature's charms admire:
> Where varied Landscapes feast the eye
>   The feet forget to tire.[14]

The last line hints at the hard walking that is to ensue. Subsequent inscriptions cover a dialogue with Neptune; the innocence of looking at the scenery; the comfort of contemplation and how it can lead to paradise; how the glory of God is reflected in the landscape, His handiwork; counselling against sin and calling on the visitor to the Hermit's Cell to be ready for death; an urn extolling the virtues of some earlier Hills; a long dialogue with Reynard the fox; reflections on hare-hunting; an encomium on the happy and devoted couple who tend the Menagerie; and some romantic lines affixed to the

10.8 The Cleft, Hawkstone, Shropshire   10.9 Stonework on Red Castle Hill, Hawkstone, Shropshire

10.10 General view of Hawkstone, Shropshire, engraved by J Walker after J Eames, 1800

Red Castle concerning its past. There was, in addition, a long prose inscription at the base of the Obelisk, commemorating Sir Rowland Hill, the first Protestant Lord Mayor of London in 1549.

The inscriptions, imputing a moral role to the landscape, were the work of Sir Richard, a Methodist and philanthropist who by ornamenting the walks and acquiring and developing additional land was praised for providing substantial local employment. It was also Sir Richard who enhanced the circuit by exhibiting aspects of many different nations and cultures, reminiscent of Parc Monceau in Paris, where the stated aim in the 1779 Prospectus was to bring together all times and all places. The entrance to the walks was through a grove containing Neptune's Whim, a cottage with a statue of Neptune behind, sitting between two large whale ribs. The cottage was in Dutch style, complemented by a windmill, functional but painted in the Dutch way: both survive but much dilapidated. A Chinese temple and a (genuine) Egyptian tent followed, but the latter soon decayed. Later on in the circuit a signpost pointed 'To a Scene in Swisserland', with 'Au Pont Suisse' on the other side. The precarious seeming, though actually sturdy, bridge spanning an abyss has been restored: in Rodenhurst's words

> For the enjoyment of this wild scene, a steady head and a steady foot are both equally necessary, especially when you cross the Bridge…Fear not, then, to pass the awful gulf, and the rock beyond it, which you are no sooner over than you turn to your left, down another deep, solemn glen or fissure, which divides the two high rocks, from whose menacing looks you have just happily escaped, and which were both almost inaccessible and unexplored till the present bridge connected them, and formed a passage over them. Those who have visited Swisserland, especially the Grissons, must be struck with the great similarity between this scene, and some in that wild romantic country.[15]

After one passes a copper-tinged 'Indian Rock' a number of different scenes are encountered, but much later on the walk the visitor comes across 'A Scene at Otaheite', comprising a hut of sticks and reeds based on illustrations in Captain Cook's published voyages, while in the surrounding hollow were displayed bows and arrows, animal horns, idols, masks, feather caps, shell necklaces and two canoes. Even plants from Tahiti were grown outside the hut.[16]

The Sublime was frequently encountered. The Cleft (Fig.10.8), a fissure between two rock faces, leads for a full hundred yards into the extensive caverns and passages of the grotto, the main chamber of which was once adorned with shells, fossils and furnace slag. It was said that the hill was mined by the Romans for copper, and therefore the eighteenth-century developments were expanding, utilising and ornamenting what was at least partly already there. Above and outside the grotto were rocks, including the high Raven's Shelf, and the views were frightening:

> Here the towering rock is lost beneath the rugged, bulging, and terrific rocks. – Next you admire the huge pending crags, highly coloured with copper, or hoary with age; and whilst the wide chasms between the rocks strike you with dread, you hear the ravens, which build upon them, croaking over your head.[17]

A Gothic Arch was built as an eye-catcher above the grotto. Dr Johnson was especially responsive to the terrifying aspects of Hawkstone: he visited in July 1774 in the company of Mrs Thrale, commenting on

> …the extent of its prospects, the awfulness of its shades, the horrors of its precipices, the verdure of its hollows and the loftiness of its rocks. The ideas which it forces upon the mind, are the sublime, the dreadful, and the vast. Above, is inaccessible altitude, below is horrible profundity.[18]

As telling a statement of the Sublime as one could wish for.

There was no lack of varied interest at Hawkstone, from the hermitage with a live hermit (subsequently replaced by a mechanical model) to the vineyard laid out as a fortification, with bastion and towers – sadly the grapes refused to ripen and the site was planted over. The vineyard was echoed by the Citadel, a mock castle erected the other side of the road for Sir Richard's steward in 1785. The castle idea for both, however, came from the Red Castle, steeped in romantic legend. This consists of a castle and keep thought to have been built in early medieval times from the native rock (Fig.10.9), the intention being (in 1227) that it should be a practical fortress with panoramic views to give warning. Stories of two giants, Tarquin and Tarquinus, long predating the actual castle, began to be woven round it, with the result that, by the eighteenth century, when embellishments were added, the Giant's Well and the Lion's Den, though based on the old castle, gave it a new romantic life. All told, the features of Hawkstone were well calculated 'to excite *astonishment* in the mind', as Richard Warner put it.[19]

The Lake District

The Lake District, with its combination of mountains and water, constitutes the most manifestly sublime scenery in England – but, of course, was not a garden. But it had profound impact on seekers after the Picturesque including those who were involved in commenting on, or designing, gardens. It shaped Gilpin's thinking and affected him permanently after being brought up there. It is also commonly taken to be the birthplace of the Romantic Movement in literature.

Individual features were recognised as particularly sublime, such as the Lodore Falls, comparable to some of the Scottish cascades. Borrowdale, just to the south of the falls, was generally regarded as the most sublime part of all; it terrified Gray. Another spectacular cascade, the Airey (now Aira) Force (Fig.10.11), was in the landscaped grounds of the Howard family's hunting lodge, Lyulph's Tower. With its two rustic bridges, as seen in the print, human presence and evidence of deliberate, or at least controlled, planting, the setting of the fall has the flavour of a garden.

The effect on landscape designers could be devastating. Repton felt it dwarfed his meagre attempts to create picturesque grounds:

10.11 Aira Force, Cumbria, print by JC Bentley after T Allom, c1820

> Shall I confess that I derived less satisfaction from this tour [to the Lake District] than I expected. It gave me a humiliating idea of the vanity of my profession. The vast lakes and their mountainous accompaniments of Nature had the effect of making me feel how little were the humble attempts of my art, which had been so often extolled, and I felt regret that Nature and Art were at such an immeasurable distance. In the aweful grandeur of the scenery there was more of the sublime than beautiful, and that sublimity was a little mixt with terror.[20]

If there were gardens where one might experience the Sublime, it was for the outward view rather than for any special internal elements. Thus Belle Isle, on an island in Lake Windermere, owed everything to its location although it had a garden landscaped by Thomas White: the outward-looking nature of the site was indicated by two small viewing pavilions. On the western shore Claife station, one of five viewing points round the lake, was itself an eye-catcher. It was designed by John Carr in the 1790s as a two-storey tower with a viewing room that had glass windows, each a different colour for the seasons or for the light. In that respect it bore some similarity to the hermitage at Dunkeld (p.126). It afforded glorious views of the whole lake and the mountains round it, from a far better vantage point than at lake level. A winding path led up to it through a Gothic arch and for the upper part of the walk visitors had their backs to the lake. Furthermore the pavilion itself screened off the view so that it came as a total surprise, a visual explosion.[21] Claife station had a small pleasure ground round it, with an Aeolian harp, and was itself built on a steep rock face. Its own interest as a garden was added to after 1800 by acquisition of a forty-five acre stretch of rock behind the pavilion which was planted up with woodland. It might be added that visiting Belle Isle and Claife by boat was a frightening and sublime experience.[22]

To the east of the Lake District lies Teesdale in the North Pennines. The waterfall with the greatest single drop in England is said to be High Force, with a plunge of towards seventy feet over and between dolerite ('whinstone') blocks – Fig.10.12. Popular with tourists from the

10.12 High Force, Teesdale, anonymous print c1780

eighteenth century, it was a natural phenomenon that was enhanced for viewing purposes by the approach path and by a 'station' facing it. The path builds up excitement from the increasing sound and in its convolutions presents a continuing kaleidoscope of views before the full spectacle is finally revealed. Although not a garden feature, it was in the grounds of Lord Barnard of Raby, and deliberately landscaped. Arthur Young was enthralled by it: 'The whole scene is gloriously romantic, for on every side it is walled in with pendent rocks an hundred feet high; here projecting in bold and threatening cliffs, and there covered with hanging woods, whose only nourishment one would imagine arose from the descending rain.'[23] His conclusion was that 'The scene is truly sublime.'

Rydal Hall

The three gardens covered in the first part of this chapter have a great deal of the Sublime in them: what follows is a group of three more that were primarily picturesque but are exceptional because of some element of sublimity. At Rydal Hall, north of Lake Windermere, the point of sublime interest was the fall, though when viewed from the summerhouse it had become narrower and less violent. The positioning resembles the hermitages at Dunkeld and the Forest of Mar. The fall had an upper reach (Fig.10.13) and a lower, the latter being more 'civilised' by the addition of a bridge. Gilpin was especially perceptive on the fall as it is seen from the hut:

> …[it] is so beautiful both in itself, and in it's accompaniments, as to deserve particular notice. – It is seen from a summer-house; before which it's rocky cheeks circling on each side form a little area; appearing through the window like a picture in a frame. The water falls within a few yards

of the eye, which being rather above it's level, has a long perspective view of the stream, as it hurries from the higher grounds; tumbling, in various little breaks, through it's rocky channel, darkened with thicket, till it arrive at the edge of the precipice, before the window; from whence it rushes into the bason, which is formed by nature in the native rock. The dark colour of the stone, taking still a deeper tinge from the wood, which hangs over it, sets off to wonderful advantage the sparkling lustre of the stream; and produces an uncommon effect of light. It is this effect, indeed, from which the chief beauty of the scene arises.[24]

It will be noticed how much Gilpin uses the language of picture-making. The summerhouse actually dates from 1668-9, which might explain why the view from it was slightly tamer and more controlled than the more turbulent reaches. It was not, therefore, prescient of the Sublime.

The Nunnery

The gardens of Nunnery House, Staffield, Kirkoswald, are a little way north of the Lakes but play an

10.13 The upper fall at Rydal, Cumbria, print by T Jeavons after H Gastineau, 1838

important part in the Cumbrian Sublime. The house was built by Henry Aglionby in 1718, and his grandson Christopher (1752-85) began to landscape the grounds on inheriting in 1770. His premature death left his sister Elizabeth to continue the work until her own death in 1822. The grounds were known in their day – Gilpin said he had heard they were 'very engaging' but could not fit them into his tight Cumbrian schedule.[25] The landscape has changed very little, as Tim Longville in a recent *Country Life* article records: 'A dark, round pool and a narrow flight of steps cut from living rock; sandstone cliffs towering above. A viewing platform which seems to hover in space, and a white waterfall thundering into the pool's darkness'.[26]

The path down from the house, on the site of an old Benedictine nunnery, leads through meadows and then woodland to the banks of the River Eden. From this westernmost point the path loops so that it travels back eastwards beside the river, with views of wooded rocks (Fig.10.14). All so far is picturesque: the Sublime mounts in intensity as one climbs northwards up the Croglin Beck which plunges into the river. William Hutchinson published an account in

10.14 River view of The Nunnery, Cumbria, anonymous print c1820

1794 and described the steep and often slippery path up from the river and how minor cascades lead up to the grand climax:

> On the banks of Croglin water, the road is gained by cutting away the rocky points in some places; in others by excavating the projecting cliffs. Here the forest rises beautifully shade above shade; not crowded with brushwood, but the long stems of straight and lofty trees form a sylvan colonnade. As you proceed up Croglin water, the walk straightens, the cliffs increase in eminence, and hang over your head in a tremendous manner, their sides and summits supporting noble oaks: here the water falls down a fine declivity, not so as to give surprise, but placidly flowing over each shelving rock; and, little agitated, glides away, till it murmurs through the pebbly channel. As you advance, the noise of a cascade strikes the ear a few moments only before it bursts upon the sight. The scene is noble and solemn; branches of trees are stretched and mingled from precipice to precipice. The water gushes in one entire spout through the parted rock. Every step you proceed from this point has new and excellent beauties. – You pass on enchanted. The sound of water-falls strikes the ear on every hand; on the path (made by a vast flight of steps) unexpectedly turning round a point of the rock, you instantly stand on the brink of a deep abyss, where the water is precipitated thirty-five perpendicular feet, into a bason of eighteen feet in depth…Though confined, the views are wild and picturesque; - romantic and unrivalled beauties attract the attention of all strangers, and the admiration of every one who has taste to admire nature in those forms, where the grand, the sublime, the romantic, and the beautiful are all united.[27]

On the way up to the great fall there are two pause points, the viewing platform and an eighteenth-century summerhouse that incorporates some fourteenth-century stone panelling from a Carlisle church. The basin into which the cascade crashes is man-made.[28] At that point one comes face to face with the Sublime.

Bolton Abbey

One of the greatest sites of all was, and still is, Bolton Abbey, park and estate in Wharfedale, North Yorkshire. The estate belonged to Lord Burlington (of Chiswick), but after his death in 1753 it passed to his daughter Lady Charlotte Elizabeth Boyle, who outlived him by only a year. Lady Charlotte had married the 4th Duke of Devonshire (based at Chatsworth), who thereby became possessed of all the Burlington properties including Chiswick and the vast Bolton Abbey estate, which covered 30,000 acres. It is likely that the 4th, 5th and 6th Dukes had most to do with such landscaping as was carried out, and although it is tempting to speculate whether Lord Burlington had any input in his time he is not known to have done so. The 6th Duke (1790-1858) contributed most: he was an avid horticulturist, becoming President of the RHS in 1838, and was Paxton's patron at Chatsworth. His work at Bolton, commencing at the age of twenty, included the laying out of paths and the construction of a waterfall on the side of the River Wharfe opposite to the ruined priory. By the early years of the nineteenth century tourism was an important consideration.

Apart from its stunning location, what is remarkable about Bolton Abbey is its sheer range of visual attractions, mostly distinctly picturesque but with touches of the Sublime. Its painterly qualities enchanted Turner and Girtin among many others, while Wordsworth was inspired by its associations. Ruins were high on the agenda and central to the visitor experience. The remains of Bolton Priory (from 1154: see Fig.10.15) – not actually an abbey – lie on a flat open stretch in the curve of the river and close to it: the ruined medieval hunting lodge Barden Tower stands above the river a couple of miles to the north as a secular counterpart. Sound, too, was an important element: the Wharfe could be heard in the surrounding woods where it was not seen.

Plantings added considerably to the scene. While there was some ancient woodland, notably the oaks in Strid Wood, there are several plots named as plantations, as reference to a modern map will show – Park, Lower Fell and Laund Pasture – as well as Westy Bank Wood. The higher reaches are more open fell and moor. One area, still known as the Valley of Desolation, was wooded before a storm laid waste the spot c1830 and gave it its name. Now

10.15 The Strid, Bolton Abbey, North Yorkshire

10.16 Cascade in Bolton Park, Bolton Abbey, North Yorkshire, print by François Vivares, 1753

it is a well-timbered combe once more, and the name seems inappropriate. It was never intended to carry the more familiar emotional connotation, though that may have added to the romantic appeal.

But it is the rockwork that leaves the strongest impression. Along the river the rocks are folded and lined at angles, and some are carved, such as the seat fashioned from a huge boulder. The Hawkstone reaches up like a spire in isolation. Away, up on the fell, are discrete rock formations such as Simon's Seat and the Cow and Calf (echoing the Cow and Calf at Ilkley Moor) and a rocking-stone. At one narrow point in the river the rocks in the water produce the authentic Sublime at the Strid (Fig.10.15), which is genuinely dangerous and has continued to claim victims up to recent times. The name is derived from 'stride' and the feature is also known as Lover's Leap, but woe betide anyone who attempts to jump across when the water is in spate, seething in hollows under the rock and churning in whirlpools.

The Sublime would also be experienced at a magnificent cascade feeding a stream which proceeds down the Valley of Desolation to the river. This is known as the Fifty-Foot Fall. It is illustrated in a superb engraving by François Vivares (Fig.10.16) dated 1753, the year of Burlington's death. The caption, 'A view…of a Beautiful & Romantic Natural Cascade in Bolton Park', emphasises the naturalness of the fall itself and the romantic appeal to the feelings, which the tourists, scrambling over rocks, are fully experiencing. However, some at least of the profuse vegetation seems arranged, and the footpaths were deliberately laid out, as one can tell today from the stepping stones to aid descent. Further upstream was another cascade swirling round a large boulder.

It appears that serious landscaping of the area occurred at the end of the eighteenth century when woods were thinned, upper and riverside paths and ridings formed and the arch thrown over the skirting road. This arch is attributed to a Mr Carr, who could be either the well-known architect John Carr of York or William the local antiquarian vicar.[29] It was William who is said to have initiated the clearance and opening up of the woods and the landscape generally, with a sequence of viewing points.[30] The 6th Duke then took the process of laying out paths further.

1 William Gilpin, *Observations, Relative Chiefly to Picturesque Beauty, Made in the Year 1772, on Several Parts of England; particularly the Mountains, and Lakes of Cumberland, and Westmoreland* (London: R Blamire, 1786), Vol.I, p.81.

2 Edward S Harwood, 'William Aislabie's garden at Hackfall', *Journal of Garden History* 7:4, 1987, pp.307-411. The whole of the issue is devoted to this article.

3 *Ibid.*, pp.376-7.

4 Gilpin, *Observations*, II, p.191.

5 Arthur Young, *A Six Months Tour Through the North of England* (Dublin, 1770), Vol.II, p.35.

6 *Ibid.*, pp.37 and 34.

7 Elisabeth Inglis-Jones, *Peacocks in Paradise* (Llandysul: Gomer Press, 1990).

8 Caroline Kerkham, 'Hafod: paradise lost', *Journal of Garden History* 11:4, 1991, p.214.

9 Quoted in Jenifer Macve, *The Hafod Landscape* (Pontrhydygroes: The Hafod Trust, 2004), p.20.

10 Kerkham, 'Hafod', p.209.

11 Quoted in *ibid.*, p.212.

12 George Cumberland, *An Attempt to Describe Hafod* [1796], ed. Jenifer Macve and Andrew Sclater (The Hafod Trust, 1996), introduction, p.8.

13 *Ibid.*, pp.42-3.

14 *Description of Hawkstone* (Shrewsbury,1818 ed.), p.8.

15 *Ibid.*, pp.19-20.

16 *Ibid.*, pp.53-4.

17 *Ibid.*, pp.16-17.

18 *Boswell's Life of Johnson*, ed. G B Hill and L F Powell (Oxford: Clarendon Press, 1950), Vol.V.p.434.

19 Richard Warner, *A Tour Through the Northern Counties of England and the Borders of Scotland* (Bath, 1803), Vol.II, p.182.

20 *Humphry Repton's Memoirs*, ed. Ann Gore and George Carter (Norwich: Michael Russell, 2005), p.84.

21 Malcolm Andrews, *The Search for the Picturesque* (London: Scolar Press, 1990), p.166.

22 Information on Claife from Karen Lynch and Sarah Rutherford.

23 Young, *Northern Tour*, Vol.I, p.345.

24 Gilpin, *Cumberland and Westmoreland*, I, pp.161-2.

25 *Ibid.*, II, p.102.

26 Tim Longville, 'Thrills and Chills in the Cumbrian Hills', *Country Life*, 23 November 2000, p.61.

27 William Hutchinson, *The History of the County of Cumberland* (Carlisle, 1794), Vol.I, pp.188-9.

28 Longville, 'Thrills and Chills', p.63.

29 Personal communication from Karen Lynch.

30 Patrick Eyres, 'Bolton Abbey: a walk through classic Picturesque terrain', *A Landscape Explored: Wharfedale at Bolton Abbey, New Arcadians' Journal* 13, 1984, no pagination.

CHAPTER ELEVEN

Repton and the Picturesque

The relationship of Humphry Repton to the Picturesque is far from straightforward. First, there were the arguments with Price and Payne Knight, particularly over the analogy between the art of the painter and that of the landscaper. Then there is the tension between theory and practice, Repton having often to side with pragmatism. Finally, Repton's own views on what was picturesque appear to change, so that by the later stages of his career he was developing almost a new genre in its own right, a 'Villa Picturesque', with elaborate series of flower gardens near the house, as at Ashridge, Endsleigh and Montreal, Kent. It could be argued that this was a move away from the Picturesque, since it is essentially inward-looking and does not relate to the wider landscape: on the other hand, it embodies intricacy and variety, which were always *desiderata* for the picturesque pundits. The separate compartments (Repton referred to them as episodes) were generally not cut off from each other, so the contrasts were manifest.

Repton clearly had a feeling for the Picturesque and welcomed the opportunity to work on a dramatic site when it arose. If natural picturesque features were lacking he might add a small-scale individual 'incident' for surprise or variety. Out of over 200 commissions (Repton said 400) the number of truly picturesque sites was small, and these will be looked at individually. But as a professional he could not afford to turn down commissions, with the result that in most cases his proposed landscaping was more consonant with Brown's parks than with the Picturesque. Repton, indeed, saw himself as taking over from Brown and would defend his predecessor against detractors who would often tar him with the Brown brush. He offended the purist theorists yet was capable of scaling picturesque heights on occasion. His importance, for the purposes of this book, is that his practice was at its peak during the very years of the apogee of the Picturesque.

What Repton considered picturesque can be gleaned from his Red Books, both from comments in the text and in some of the watercolours with which he illustrated the books. In addition, his published volumes contain a good deal of opinion, often taken from the Red Books (as indeed are some of the illustrations). The Red Books were intended as 'persuaders', and the commentary is of a polite but exhortatory tone. But in placing what he called Convenience above other considerations, the hired consultant Repton often had to compromise in order to suit the wishes of his client. It is reckoned that very few commissions were carried out according to Repton's plans in full – much more common, in fact, was the adapting of some of his ideas by others at a later date.

Long before he actually became a landscape gardener, at the age of thirty-seven, he had, or so he maintained, studied the picturesque results of landscaping. In his *Prospect* (or prospectus) of 1789 he proclaimed:

H. REPTON having for many years (merely as an amusement) studied the picturesque effect resulting from the art of LAYING OUT GROUND, has lately been advised by many respectable friends (to whom he has occasionally given sketches for the improvement of their own places) to enlarge his plan, and pursue professionally his skill in LANDSCAPE GARDENING.[1]

So, quite apart from announcing his professional arrival, Repton hints at his prime method of drawing up plans, viz. by sketches.

At the same time Repton issued a trade card (Fig.11.1) which is instructive both about his professional intentions and about his notion of a desirable landscape of a distinctly picturesque kind. He depicts himself as a man of action, surveying with a theodolite, but as his career evolved he became less of a practitioner and more of a theorist and delineator of ways to improve an estate. The landscape on which he is working contains a number of features that he would continue to cherish. There is dense planting down to the edge of the water, contrasting with the bare banks usually preferred by Brown. Labourers toil by the edge to increase the sense of needful activity in improving an estate. The planting generally is profuse and tending to wild. The lake is naturalistic in shape and outline. There is a tower rising above the trees, a motif beloved of more than one designer (e.g. Hamilton at Painshill) and prophetic of Repton's future commission at Blaise. This in itself echoes Milton's oft-quoted (more than once by Repton himself) lines from *L'Allegro*: 'Towers and battlements it sees Bosom'd high in tufted trees'.

His chosen medium of the Red Books, so-called from being bound often (but by no means always) in red morocco leather, combined text with illustrations of an alluring nature for his clients. By means of a flap, or slide as Repton called it, a scene could be viewed as it currently

11.1 Humphry Repton's trade card, engraved by Thomas Medland after Repton, 1788

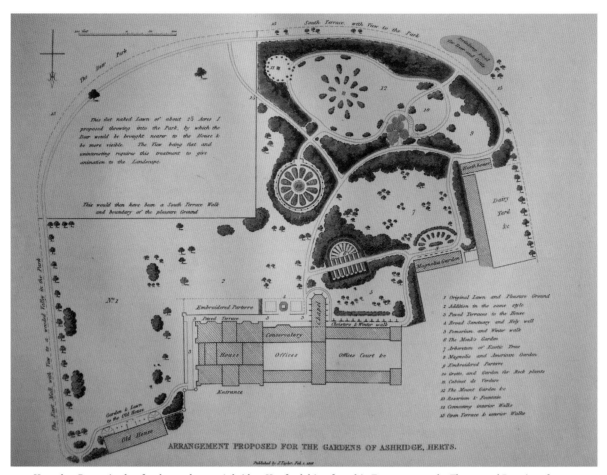

11.2 Humphry Repton's plan for the gardens at Ashridge, Hertfordshire, from his *Fragments on the Theory and Practice of Landscape Gardening*, 1816, second plate following p.144

existed (flap down) and as it would be when 'improved' by Repton (flap lifted). Perversely Tom Stoppard in his play *Arcadia* reversed these two positions, which seems psychologically wrong. Thus, even if the scenery itself was not especially picturesque at a given site, Repton's method, of creating pictures, *per se* rendered the views worthy of illustration and therefore in a simple sense picturesque. Repton used watercolour as a fashionable means of conveying his message, in a tradition already established by Sandby, Hearne and Rooker. It enabled him to communicate two things, overtly the results of what his improvements would bring to the scene, and, subliminally, a philosophy of what constituted the Picturesque. In addition to the watercolours, some illustrations were sketches in pencil, ink and grey wash.

André Rogger has considered at length and in depth the images of the Red Books. He conducts a penetrating analysis of their relation to the Picturesque in chapter six of *Landscapes of Taste: The Art of Humphry Repton's Red Books*. Repton himself claimed that the illustrations were complementary to the text, which was in itself often didactic, though sometimes they seem to give out a different message to the words. Many of the images had a life beyond that confined to a Red Book, which would at the time be seen only by the owners and their friends or visitors. Some of the illustrations found their way into his published books, but a great many more were re-drawn and engraved in miniature for the annual almanac Peacock's *Polite Repository* between 1790 and 1811, in which they appeared as vignettes, generally focusing on the house. Some of the non-site-specific images used for the

11.3 Rosary at Ashridge, Hertfordshire, from Humphry Repton, *Fragments on the Theory and Practice of Landscape Gardening*, 1816, opposite p.140

frontispieces acted rather like Repton's tradecard, with illustrations such as a classical temple or arch in an idealised setting: others included ruins and a dense but varied planting with lake and mountain in the distance. In this way Repton's ideas about landscaping could reach a much wider audience.

Rogger has also discussed the careful way in which the images were managed and positioned in the Red Books so as to maximise their impact.[2] In many cases the impact would be of a specifically picturesque kind, certainly at sites where such effects were possible. But the message had to be hammered home by the text, whether in Repton's elegant calligraphy in the Red Books or in the subsequently published works. It was only in the *Polite Repository* vignettes that the images had to stand alone.

While Repton could express his opinions or general ideas as applied to the particular site in a Red Book, it was in his three major volumes that he could expatiate at more length, categorise his thinking, and bring together the material contained in a large number of Red Books. The three works – *Sketches and Hints on Landscape Gardening* (1795), *Observations on the Theory and Practice of Landscape Gardening* (1803) and *Fragments on the Theory and Practice of Landscape Gardening* (1816) – span more than twenty years of his career and thus give him the chance to develop and modify his ideas, as well as respond to the demands made by the practicalities of his trade and the wishes of owners. He himself, though, denied that he had changed and said he was true to his earlier principles. The title of the last work betrays a slight weariness and disillusion, the author being unwell, at the end of his career and, overall, a disappointed man. Further, by 1816 the battles over the Picturesque were largely over, and it was even becoming unfashionable and the subject of mockery (see p.30), owing, in part at least, to Repton's own late designs, which exhibit a change of direction (a neo-Picturesque?).

In the opening chapter Repton's forceful arguments for differentiating between landscape painting and garden design were set out. He was not, therefore, in tune with Price's dogged insistence on the analogy, yet in some ways his practice, which after all consisted in presenting scenes in the form of pictures, belied his stance. But, ever the pragmatist, Repton knew that he had to sell his ideas and that the visual medium was the most effective way of doing so. It also suggests that those he was trying to impress and convince, the owners, were themselves susceptible to a picturesque means of expression, and confirms the Picturesque as a dominant fashion of the day.

Although the majority of Repton's images cannot be classified as picturesque, there are a significant few that can, especially for the relatively small number of picturesque locations at which he was consulted. Repton's overall definition of the art of landscape gardening was 'The pleasing combination of Art and Nature adapted to the use of Man',[3] which did not in itself carry any picturesque implications, yet he did not hesitate to promulgate his opinions on a desirable end-product in which any potentially picturesque effects would be pointed up. For Repton, the house would often set the tone for the garden improvements: if the setting was, or was to be made, picturesque, then Gothic was preferable to classical for the architecture of the mansion. Repton illustrated a contrasting presentation of a Grecian (=classical) house with a restrained setting and a Gothic pile with wilder surroundings. Gothic was preferred because of its irregularity of outline, though for full effect it needed plants and weathering:

> After all, no building can appear truly picturesque, unless in its outline the *design* can be enriched by vegetation (such as ivy or other creeping plants); and the *colouring*, by those weather stains, which time alone can throw over the works of Art, to blend them with the works of Nature, and bring the united composition into pleasing harmony.[4]

Repton himself realised that the Red Books were a marketing tool and that the pictured improvements were often fanciful and unlikely to be implemented in full. Even so, he was disappointed that so few of his plans were taken up at once, or even at all. He was not above distorting and exaggerating the topography in his views, so he must have recognised that what he depicted would be unattainable anyway. As an aside, Richard Gorer has pointed out that Repton's proposal for the rose garden at Ashridge was unachievable, given the varieties of rose available at the time (Fig.11.3).[5] The Red Book for Glemham Hall, Suffolk, has been published, and the introduction by Stephen Daniels indicates Repton's repertoire of trickery and illusion to change the appearance and lie of the land.[6] The basically flat Suffolk terrain is rendered picturesque by the use of a double flap – the first one removes a building that more resembles a dwelling than a stables, and the overlay beneath reveals a scene very much in keeping with the tradecard of a couple of years earlier: there is a lake (never executed) and a finely wooded hill in the background with the obligatory tower rising from the wood.

Perhaps because he always considered the 'convenience' of his clients, Repton's idea of the Picturesque was often more cosy and decorative than, say, the wilder naturalism of Downton. Even where he had the opportunity to exploit a picturesque site, as at Endsleigh, he would – in addition to grander sweeps and views – incorporate small-scale intimate effects near the house. Where the site was not in itself dramatic or extensive, such effects would become more important, and variety can be seen as the keynote and link with the Picturesque. Thus what we might call the Villa Picturesque came into being, a principally Reptonian development that would lead to the suburban gardens of Loudon and his successors.

Repton created quite a number of 'compartments', generally near the house. Thus, complementing the Indian architecture at Sezincote, Gloucestershire, there is an Indian-style garden within an area known as the thornery, including a bridge with Brahminee bulls, a column with a coiled serpent round it and a temple to the god Souriya. Another thornery, this time well away from the house, was in a grove of thorns at Woburn Abbey, centred on a cottage. A vignette was published in the *Polite Repository* for 1810: Repton desired the cottage to be surrounded by every type of thorn that could endure the climate. At Ashridge, Hertfordshire, he devised a series of gardens around the house (Fig.11.2), but his plans were subsequently taken up and modified by Wyatville (see p.174). However, it is clear that he was alert to the historicist associations of the (mock Gothic) house, and conceived a Monks' Garden with a central conduit (Fig.11.4), while to one side a *souterrain* leads through a mount. A geometrical rose garden, clear forerunner of several such in the Victorian garden, was also planned (Fig.11.3).

Repton would often present his illustrations as from the windows of the house. Not only was this the most common view the owner would have of the grounds, but it was crucial to the design. In Repton's client-centred world the house was the basic viewing point, and the maximum had to be derived from the appearance of the gardens seen from it. There were, however, two other important viewing strategies. One was the approach, as Repton termed what we would call a drive, leading to the house. This could be winding and circuitous, but once the house was glimpsed he insisted it should not then leave the sight. The house could, however, be masked until the last moment, when it emerges unexpectedly, as at Kenwood, approached from the north. Second, what Repton referred to as a drive was precisely that, a circuit for driving horse and carriage around but within the estate, to encompass points of particular interest. Jane Bradney has written a perceptive account of how Repton's carriage-drives controlled the way in which the landscape was seen and experienced. Her article covers the clientele and what they saw, or were allowed to see, with secondary agendas such as the blocking out of views of other owners' properties, and demonstrates that Repton had an evolutionary and varied (though pragmatic) approach to the art of laying out a drive.[7]

In *Fragments* Repton declares that the word Picturesque is more easily understood than defined. He does not believe it covers all subjects capable of being represented in a picture, and should be confined to those which are 'beautiful'. Repton goes on to inquire into picturesque circumstances in actual landscape: he classifies them under three heads – steepness of ground, abrupt rocks and water in rapid motion, 'for, we may consider wood, and lawn, and smooth water, as common to all landscapes, whether in Cornwall or in Lincolnshire'.[8] After proposing that 'romantic rocks' should be brought into view, he concludes that 'of all picturesque objects, there is none so interesting as Water in rapid motion; and it is the duty of art to avail itself of every opportunity to force it into notice'.[9]

Unlike Price and Payne Knight, Repton believed firmly in the hand of art controlling nature. This was linked to his central conviction (obligatory in his profession) that people should be comfortable in their homes, which extended to their gardens. As he commented in his observations on improvements to be made at Blaise Castle, 'Where man resides nature must be conquered by art: it is only the ostentation of her [art's] triumph, and not her victory, that ought to offend the eye of taste'.[10] In this instance the conquering was achieved by gunpowder, blasting away the rock to make it passable by carriage. In similar vein, Repton (in relation to Endsleigh) maintained that 'without the aid of art, the most romantic or picturesque scenery in nature is a desert, and only fitted to the habitation of wild beasts'.[11]

Blaise Castle

Repton's most picturesque site was at Blaise Castle, near Bristol. The owner, by recent purchase in 1789, was John Scandrett Harford, a Quaker interested in gardens as so many were, including Thomas Goldney as the most famous local example. Repton visited Blaise over the years 1795 and 1796, and found a site that was not only spectacular in itself, with gorges, swelling heights and views, but even had a pre-existing tower rising from the trees in his favourite approved fashion. This was Blaise Castle, a sham castle erected in 1766 for Thomas Farr as a prospect tower (but also to be seen).

The castle set the tone for the estate, not only by name but by its dominant position (Fig.11.5). Repton recognised this, and proposed an entrance lodge where previously there had been just a gate in the fence (Fig.11.6). The lodge was to be castellated, to reflect and foreshadow the castle deep within the estate. It did, however, cause him some disquiet because the house was neo-classical. But since it could not be seen from the road, Repton concluded that a Gothic castle lodge would be more appropriate in this instance.[12] His Red Book has survived and has been published in a monochrome format by the Friends of Blaise.

From the lodge, Repton's approach proceeded in a tortuous, looping line to accommodate the violent changes in level. This necessitated cutting rock in some places and building up the foundation of the road in others. Repton keeps returning to the word 'romantic' to describe Blaise: 'the approach will be in strict character with the wildness of the scenery, and excite admiration and surprize without any mixture of that terror which tho' it partakes of the sublime, is very apt to destroy the delights of romantic scenery'.[13] Repton shows that, as always, convenience takes priority over the extremes of feeling. He is not entirely consistent, however, and refers to the 'grand and sublime combination of rocks and trees' which he was anxious to promote: dense hanging woods and caverns and scars of rock are the essence of the place. And far away were views of the Welsh mountains across the mouth of the Severn.

The one great lacuna at Blaise was water. Various attempts were made or suggested to rectify the situation, and Repton intended a pool and stream in the bed of the gorge. However, the water, then as now, sometimes dried up. But to compensate there were at least distant views of the Bristol Channel.

Repton's approach took the visitor through thoroughly picturesque scenery, including a deep ravine, and ended at the house, in a much more tranquil setting, later adorned with Nash's pretty dairy with pool in front of it (Fig.11.7). In addition there was a Reptonian drive, which

11.4 Design for conduit at Ashridge, Hertfordshire, from Humphry Repton, *Fragments on the Theory and Practice of Landscape Gardening*, 1816, third plate following p.144

11.5 Blaise Castle, Bristol, in picturesque setting, lithograph by JS Prout c1820

11.6 The proposed lodge at Blaise, from Humphry Repton, *Observations on the Theory and Practice of Landscape Gardening*, 1803, p.145 (flap lifted)

11.7 John Nash's dairy at Blaise, Bristol

took visitors already staying at the house round particular points of interest within the wild landscape, and, further, a route for walkers. No picturesque corner was to be unexplored. The approach zig-zagged past a thatched Timber Lodge, now much altered, and then Woodman's Cottage (1797), where the plantings opened up in front to afford a view from a distance. This sign of rural habitation was vital to Repton's concept of a picturesque landscape, and he depicts it in his Red Book with smoke curling up from the chimney as he did elsewhere: the smoke indicated an inhabitant and itself provided motion or animation in the view. From the house both the cottage and the castle rearing up among the trees were to be visible. The choice of a cottage was deliberate: its 'cheerfulness', as Repton put it, was to alleviate the sombre feeling of the castle.

The point of the drive was to allow those who might be less mobile on foot to see the splendours of the 'deep romantic glens'. For those who were active (and agile) the walk took in some more perilous points, such as the Lover's Leap or a cavern opening on to a hill opposite. It is clear that, having got so many picturesque snapshots within his grasp, Repton was going to milk them for all they were worth.

In 1812 Repton's son George collaborated with John Nash to produce a complementary scene, a picturesque village, on the far side of the house. This was the enchanting set of *cottages ornés* constituting Blaise Hamlet (Fig. 11.8), each one different. In a sense this accords with Repton's later thinking (and he was still active in 1812 despite ill-health) and contrasts with the wild gorge, yet preserves the irregularity and variety demanded by the Picturesque.

Oldbury Court

Not all that far from Blaise, at Oldbury Court, on the steep banks of the River Frome, Repton was called in by Thomas Graeme in 1799 to improve a site that was already replete 'with such a variety of sublime and beautiful scenery as seldom occurs in places of much greater extent'.[14] Cliffs had been formed by the workings of quarries, and woods covered the sides of the gorge in this unsung site. Repton devised walks with superb views as the ascent rose, together with a rotunda and various rustic buildings. There were pools, bridges, waterfalls and rustic bridges, and much of Repton's woodland has survived.[15] There were two views of Oldbury in the *Polite Repository*. Repton cleared the view by moving a ridge of earth as he had done at Moccas: 'At OLDBURY COURT the view is opened into a romantic glen by the same kind of operation.'[16]

Ferney Hall

One of Repton's earliest commissions (1789) was at Ferney Hall, near Ludlow, Shropshire. This brought him into close proximity with Downton, and indeed Repton consulted Payne Knight, being at that time on good terms with him. Advice was sought particularly on the landscaping of a dell, which Repton ornamented in his Red Book with a 'picturesque bridge over the narrow part of the pool', an intimate romantic scene. However, Repton had to oblige the owner, Samuel Phipps, in respects that dismayed Payne Knight, and set in train the rift between them. All work on the project was halted in 1790, however, by the death of Phipps.[17]

11.8 One of the cottages at Blaise Hamlet, Bristol

Thoresby

The imported rock from Creswell Crags has been mentioned (p.90). It formed the ragged cascade prescribed by Repton at Thoresby to replace an earlier formal structure. Repton drew the cascade to be engraved in the *Polite Repository* for 1801 and it formed the focal point in his landscaping.[18] Repton thought highly of the cascade and was gratified by the impression it made on the owner, who declared, 'scarce a day passed that I do not cross the 'Nature's Bridge' [a large flat slab placed across the cascade] to see and hear the roaring flood. The very rocks appear to shake!'[19]

Commissions in Wales

Repton's Welsh practice was a varied one, and perhaps did not exploit as much of the picturesque possibilities as he could. At Rug, Clwyd, he contented himself with adding a large lawn, claiming that comfort came before an extensive prospect.[20] But at Plas Newydd, on Anglesey, he could hardly have avoided the superlative views across the Menai Strait inland as far as Snowdon. In 1799 he produced his recommendations in the usual Red Book, and 'By 1803 most of his suggestions had been carried out; the woods were filled out to screen the house from the road, the main drive was reorientated, and additional plantings of fir, oak and birch were made.'[21]

But it was at Stanage Park, Powys (1803), that Repton spread his picturesque wings most freely. The house was designed partly by Repton himself and his son John Adey Repton, and was modelled on the castellated pile at Downton. In the Red Book Repton looks back to the Picturesque controversy as if it were a thing of the past and appears to approve of Payne Knight's condemnation of Brown. Repton says that the character of a castle would be best fitted for the situation, and admits that the example of Downton would be the best to follow but that he dare not recommend it because of extravagance.[22] In the event, however, the owner, Charles Rogers, overcame Repton's scruples by commissioning such a castle. Repton deliberately introduced some artificiality near the house in the form of walls and terraced lawns, but created two picturesque drives, a pond and an extensive plantation especially of larch.[23] The surroundings were described by Repton as wild and shaggy.

Repton in Cornwall

Repton made two sorties into the naturally picturesque county of Cornwall, early and late in his career. The first tranche came in autumn 1792, with four visits (Antony, Catchfrench, Trewarthenick and Port Eliot), and a later pair, Pentillie and Tregothnan, followed in 1809. One might have expected his 'picturesque' Muse to soar here, yet, as with the Welsh commissions, there is nothing to compare with his work at Blaise and Endsleigh. At Antony, he proposed a scheme that created a triple vista down to the Lynher estuary, accessing the outward view but not as a panorama. Catchfrench, overlooking the Seaton valley, was somewhat enclosed, but Repton was able to open a view to the west by means of lowering a meadow ridge. Trewarthenick was an inland property with no remarkable views, but Repton proposed deep plantations to allow walks to be cut through that would permit sight of the best of what was there. Port Eliot, however, proved the Cornish commission with the most 'capabilities', which Repton attempted to exploit. Some work had already been done, such as The Craggs, a quarry garden with 'sublime horrors' of cliff and protruding rock, but the location provided views of the sea, the Tiddy estuary and other creeks, and a swarm of small hills. Repton's art consisted in planting in such a way as to heighten the hills.[24]

Of the two late commissions, Pentillie had a castle perched on a steep hill above the Tamar, but although a Red Book was produced, and survives, it is not known what Repton's proposals amounted to, or whether they were executed. At Tregothnan, as at Port Eliot, much had already been accomplished to accentuate the picturesque elements of a wooded peninsula between the rivers Fal and Truro. There were several miles of scenic drives, and all Repton was able to do was to adjust the planting to admit varied and briefer glimpses of the water.[25]

Attingham

This was a case of Repton attempting to create something picturesque for a site that did not have much potential. A distant view of the Wrekin gave some character to this Shropshire property which was on the whole rather flat. Repton considered that the park should be extended and then:

> Secondly, some striking and interesting features should be brought into notice, such as the junction of the Severn and the Terne, which may be actually effected within the limits of the park; and particularly the great arch across the Terne, of which no adequate advantage is at present taken. There are also some large trees, and many interesting points of view, which well deserve attention in a plan professing to increase the number of beautiful circumstances, rather than the number of acres in the park.[26]

Repton observed that there was already a picturesque scene comprising 'some fragments of an old mill and brick arches' that created a composition not unlike a painting by Ruisdael in the house. However, their juxtaposition in front of the colonnade and portico of the house (Fig.11.9) suggested a ruined ancient temple rather than the modern mansion: since this was not the case, the ruins in the foreground 'however picturesque in themselves, are incongruous and misplaced' so close to the house.[27]

Valleyfield

Repton's work at Valleyfield, Fife, attracted some controversy. For a start, Repton never visited Scotland, the commission being undertaken by his two sons though Repton drew up the

11.9 View of Attingham, Shropshire, from Humphry Repton, *Observations on the Theory and Practice of Landscape Gardening*, 1803, p.116

proposals in a Red Book. Loudon clearly resented this and attacked Repton for being ignorant of the special qualities of the Scottish landscape and for destroying some of its beauties.[28] Repton himself claimed that he had taken advantage 'of the deep romantic glens and wooded banks of the river which flows through the grounds, and falls into the Frith [sic] of Forth at a short distance from the house, an approach has been made, which, from variety, interest, and picturesque scenery, may vie with any thing of the kind in England'.[29] While Repton had indeed spoiled a particularly attractive dell by the construction of an approach to the house, the approach itself provided a range of picturesque views and was carried over two rustic bridges devised by Repton, one of which was composed of rugged rocks similar to those along the road.[30] One problematic feature, which might have appeared to be out of place in such a spectacular location and which predictably incurred Loudon's ire, was a flower garden with a formal canal. However, the owner, Sir Robert Preston, was interested in plants and was likely to have requested such a facility for his collection. The flower garden was enclosed by walls and hidden from the house so did not obtrude on the view.

Endsleigh

A richly promising location was at Endsleigh, on the Tamar that separates Devon and Cornwall. Repton lamented that this, the most picturesque site at which he had been consulted (had he forgotten Blaise?), had come so late in his career (and life) and at a time by which he was virtually immobile. A country retreat of the Duke of Bedford, it comprised a *cottage orné* by Wyatville surrounded by Repton's flower gardens, reminiscent of the layout at Ashridge, and with exceptional views down to the river and across into Cornwall. Georgina, Duchess of Bedford, was the driving force behind the flowering of Endsleigh. It was the last full commission of Repton (1814), and although partially realised much of the planning and design

11.10 Proposed weir at Endsleigh, Devon, from Humphry Repton, *Fragments on the Theory and Practice of Landscape Gardening*, 1816, p.221

was taken over by Wyatville (see p.174). Repton contrasted its inland position on the Tamar with the 'romantic Banks' nearer the mouth of the river: 'Here [at Endsleigh], Solitude, embosomed in all the sublimity of umbrageous majesty, looks down on the infant River struggling through its rocky channel, and hurrying onwards with all the impetuosity of ungoverned youth, till it becomes useful to mankind.'[31] The usefulness in this case meant Plymouth as a centre of commerce and a dockyard for the fleet.

Repton's sketch of the house, with a weir in the foreground that was intended to be fordable, is shown in Fig.11.10. Below the house it was proposed to have a flat walk, with a pierced wall on its northern side, and an uninterrupted view down a steep slope to the river. Opposite, on land which was brought into the Endsleigh estate, Repton intended to place his favourite device of a cottage with smoke curling up to animate the scene, and likewise with the introduction of cattle and pasture on both sides of the river. The wood on the far side was to have clearings to break the density of the existing solid block.

Repton had in fact submitted designs for the house (with the help of his sons) in 1809, but Wyatville's version had been adopted, on a slightly different site, from 1810. In a reverse of the situation at Ashridge, Wyatville actually preceded Repton in laying out the grounds, though Repton was brought in seemingly as a result of the Duke's dissatisfaction, especially with regard to the slope to the south.[32] Repton had suffered a severe accident in 1811, when a carriage had overturned on ice, and was by 1814 a cripple, carried about in an invalid chair. He proposed winter gardens, a children's garden, a gravel walk, development of a dell and the removal of a wall. Wyatville, having been temporarily ousted, returned and took up some of these ideas, modifying them in his own way.

The drives through Leigh Wood, on the hill, were according to Repton laid out by an employee of the Duke's at Woburn Abbey, a Mr Salmon, rather than Wyatville. He considered that these steep drives were too sublime to be picturesque and should be amended accordingly: 'In the Drives through Leigh Wood, some advantage has been taken of the steepness; but it should be shewn as an object of beauty from the precipitous side of the road, and not as an object of terror, by making the roads too steep.'[33] He also thought that those 'romantic rocks' that were hidden by scrub should be brought into view and that the river should be agitated to make it more interesting (hence the proposed weir).

A particular instruction was to pay attention to the slope down to the river. The reason for a plain, unplanted slope was that Repton found that any tree or shrub more than six feet high would obscure the view of the river. By no means all Repton's proposals were implemented – those that were not included a walled kitchen garden and conservatory wing, a viaduct, a mill and a cascade on the hill. On the other hand, many of his plans did come to fruition (even if mediated by Wyatville), as can be seen in a series of watercolours of 1841 by John Cook Bourne. As well as the set of gardens round the house there was a 'Dairy Dell' to complement Wyatville's rustic dairy, including a chain of pools with paths arranged to view them to best advantage.[34]

By the time of *Fragments*, Repton seems to have edged more towards Price and, whether willingly or consciously, moved towards an acknowledgment of at least some connection between painting and gardening. This was recognised by Loudon when he edited and republished Repton's works in 1840. It also shows in the heavily decorative Red Book views of the later years. Loudon himself had changed too, from attacking Repton in the early 1800s to accepting that some at least of his opinions were sound and had lasting value. His tributes to Repton in the 1840 edition are both handsome and genuine.

1 Cited in André Rogger, *Landscapes of Taste: The Art of Humphry Repton's Red Books* (Abingdon and New York: Routledge, 2007), p.1.

2 *Ibid.*, especially pp.79-83.

3 Humphry Repton, *Fragments on the Theory and Practice of Landscape Gardening* (London: J Taylor, 1816), p.viii.

4 *Ibid.*, p.20.

5 Richard Gorer, 'The Puzzle of Repton's Roses', *Country Life*, 11 March 1982, pp.654-6.

6 Humphry Repton, *The Red Books for Brandsbury and Glemham Hall*, intro. Stephen Daniels (Washington, DC: Dumbarton Oaks, 1994), p.ix.

7 Jane Bradney, 'The Carriage-Drive in Humphry Repton's Landscapes', *Garden History* 33:1, 2005, pp.31-46.

8 Repton, *Fragments*, p.218.

9 *Ibid.*

10 Humphry Repton, *Observations on the Theory and Practice of Landscape Gardening* (London: J Taylor, 1803), p.145n.

11 Repton, *Fragments*, p.220.

12 Repton, *Observations*, p.145.

13 *Humphry Repton's Red Book for Blaise Castle* (Friends of Blaise, n.d.), 'The Approach'.

14 Quoted in *Parks and Gardens of Avon*, ed. Stewart Harding and David Lambert (Bristol: Avon Gardens Trust, 1994), p.63.

15 *Ibid.*, pp.62-3.

16 Repton, *Observations*, p.10.

17 Stephen Daniels, *Humphry Repton: Landscape Gardening and the Geography of Georgian England* (London and New Haven: Yale University Press, 1999), pp.109-10.

18 *Ibid.*, pp.161-3.

19 *Humphry Repton's Memoirs*, ed. Ann Gore and George Carter (Norwich: Michael Russell, 2005), pp.115-116.

20 Elisabeth Whittle, *The Historic Gardens of Wales* (London: HMSO/Cadw, 1992), p.61.

21 *Ibid.*

22 Repton, *Fragments*, p.35.

23 Whittle, *Gardens of Wales*, p.62.

24 See Timothy Mowl, *Historic Gardens of Cornwall* (Stroud: Tempus, 2005), pp.81-90 and 93-5.

25 *Ibid.*, pp.96-7.

26 Repton, *Observations*, p.115.

27 *Ibid.*, p.116.

28 A A Tait, *The Landscape Garden in Scotland 1735-1835* (Edinburgh: Edinburgh University Press, 1980), p.182.

29 Repton, *Observations*, p.100n.

30 Tait, *Landscape Garden in Scotland*, pp.180-1.

31 Repton, *Fragments*, pp.213-14.

32 Daniels, *Repton*, p.186.

33 Repton, *Fragments*, p.218.

34 See Richard Stone, 'The Creation of Endsleigh: A Regency Picturesque Masterpiece', *Devon Gardens: An Historical Survey*, ed. Steven Pugsley (Stroud: Alan Sutton/Devon Gardens Trust, 1994), pp.76-90.

CHAPTER TWELVE

The Wyatts, Nash and a New Look

Late in the eighteenth century and early in the nineteenth there was a change of attitude towards decoration in gardens, in terms of both buildings and design, which can be seen as complementary to the Picturesque though running counter to the wild and the natural. We have already seen this in respect of Repton, and it is also true of architects he worked with – his sons; James and Jeffry Wyatt; and John Nash. They helped to create a sometimes cosier, more client-friendly romanticism (often Gothic) in gardens, manifested in architecture but also in garden design and in any case colouring the landscape and people's responses to it.

The Wyatts and Nash were primarily architects and are remembered as such, but they were responsible also for garden plans to an extent that may not always be appreciated. Furthermore, they were often engaged to work at sites at the very heart of the Picturesque, as covered in this book, and thus were party to the vision and approach of the owner: this would inevitably have involved discussion with him. Even where their input was purely architectural – usually the house – it could set the tone for the property as a whole and determine how visitors should react. At this time, moreover (and this was in keeping with Price and Payne Knight), there was a move to integrate the house and garden buildings more fully into their setting to produce an overall composition.[1] So their own creative ideas would undoubtedly have enhanced what the owner was trying to do. James Wyatt and Nash spanned both the wild Picturesque and the 'New Look'.

The Villa Picturesque of the mainly post-1800 Wyatts and Nash can also be seen in relation to the romantic. Appreciation of what they were doing was an aesthetic matter, subjective, visual and emotional rather than cerebral. Decoration, whether floral or architectural, was uppermost, and often rural in style. This was the golden age of the *cottage orné*, with surrounding gardens usually of a formal layout, though planting might be luxuriant. The cottage garden as such, however, would not arrive till the end of the nineteenth century. For this early period, the first years of the century, the term Regency gardening has come into use to describe the emphasis on decoration and the close bond between house and garden (floral and plant embellishments were often to be found in the house, and conservatories attached directly to it). Window boxes arrived, and trellis could be found both on outside walls and inside the conservatory.

Italianate architecture began to creep in, alongside a neo-Gothic which was softer and less severe than its earlier eighteenth-century counterparts. Even where classicism was involved, following Adam it was often more decorative than the sometimes plain Palladianism of former days. Orientally-inspired architecture appeared as well, with the mansion at Sezincote, Gloucestershire, inspiring the Royal Pavilion at Brighton. In such cases the plantings and gardens were intended to complement the building, as witness Repton's proposal for Chinese plantings in front of the Chinese dairy at Woburn.

James Wyatt

James (1746-1813), the most distinguished of the unparalleled Wyatt dynasty which ran to twenty-five architects of note, was brought up at the time of the English Landscape Garden, saw the Picturesque flourish and then assisted in the creation of the Regency garden. His own building styles varied from classical to Gothic, though he favoured the latter. He was perhaps unfortunate to be working at a time when competitors included Adam, Chambers, Robert Taylor and Nash, but on Chambers' death in 1796 he was appointed Surveyor General to the Board of Works, in effect official principal architect. He has had his share of detractors, some seeing him as a weathervane adapting his style to suit circumstances in a facile manner, and Pugin labelled him 'Wyatt the Destroyer'. Undoubtedly he had faults, particularly in lack of efficiency, being late, not replying to letters and not planning properly, but what he produced, much of which survives, is pleasing or stimulating to the eye and enlivens the surroundings, giving them a particular feeling through the lustre of the buildings.

An early commission, the Gothic mansion at Sheffield Park, Sussex, showed Wyatt's propensity for surprise and irregularity in the front that looks over the gardens. This façade is irresistibly eye-catching and demonstrates Wyatt's response to the Picturesque, which by then was the coming force. Another Gothic concoction, Lee Priory, Kent (c1785-90), was praised by Walpole as 'a child of Strawberry prettier than the parent'.[2] It shared the asymmetricality and pseudo-monastic style of Sheffield Park, and in its central spire owed something to the mausoleum at Batalha in Portugal.[3] Both Lee Priory and Batalha, which William Beckford knew well from his sojourn in that country, were heavily influential in the ill-starred Fonthill Abbey, at once Wyatt's supreme creation and his shame.

Wyatt's Gothicism has been criticised as unscholarly, but authenticity was not his purpose, although he did utilise ecclesiastical sources. Repton explained that Wyatt preferred Gothic to classical because it suited the English climate better in terms of weathering, and that Wyatt's brand of Gothicism was his own invention: 'In his Gothic buildings, to unite modern comfort with antiquated forms, he introduced a style which is neither Grecian [classical] nor Gothic, but which is now become so prevalent, that it may be considered as a distinct species, and must be called *Modern Gothic*.'[4]

The ultimate Gothic building, which would have entitled it to be ranked with the Seven Wonders of the World, was of course Fonthill Abbey. The story of Wyatt's monumental folly (in both senses of the word) has often been told but is always fascinating. If ever a building could be described as sublime, this was it. The vast pile comprised an irregular cruciform arrangement of galleries and halls of unequal size and height, with an octagonal tower rising 276 feet high in the centre. A spire, which would have reached 450 feet in height, was planned but not executed. The furnishings and decoration within were equally extravagant and breathtaking. But it was not always planned thus. The partnership of Wyatt and Beckford dated back to about 1781, the year of Beckford's majority, and the road to constructing the Abbey was an uneven one. The first thought was the erection of a tower at Stops Beacon on the foundations once laid by Alderman Beckford, but that scheme was soon abandoned.

Next came the idea of a pavilion in the form of a medieval convent which was partly intact and partly in ruins to one side – prophetic as to what was to happen to the Abbey. John Rutter

12.1   Fonthill Abbey, Wiltshire, from Beacon Terrace, engraved by T Higham after G Cattermole, from John Rutter, *Delineations of Fonthill and its Abbey*, 1823, opposite p.90

described how Wyatt was commissioned to build the convent in 1796, and even illustrated what it would have looked like had it been brought into being.[5] The purpose was clearly to create a highly picturesque garden building. Although that particular project went no further, the idea was burning away in Beckford's mind, and the following winter the basis of what would eventually go up was planned and designed. But even though the conception was from the start gigantic, for several years, while it was growing, the Abbey was still regarded as a building for show rather than habitation. Only in 1807 did Beckford knock down his father's house Fonthill Splendens and move into the Abbey as his residence.

The Abbey was so enormous it dominated the landscape of Fonthill and could be seen for miles around. This meant that the gardens were touched by its awesome presence, though sometimes obscured from view by woodland: and in return the gardens, in particular the plantings, provided an important background against which to savour the Abbey (Fig.12.1, taken from the terrace avenue which led to where the initial tower had been planned). Between them, then, Beckford and Wyatt had created an integrated picturesque/sublime vision.

The story of the Abbey shows the dream turning sour. The central tower collapsed twice even before the final catastrophe in 1825, when it imploded, leaving the wings mostly unharmed but effectively spelling the end of the building. Wyatt had, under pressure from Beckford, had to rush his work and tried out a composition cement which did not last, and the mason is said to have confessed on his deathbed that the foundations had not been properly laid. Wyatt himself was killed in a carriage accident in 1813, and it is not clear who was responsible for continuing residual work on the Abbey, although Wyatt's sons and his nephew Jeffry have been canvassed as possible helpers.[6]

The Abbey has tended to dwarf or sideline Wyatt's earlier connection with Fonthill. There are two drawings by him which can be dated to c1781, one of which was a landscape plan for the Old Park, including a new road, a cascade, islands in the lake, plantations and a bridge.[7] Though not implemented, this plan demonstrates first that Wyatt was involved in garden design as well as architecture, and second that he adopted a naturalistic approach to design, with a picturesque sensibility. In 1792 he designed the sham Gothic ruins at Frogmore, part of the great Windsor estate, for Queen Charlotte, almost a trial run for the convent at Fonthill.

Wyatt worked at several key sites. He built offices at Strawberry Hill for Walpole in 1790 and a church for Johnes at Hafod in 1801-2, set in the landscape not far from the Peiran Falls. At Croome Court he was responsible for some late additions and modifications in a basically Brown landscape that was, unusually, well-ornamented: he made Brown's Dry Arch of 1765, a sort of underpass, more picturesque in 1797 and designed the pedestal for a Coade stone Druid nearby. Further out from the pleasure grounds were his 'Saxon' Broadway Tower of 1794 and the classical Panorama Tower, designed in 1801 but not built till a few years later, on the irregular outer circuit. Pirton Castle (1797) is also usually attributed to Wyatt, but his drawing is dated 1801.[8] The Panorama Tower illustrates Wyatt's softening and romanticising of original forms – the plain lines of the Temple of Vesta at Tivoli, the model for so many garden temples, has been prettified by a balustrade above the colonnade and the raising of the central dome to form an upper storey (a dining/prospect room).

Wyatt was George III's favourite architect and carried out a number of commissions at Windsor (including Frogmore and Cumberland Lodge), also designing the castellated palace at Kew.

12.2 James Wyatt's dairy at Cobham Hall, Kent

With Princess Elizabeth he was responsible for a number of garden celebrations at Frogmore involving temporary picturesque structures and masses of floral embellishment.

Two crenellated Gothic mansions, Ashridge and Lasborough Park, Gloucestershire, bore some relation to their gardens. In the case of the abbey/palace of Ashridge, which owed something to Fonthill in its central tower, Wyatt was building on the site of a medieval college, and Repton accordingly devised a scheme of fifteen small garden compartments to reflect the sort of plots that could have been found there originally. Lasborough Park (1794-7) was a castellate mock fort built for Edmund Estourt and was set in the middle of a park developed from an old deer park in Brownian style with belts and clumps contemporary with the house. Unlike Brown, however, the gardens adjacent to the house were not bare grass but proper pleasure grounds and a terrace in the newer taste.

Wyatt worked with Repton on a number of occasions, but his unbusinesslike ways dismayed the conscientious Repton, who turned to Nash instead. But, as with many partnerships between architect and landscape designer, the chronology must be checked, since one or other may have been on the scene first, or afterwards, working independently. Such was the case at Cobham Hall, Kent, where Wyatt had already erected the Mausoleum for Earl Darnley. Repton worked there off and on for over twenty years from 1790, planning extensive changes to the gardens, which were embellished by Wyatt's Gothic Dairy of 1795 (Fig.12.2), a functioning dairy in the form of a chapel. It had cloisters and vaulting, and the chimney was disguised as a bell tower. The Pump House, built in 1789 to raise water from the pond for the use of the Hall, was modified by Wyatt in 1804 to add an upper castellate storey (Fig.12.3). The surroundings were landscaped by Repton accordingly, serpentising the old fish ponds. In both cases, Wyatt's architecture was idiosyncratic, not to say whimsical, given the practical functions that the buildings served. They would certainly have surprised, as they still do.

The Mausoleum at Cobham Hall, 1783 (Fig.12.4), was constructed for the 3rd Earl Darnley, who had died in 1781 but had specified it in his will. It is in the form of a pyramid on a square, with a chapel in the upper part and sixteen recesses for sarcophagi in the lower: it was,

12.3 Pump house, modified by James Wyatt, at Cobham Hall, Kent   12.4 James Wyatt's Mausoleum at Cobham Hall, Kent

12.5 James Wyatt's Mausoleum at Brocklesby, Lincolnshire,   12.6 James Wyatt's classical bridge at Chiswick, Middlesex
engraved by JF Dauthermare after JC Nattes, 1803

however, never consecrated or used. The siting is well away from the house, on a hill, giving it
the prominence that a mausoleum, the most ostentatious of monuments, normally demands.
Seven years later Wyatt built another, very different mausoleum at Brocklesby, Lincolnshire,
to commemorate the death of Sophia Pelham in 1786. It is a smaller, more decorative version
of Hawksmoor's rather severe mausoleum at Castle Howard, and shows the change of taste
between 1730 and 1790. It is more attractive as a building (Fig.12.5), on a smaller-scale knoll
than its Yorkshire counterpart, and shows picturesque taste moving towards something neater
and more appealing, perhaps to accord with the sense that it was a monument to Sophia.

Wyatt himself was steadily moving towards the decorative. Even the massive behemoth of
Fonthill had an excess of ornamentation within, mostly designed by Wyatt, and there is a
romantic feeling about his mature work. Sometimes he implemented or modified the work of
earlier architects, such as realising Henry Keene's bridge at Hartwell House, Buckinghamshire,
or replaced a previous structure, as he did with an iron bridge at Syon House, superseding one
by Adam. It can also be seen in his classical creations, such as the attractive Adamesque bridge
at Chiswick (Fig.12.6), dating from 1788. And at Wilton he designed a terrace garden with
flowers and a central walk next to the house which seems to have been turned into more of an
Italian garden by Lady Catherine, wife of the 11th Earl of Pembroke, and Richard Westmacott.

One of the finest picturesque sites Wyatt was employed at was Badger Dingle (pp.45-6). Having
designed Badger Hall, Wyatt went on to build the temple (1783: fig.2.14) and the rotunda,
and possibly the other buildings which included an ice house and three different boathouses,
one for each level of the water. Whether he had any say in the layout of the picturesque dell
is moot, since a professional, William Emes, was called in for garden planning, but the two
follies made it very different from, say, Downton or Hafod. There is the sense of circuit, if not
a complete one, and almost a harking-back to the incident-studded pictorial gardens of a few
decades earlier, but within a wilder setting.

Wyatt's versatility, and his attachment to the decorative, can be seen in the range of orangeries
that he designed, including Bowden House, Wiltshire; Ammerdown Park, Somerset;
Goodwood, West Sussex; and Dodington, Avon. All were very different; some were attached
to the house; some were Gothic and some were faced with flint.

Samuel Wyatt

Samuel (1737-1807), the elder brother of James, trained at Kedleston, initially as a carpenter (he was known as 'the wonder-working Chip'). At twenty-three he became Clerk of the Works there, at the same time that Robert Adam was working on both house and gardens. In later years he became an architect in his own right, and was probably responsible for the superb orangery at Blickling, Norfolk. He designed the Vinery at Holkham in the same county, but is most remembered for his model farms, where farm buildings of various kinds were given proper architectural form, thereby giving a new twist to the by then outmoded *ferme ornée*. Thus at Holkham he designed over fifty such buildings; at Shugborough five lodges, a dairy in the Tower of the Winds, and a model farm; the Demesne Farm at Doddington, Cheshire; a poultry house at Winnington Hall, Cheshire; and model estate buildings at half-a-dozen more properties.[9]

Sir Jeffry Wyatville

Wyatville, born Jeffry Wyatt (1766-1840), was the nephew of Samuel and James, and trained under both. In 1824 he was permitted to change his name to Wyatville: George IV is supposed to have said *à propos* the suffix, 'Veal or mutton, call yourself what you like.'[10] For convenience he will be referred to throughout as Wyatville. He worked at Repton sites such as Ashridge and Endsleigh, but usually before or after Repton, in both these instances modifying Repton's designs. In general he was responsible for much more garden design than James, and can be seen as developing Repton's Villa Picturesque in respect of gardens near the house though (as an architect) working on a much larger scale as well. His most famous achievement was the remodelling of Windsor Castle in romantic style, for which he was knighted in 1828.

12.7 Endsleigh house and garden, Devon, anonymous print c1820

12.8 Terrace and wall at Endsleigh, Devon   12.9 Jeffry Wyatville's Orangery at Belton, Lincolnshire

At Ashridge Wyatville took over as architect for the house on the sudden death of James Wyatt. Furthermore, although Repton had drawn up plans for numerous garden compartments, they were already being altered prior to Repton's death. Wyatville, in implementing Repton, drew up proposals of his own, based on the earlier ideas. Both Repton's overall plan (1813) and Wyatville's revised plan (1823) survive, so one can make a comparison and discern Wyatville's modifications. Not only did he redesign artefacts such as the cross in the Monks' Garden but planned a flower parterre in that garden and filled other compartments with seats, fountains and orange tubs. He also built an orangery as a wing extension to the house.[11]

Endsleigh, discussed in the previous chapter, has a curious chronology. Repton was actually chosen ahead of Wyatville to design the house (a *cottage orné*), but his proposals were rejected in favour of Wyatville, whose picturesque *jeu d'esprit* survives. In the case of the gardens, however, it seems that Wyatville had already created the terraces, some walks and probably some shaping of the water features in the Dairy Dell before Repton's arrival in 1814.[12] Repton drew up proposals, as set out in a Red Book, which must have been founded on what was already there rather than *de novo*, though it appears his proposals were largely put into effect. However, just as at Ashridge, Repton's ill health and demise in 1818 meant that Wyatville took over in charge of their implementation and, as very much his own man, altered Repton's designs, particularly where architecture was involved. Drawings by Wyatville for garden features and settings exist. It appears that he designed the Wisteria and Yew Walks, the original terrace (Fig.12.8), the Children's Garden next to the house, the quarry steps and arbour, and many rustic buildings including the dairy and a shell house grotto. He further designed a Swiss cottage with complementary Alpine garden.[13]

At Belton Wyatville designed the beautiful orangery (Fig.12.9), which stands in front of the Italian Garden, laid out by him in 1810-11. Although the garden was modified later, the terrace wall, steps and urns were all by Wyatville, as is the exedra facing, although that was moved from another part of the garden in 1921. As an Italianate garden it is remarkably early, showing how much of a pioneer he was in garden design. At Burley-on-the-Hill, Leicestershire, he re-designed Repton's terrace in 1801 to give it a termination.[14] He turned St Ann's Cliff at Buxton, Derbyshire, into a steep if formal garden known as The Slopes with urns, fronting the Crescent, though what we see now probably reflects Paxton's later work just as much. Trees shade the slopes today, but were originally confined to the perimeter boundary. He worked also at

Chatsworth, remodelling the house, building gates and lodges and restoring 'Queen Mary's Bower' with cast-iron trellised arches and pavilions: other features included a new lower end to the cascade in 1822 and eight formal stone baskets or parterres thirty-two feet square for the western garden.[15]

A late commission was at Kew, where, apart from an unexecuted Palm House, he designed King William's Temple (1836). This was dedicated to various past military victories, thereby picking up on the rash of classical temples by Chambers around 1760, especially the (now lost) Temple of Victory. But, following the work on Windsor Castle, he accomplished his greatest garden works in the Great Park, especially in the area around Virginia Water. His creation of the forum-like Temple of Augusta using genuine classical columns has been covered in the chapter on ruins (p.78), but shows that his picturesque approach was still alive. Jane Roberts, in her monumental book on Windsor's royal gardens and parks (1997), has shown the enormous extent of Wyatville's input: he remodelled Flitcroft's triangular Belvedere of c1750, designed the fishing pavilion (subsequently further orientalised by Frederick Crace) and built a boathouse near the fishing pavilion which also had some Chinese touches added. There were wooden bridges and one of rock at the foot of the grand cascade, a rustic gazebo, a Swiss cottage, gates, lodges, a boatman's house, and a hermitage above a small cascade. The magnificent Five-Arch Bridge which still spans the lake was Wyatville's rebuilding of an earlier bridge by Thomas Sandby that had deteriorated. All were calculated to enhance the decorative appeal of this part of the grounds. Wyatville was also in charge of some of the gardens at Windsor, though detailed designs were probably left to others. He did, however, draw up a plan for plantations north of the castle.[16]

Lewis Wyatt

Another nephew of Samuel and James, Lewis Wyatt (1777-1853) has been considered to be a superior architect to Jeffry. Samuel had rebuilt the house at Tatton Park, Cheshire, towards the end of the eighteenth century, and further alterations were subsequently made by Lewis. Repton had in the meantime landscaped the park, but in 1818 Lewis built the Conservatory, which survives although it has lost its connecting corridor to the house. He was also responsible for 'Charlotte's Garden', designed for Lady Charlotte Egerton in 1814. The centrepiece, which matches the Wyatts' carpet design in the house, was a pattern of petal-shaped beds on a slight rise in the lawn that originally contained unusual plants. This area also embraced an arbour, a rockery and a serpentine path,[17] all in the Villa Picturesque style. Also in Cheshire, the most rewarding county for both Lewis and Samuel, Lewis carried out his most extensive garden work at Lyme Park for the Legh family. He made considerable, though discreet, alterations to the house and restored the Cage out in the park, the name suggesting it was a temporary gaol, though it was later used as a banqueting house. During his period of commission, 1814-18, Lewis converted the formal pond into a naturalistic lake, laid out the North Garden and commenced construction of the orangery.[18] He built the west terrace walk, which afforded views over the Dutch Garden (not formed till 1860) and the lawns to the park and moor beyond. The panel beds in the garden in front of the orangery, though dating from c1860 and containing modern plants, bear some resemblance to the patterns at Tatton. He also constructed a stone walkway with a bastion looking down on his North Garden, a regular design with long beds, accurately restored in 2000-1 (Fig.12.10). The revival of formality was complete.

12.10 Walk by Lewis Wyatt at Lyme Park, Cheshire

John Nash

John Nash (1752-1835), born in the same year as Repton, was also one who lived through the phases of the Picturesque. After a distinctly shaky start to his career (he was declared bankrupt in 1783) he licked his wounds in Wales, gradually establishing a successful country house practice there. He designed several houses in the 1790s and altered Dolau Cothi, the family home of the second wife of Thomas Johnes of Hafod. He then worked at Hafod itself, re-facing the main front in Gothic style and adding an octagonal library in 1793-4. He was therefore exposed to first-hand experience of the wonders of Welsh scenery, and the Picturesque was reflected in his work. He designed Castle House, Aberystwyth, c1794 for Uvedale Price, a triangular and battlemented essay in Gothic castle style with three towers. Price used Castle House as a summer retreat, and no doubt harangued Nash with his views on the Picturesque. Nash's Gothic was always for spectacle rather than authenticity.

The partnership between Nash and Repton commenced in 1796 and lasted for about four years, after which they fell out, though Nash subsequently worked with both Repton's sons. They collaborated at Blaise and at Luscombe (Fig.3.6), where house (a castle based on Downton) and intimate garden were unified. At Cassiobury, Hertfordshire, Nash and Repton devised a set of different flower gardens divided by shrubberies. At Blaise Nash, together with the young Reptons, created first the thatched dairy (Fig.11.7) and then, in 1810, the stunning complex of nine rustic cottages, all different, that comprised Blaise Hamlet, grouped round a green. Not only were the cottages ornate, with varied chimneys, but they were given floriferous trappings of clematis, roses and honeysuckle.

Nash's castle manner proved to be as successful and popular as Adam's or Wyatt's, and totalled about a dozen. Irregular in shape and outline, the best example is probably his own house at East Cowes Castle, Isle of Wight (1798), though Caerhays Castle, Cornwall, runs it close with its demonstration of Nash's 'episodic, scenic composition'.[19] But it was not his only style, and he also introduced an Italianate villa mode in a few instances mostly in the first decade of the nineteenth century, though still irregular in form. In the first twelve years of the century he built twenty country houses, transformed half a dozen more and enlarged or modified many: in addition cottages, lodges, park entrances and dairies flowed from his draughtsman's board.[20]

Like James Wyatt before him, Nash was involved with royal commissions, and was said to be the Prince Regent's architect of choice. His engagement at Windsor Great Park led him to being appointed one of four Commissioners or Keepers of the Great Park, and he submitted various designs, e.g. for a neo-Norman bridge (not built) over the Long Walk, though Wyatville took over from him in 1823. Nash and William Townsend Aiton, the Royal Gardener, together designed the garden of the Royal Cottage in the park.

Nash now turned to garden planning, in the new Regency manner, usually in relation to the house, although in the case of St James's Park in 1827 it involved ornamental shrubberies within the park. With Nash it was more a case of design than horticulture, and he had to work with, in particular, Aiton when it came to plants. Nash became Architect to the Office of Woods and Forests, which made him officially the master of picturesque planning of scenery and architecture in combination. One result was the Royal Pavilion at Brighton, not intended by Nash to be authentic Indian but picturesque, and set in gardens that he designed to balance it, consisting of winding paths, lawns and shrubberies. Mavis Batey has described this approach as 'forest lawn' scenery, derived from the glades in the New Forest where bushes drift and project into the clearings, and has compared it to Nash's London plans for St James's Park and Regent's Park.[21]

Nash's greatest scheme was Regent's Park with, originally, the idea of a massive curving way linking the park and St James's Palace and park, though in the event it petered out at Regent Street, and Nash was sidetracked by the commission to build Buckingham Palace. The park itself, conceived as a unified entity, was bounded by rows of town houses and interspersed by elegant villas in their own grounds. But the open ground was considerably varied in character and purpose, including a zoo, archery area and lake. Some walks and compartments were regular and formal: others were in free, landscape form by way of contrast.

Other architects

There were others who propelled the garden in the direction of the ornamental and adopted Repton's ideas of the Villa Picturesque. Chief among them were his sons George Stanley and John Adey, who worked with Nash as well as with their father. Apart from Blaise Hamlet they were involved in various projects from the Thornery at Woburn Abbey to the ladies' bath house at Adlestrop, Gloucestershire, and even some initial work on Regent's Park.
One man who owed much to Repton was John Plaw, the architect of the stunningly-located Pantheon-style house on the island, Belle Isle, in Lake Windermere. Plaw often quoted from Repton and declared that he designed his houses to fit the scenery.[22] The title of his book *Ferme Ornée; or Rural Improvements* (1795) suggests a return to a fashion that was long obsolete, but he had something new in mind, the creation of an entire farm complex unified by Gothic or other picturesque architecture.[23] This had been done in the past in isolated cases, the self-conscious

approach of the rococo, but Plaw sought a harmonising of all the farm buildings. It can be seen as a parallel to Samuel Wyatt's model farms.

Plaw (c1745-1820) had in fact started before Repton. Belle Isle was built in 1774-5, and his book *Rural Architecture; or Designs from the Simple Cottage to the Decorative Villa* had come out in 1785. It would appear, then, that Repton shaped Plaw's thinking largely by confirming the direction he was already taking. His other major volume was *Sketches for Country Houses, Villas and Rural Dwellings* (1800).

William Atkinson (c1773-1839), a pupil of James Wyatt, tended to work in Gothic and designed a castle house at Twyford Abbey, Ealing, 1807-9, set in 268 acres of wooded parkland. He worked for Thomas Hope at Deeepdene, probably Gothicising the mansion, and is significant because he was both an architect in the romantic style and a horticulturist. He published *Views of Picturesque Cottages with Plans* in 1805.

John Buonarotti Papworth (1775-1847) was a pupil of Plaw and was equally given to quoting from Repton. An elderly William Chambers had encouraged him to take up architecture,[24] and when it came to gardens Papworth focused on decorative buildings. His designs were published in Ackermann's *Repository of Arts* and in *Hints on Ornamental Gardening* (1823). Houses and small villas were covered in *Rural Residences* (1818). His great range of exuberant designs has led him to be called 'perhaps the most prolific and versatile exponent of the lighter side of Regency Picturesque taste', as a result of which his friends encouraged him to adopt his middle name from Michelangelo.[25] Among his many commissions was the seven-arched bridge at Alton Towers, and his published designs would often influence garden buildings even where he was not directly employed. For example, the classical temple surmounting a bridge at Leigh Park, Hampshire, was based on a design in his 1823 book.

1 Mavis Batey, *Regency Gardens* (Princes Risborough: Shire, 1995), p.7.

2 Horace Walpole, *The Yale Edition of Horace Walpole's Correspondence*, ed. WS Lewis and AD Wallace (New Haven and London: Yale University Press and Oxford University Press, 1944), Vol.XII, p.111.

3 David Watkin, *The English Vision: The Picturesque in Architecture, Landscape & Garden Design* (London: John Murray, 1982), p.103.

4 Humphry Repton, *Fragments on the Theory and Practice of Landscape Gardening* (London: J Taylor, 1816), p.17.

5 John Rutter, *Delineations of Fonthill and its Abbey* (Shaftesbury: author, 1823), pp.108-9.

6 Megan Aldrich, 'William Beckford's Abbey at Fonthill: From the Picturesque to the Sublime', *William Beckford, 1760-1844: An Eye for the Magnificent* (New Haven and London: Yale University Press, 2001), p.130.

7 Robert J Gemmett, *Beckford's Fonthill: The Rise of a Romantic Icon* (London: Michael Russell, 2003), pp.62-3.

8 Archival references provided by Mike Cousins.

9 J M Robinson, *The Wyatts: An Architectural Dynasty* (London: Oxford University Press, 1979), p.33.

10 Quoted in Watkin, *The English Vision*, p.120.

11 Kay Sanecki, *Ashridge: A Living History* (Chichester: Phillimore, 1996), p.51.

12 Richard Stone, 'The Creation of Endsleigh: A Regency Picturesque Masterpiece', *Devon Gardens: An Historical Survey*, ed. Steven Pugsley (Stroud: Alan Sutton/Devon Gardens Trust, 1994), p.82.

13 *Ibid.*, p.89.

14 Derek Linstrum, *Sir Jeffry Wyatville: Architect to the King* (Oxford: Clarendon Press, 1972), p.232.

15 *Ibid.*, p.160.

16 Jane Roberts, *Royal Landscape: The Gardens and Parks of Windsor* (New Haven and London: Yale University Press, 1997), p.188.

17 *Tatton Park, Cheshire* (Tatton Park: Cheshire County Council, 1998), p.9.

18 *Lyme Park, Cheshire* (Swindon: The National Trust, 2009), p.40.

19 Watkin, *The English Vision*, p.115.

20 John Summerson, *The Life and Work of John Nash, Architect* (London: George Allen and Unwin, 1980), p.43.

21 Batey, *Regency Gardens*, p.70.

22 *Ibid.*, p.15.

23 *Ibid.*, p.17.

24 *Ibid.*, p.37.

25 Watkin, *The English Vision*, p.191.

Coda

With their attention to smaller-scale varied and colourful gardens round the house, and some Italian-style villa building, Repton, the Wyatts and Nash heralded a new approach to garden design as well as modifying the Picturesque. The enormous changes in design that were to become ever more apparent in the nineteenth century were linked to the rise of the middle class and of suburbia. The Picturesque, certainly in its application to gardens, was bound to fade because of scale if nothing else. Very few had vast new tracts of land to manage, and the emphasis would henceforth be on gardens of small area. While this might, and did, incorporate some picturesque principles, those of intricacy and variety, the large-scale effects beloved of the old picturesque tourists were no longer being created. One exception, though, was Alton Towers, Staffordshire, where the 15th Earl of Shrewsbury harked back to the pictorial garden in creating a building-studded landscape in a steeply undulating setting 1814-27. New materials were used – a cast-iron pagoda and prospect tower – together with associational structures such as a Druid's Temple and a Swiss cottage for a blind Welsh harpist. Loudon disapproved, saying that Shrewsbury had carried out his scheme with more fancy than judgement.[1] His view may have been coloured by the fact that his own involvement had been rejected.

Italian influence made itself steadily more felt, to come to a climax with royal Osborne on the Isle of Wight. Thomas Hope's Deepdene, near Dorking, Surrey, its plan based on an earlier Italianate structure, led a procession of architecture, urns and sculpture down a series of uneven terraces: this time Loudon was delighted and was sure that Uvedale Price would be too.[2] It may be surprising that Price should be thought to approve of such artefacts, but we have seen that Payne Knight had already declared that an Italian parterre was perfectly acceptable as a contrast to a more untamed park outside. Italianate terraces became more and more popular, thanks to the work of the Kennedys and later Charles Barry.

An example of a Regency garden with an aura of the late Picturesque is Worcester College, Oxford. In 1817 the irregular lake was created, together with a lawn bordered by a Regency shrubbery with bays and bulges. The picturesque feeling was apparent in the lake; a type of *cottage orné* with a raised garden in front of it; and glimpses through the trees of the Provost's lawn and garden leading to a façade that looked like a Palladian mansion but was in fact the end of a range of rooms.

J C Loudon (1783-1843) brought utilitarian and environmental concerns to bear on his long career, which reflected landscape gardening early on (albeit in reaction to Repton), through suburban gardens and ornamental shrubberies to a full-circle return to some at least of eighteenth-century landscaping principles when he published an edition of Repton's work in 1841 two years before his death. His portfolio, and his interests, over the years covered public parks for health and education (trees were to be labelled), small-scale gardens and the creation of the 'gardenesque', a plant-centred philosophy to display trees, shrubs and flowers to their best advantage and allowing them to grow naturally. His main disagreement with the Picturesque was that it was not horticultural.

William Sawrey Gilpin (1762-1843) was the nephew of William Gilpin, and owed much of his thinking to his uncle though probably more to Price. His initial career was as a landscape artist, but around 1820, when he would have been fifty-eight, he took up landscape gardening, having been encouraged by Price over many years.[3] He designed some small-scale parterres, as at Audley End, Essex, and terraces such as Clumber, Nottinghamshire, as well as laying out the arboretum at Nuneham Courtenay. But the Picturesque had one final, splendid flourish in Gilpin's work at Scotney Castle, Kent, from 1834, where a romantic castle sits in a lake. It served as the inspiration for Christopher Hussey's book, since it was the Hussey family home.

1 John Claudius Loudon, *In Search of English Gardens* (London: Century, 1990), p.59.
2 *Ibid.*, p.44.
3 Sophieke Piebenga, 'William Sawrey Gilpin (1762-1843): Picturesque Improver', *Garden History* 22:2, 1994, pp.177-8.

Acknowledgements

In attempting to tackle the Picturesque, of all subjects, one is heavily dependent not only on what has been written before but on the wisdom, knowledge and guidance of others, in this case those who have been consulted in the preparation of this book. Chief among them have been Michael Cousins, whose immense research in archives has enabled him to put me straight on various factual details, and Karen Lynch, based in Yorkshire, who has been very helpful in respect of several 'sublime' sites. Christopher Dingwall has been greatly supportive in all matters Scottish, and the chapter on the Scottish Picturesque would not have been possible without his help. Jane Bradney has given valuable advice on Repton and some of his contemporaries.

The opening chapter, in which a vast acreage had to be compressed, was read by Katy Myers, Tim Richardson and Martin Wood, and I have profited much from their comments. Others who have helped include Charles Boot, Patrick Eyres, Sarah Rutherford, Steffie Shields and Sophie Seifalian. I am most grateful to all.

Illustrations are reproduced by kind permission of: The Bridgeman Art Library/The Earl of Harewood (cover picture); The University of Bristol Special Collections (1.4, 1.5); Jochen Müller (2.14); The Bodleian Library, Oxford (3.4); Shrewsbury Museums Service (8.1); Science Museum, London (8.2); and National Library of Wales (10.5, 10.6). All other illustrations have been photographed by the author or are from his collection.

The comprehensive index has been prepared by Douglas Matthews.

It has been a pleasure to work with John Sansom and Clara Hudson of Redcliffe Press.

Select Bibliography

Contemporary publications and writings (up to 1832)

Edmund Burke, *A Philosophical Enquiry into the Origin of our Ideas of the Sublime and Beautiful*, R & J Dodsley, 1757, amplified 1759

William Chambers, *A Dissertation on Oriental Gardening*, W Griffin, 1772

William Combe, *The Tour of Dr Syntax in Search of the Picturesque, a Poem*, 1812

George Cumberland, *An Attempt to Describe Hafod*, 1796 (bicentenary edition, ed. Jennifer Macve and Andrew Sclater, Hafod Trust, 1996)

John Dalrymple, *An Essay on Landscape Gardening* [c1760], Bolton Corney, 1823

(William Gilpin), *A Dialogue upon the Gardens…at Stow*, B Seely, 1748

William Gilpin, *Observations on the River Wye, and several parts of South Wales, &c…*, R Blamire, 1782

William Gilpin, *Observations…Made in the Year 1772, on Several Parts of England, particularly the Mountains, and Lakes of Cumberland, and Westmoreland*, R Blamire, 1786

William Gilpin, *Remarks on Forest Scenery, and other Woodland Views…*, R Blamire, 1791

William Gilpin, *Three Essays: On Picturesque Beauty; On Picturesque Travel; and on Sketching Landscape*, 1792

William Gilpin, *Observations…Made in the Year 1776 on Several Parts of Great Britain; particularly the High-Lands of Scotland*, R Blamire, 1789

William Sawrey Gilpin, *Practical Hints upon Landscape Gardening*, T Cadell, 1832

Richard Payne Knight, *The Landscape*, W Bulmer, 1794, annotated 1795

Richard Payne Knight, *An Analytical Inquiry into the Principles of Taste*, T Payne and J White, 1805

William Marshall, *Planting and Ornamental Gardening: A Practical Treatise*, J Dodsley, 1785, reissued as *On Planting and Rural Ornament*, 1796

George Mason, *An Essay on Design in Gardening*, B&J White, 1795

(William Mason), *An Heroic Epistle to Sir William Chambers, Knight*, J Almon, 1773

John Matthews, *A Sketch from the Landscape*, R Faulder, 1794, amplified c1795-6

Uvedale Price, *An Essay on the Picturesque*, J Robson, 1794

Uvedale Price, *Essays on the Picturesque*, J Robson, 1798

Humphry Repton, *Sketches and Hints on Landscape Gardening*, J & J Boydell, 1794

Humphry Repton, *Observations on the Theory and Practice of Landscape Gardening*, J Taylor, 1803

Humphry Repton, *An Enquiry into the Changes of Taste in Landscape Gardening*, J Taylor, 1806

Humphry Repton, *Fragments on the Theory and Practice of Landscape Gardening*, J Taylor, 1816

Humphry Repton, Memoirs (mss), published as *Humphry Repton's Memoirs*, ed. Ann Gore and George Carter, Michael Russell, 2005

John Rutter, *Delineations of Fonthill and its Abbey*, author, 1823

Horace Walpole, *The History of the Modern Taste in Gardening* [1770], reprinted by Ursus Press, 1995

Claude-Henri Watelet, *Essai sur les Jardins* [1774], ed. and trans. Samuel Danone, University of Pennsylvania Press, 2003

Thomas Whately, *Observations on Modern Gardening*, T Payne, 1770

Arthur Young, *A Six Weeks Tour Through the Southern Counties of England and Wales*, W Nicoll, 1768

Arthur Young, *A Six Months Tour Through the North of England*, 1770

Modern publications (books and articles from 1925)

Malcolm Andrews, *The Search for the Picturesque*, Scolar Press, 1989 (pbk 1990)

Andrew Ballantyne, *Architecture, Landscape and Liberty: Richard Payne Knight and the Picturesque*, Cambridge University Press, 1997

Carl Barbier, *William Gilpin: His Drawings, Teaching, and Theory of the Picturesque*, Clarendon Press, 1963

Mavis Batey, 'The Picturesque: An Overview', *Garden History* 22:2, 1994, 121-32

Mavis Batey, 'The English Garden in Welsh', *Garden History* 22:2, 1994, 157-61

Mavis Batey, *Regency Gardens*, Shire Publications, 1995

Mavis Batey, *Jane Austen and the English Landscape*, Barn Elms, 1996

Jane Bradney, 'The Carriage-Drive in Humphry Repton's Landscapes', *Garden History* 33:1, 2005, 31-46

David Coffin, *The English Garden: Meditation and Memorial*, Princeton University Press, 1994

Stephen Daniels and Charles Watkins, *The Picturesque Landscape: Visions of Georgian Herefordshire*, University of Nottingham, 1994

Stephen Daniels, *Humphry Repton: Landscape Gardening and the Geography of Georgian England*, Yale University Press, 1999

Christopher Dingwall, 'Gardens in the Wild', *Garden History* 22:2, 1994, 133-56

Christopher Dingwall and Don Aldridge, 'The Hall of Mirrors: Reflections on the Sublime and on the Iconography of Ossian at the Hermitage, Dunkeld,' ed. Patrick Eyres, *New Arcadians Journal* 47/48, 1999

Nigel Everett, *The Tory View of Landscape*, Yale University Press, 1994

Hazel Fryer, 'Humphry Repton's Commissions in Herefordshire', *Garden History* 22:2, 1994, 162-74

Robert J Gemmett, *Beckford's Fonthill: The Rise of a Romantic Icon*, Michael Russell, 2003

Edward Harwood, 'William Aislabie's garden at Hackfall', *Journal of Garden History* 7:4, 1987, 307-411 (whole issue)

Walter J Hipple, *The Beautiful, Sublime, and the Picturesque in Eighteenth-Century British Aesthetic Theory*, Southern Illinois University Press, 1957

John Dixon Hunt, *The Figure in the Landscape: Poetry, Painting, and Gardening during the Eighteenth Century*, The Johns Hopkins University Press, 1976 (pbk 1989)

John Dixon Hunt, *Gardens and the Picturesque: Studies in the History of Landscape Architecture*, Massachusetts Institute of Technology, 1992

John Dixon Hunt, *The Picturesque Garden in Europe*, Thames & Hudson, 2002

Christopher Hussey, *The Picturesque: Studies in a Point of View*, G P Putnam's Sons, 1927

David Jacques, *Georgian Gardens: The Reign of Nature*, Batsford, 1983

Caroline Kerkham, 'Landscaping the Sublime' [Hafod], *Country Life,* 29 November 1990, 48-51

Caroline Kerkham, 'Hafod: paradise lost', *Journal of Garden History* 11:4, 1991, 207-16

Mark Laird, *The Flowering of the Landscape Garden: English Pleasure Grounds* 1720-1800, University of Pennsylvania Press, 1999

David Lambert, '"The Poet's Feeling": Aspects of the Picturesque in Contemporary Literature, 1794-1816', *Garden History* 24:1, 1996, 82-99

'A Landscape Explored: Wharfedale at Bolton Abbey', *New Arcadians' Journal* 13, 1984

Derek Linstrum, *Sir Jeffry Wyatville: Architect to the King*, Clarendon Press, 1972

Tim Longville, 'Thrills and Chills in the Cumbrian Hills' [The Nunnery], *Country Life*, 23 November 2000, 60-3

Karen Lynch, '"Extraordinary convulsions of nature": The Romantic Landscape of Plumpton Rocks', *With Abundance and Variety: Yorkshire Gardens and Gardeners across Five Centuries*, ed. Susan Kellerman and Karen Lynch, Yorkshire Gardens Trust, 2009, 123-42

Jennifer Macve, *The Hafod Landscape: An Illustrated History and Guide*, The Hafod Trust, 2004

Elizabeth Wheeler Manwaring, *Italian Landscape in Eighteenth Century England,* Frank Cass, 1925

Alexander Marr, 'William Beckford and the Landscape Garden', *William Beckford, 1760-1844: An Eye for the Magnificent*, ed. Derek Ostergard, Yale University Press, 2001, 137-54

Jennifer Meir, *Sanderson Miller and his Landscapes*, Phillimore, 2006

Timothy Mowl, *Gentlemen & Players: Gardeners of the English Landscape*, Sutton Publishing, 2000

Timothy Mowl, *Historic Gardens of Gloucestershire*, Tempus Publishing, 2002

Timothy Mowl, *Historic Gardens of Worcestershire,* Tempus Publishing, 2006

Timothy Mowl and Marion Mako, *The Historic Gardens of England: Cheshire*, Redcliffe Press, 2008

Paul Sandby: Picturing Britain [exhibition catalogue], Royal Academy of Arts, 2009

Joan Percy, *In Pursuit of the Picturesque: William Gilpin's Surrey Excursion*, Surrey Gardens Trust, 2001

The Picturesque in Late Georgian England, ed. Dana Arnold, The Georgian Group, 1995

Sophieke Piebenga, 'William Sawrey Gilpin (1762-1843): Picturesque Improver', *Garden History* 22:2, 1994, 162-74

The Politics of the Picturesque, ed. Stephen Copley and Peter Garside, Cambridge University Press, 1994

Tim Richardson, 'Hawkstone Park, Shropshire', *Country Life*, 23 January 2003, 62-7

Jane Roberts, *Royal Landscape: The Gardens and Parks of Windsor,* Yale University Press, 1997

John Martin Robinson, *The Wyatts: An Architectural Dynasty*, Oxford University Press, 1979

Sidney K Robinson, *Inquiry into the Picturesque*, University of Chicago Press, 1991

André Rogger, *Landscapes of Taste: The Art of Humphry Repton's Red Books*, Routledge, 2007

Richard Stone, 'The Creation of Endsleigh: A Regency Picturesque Masterpiece', *Devon Gardens: An Historical Survey*, ed. Steven Pugsley, Alan Sutton/Devon Gardens Trust, 1994, 76-90

John Summerson, *The Life and Work of John Nash, Architect,* George Allen and Unwin, 1980

Michael Symes, *William Gilpin at Painshill*, Painshill Park Trust, 1994

Michael Symes, *Mr Hamilton's Elysium: The Gardens of Painshill*, Frances Lincoln, 2010

Michael Symes and Sandy Haynes, *Enville, Hagley, The Leasowes: Three Great Eighteenth-Century Gardens*, Redcliffe Press, 2010

A A Tait, *The Landscape Garden in Scotland 1735-1835*, Edinburgh University Press, 1980

Nigel Temple, *John Nash & the Village Picturesque*, Alan Sutton, 1979

Christopher Thacker, *The Wildness Pleases: The Origins of Romanticism*, Croom Helm, 1983

David Watkin, *The English Vision: The Picturesque in Architecture, Landscape and Garden Design*, John Murray, 1982

Elisabeth Whittle, '"All These Inchanting Scenes": Piercefield in the Wye Valley', *Garden History* 24:1, 1996, 148-61.

Tom Williamson, *Polite Landscapes: Gardens and Society in Eighteenth-Century England*, Sutton, 1995

Kenneth Woodbridge, *The Stourhead Landscape*, National Trust, 1982

Christopher Woodward, *In Ruins*, Chatto & Windus, 2001

Index

About Redcliffe

Redcliffe Press publishes a wide range of books from Bristol art and architecture to poetry and from biography to historic gardens. An associated company, Sansom & Company publishes books on British art and artists, specialising in the twentieth century and contemporary. It has a growing sculpture list.

For more information, please see our websites:

www.redcliffepress.co.uk
www.sansomandcompany.co.uk

or for a 48-page catalogue of our current and forthcoming art titles email info@sansomandcompany.co.uk or write to:

Sales Department, Sansom & Company Ltd., 81g Pembroke Road, Bristol BS8 3EA

Enville, Hagley and The Leasowes

Three great 18th-century gardens

Michael Symes and Sandy Haynes

Enville, Hagley and The Leasowes were the three great eighteenth-century landscape gardens of the West Midlands. They had much in common yet, viewed individually, had their own distinctive character.

The authors examine each to bring out its original appearance and reception by contemporary visitors, and the three are also considered as a trio – as they often were at the time – bound together by topography and a remarkable networking of those involved in their creation. An intriguing chapter discusses the history of the *ferme ornée*, which The Leasowes is traditionally considered to embody.

The gardens were not only local treasures, but stand out prominently in any survey of the eighteenth-century English garden, reflecting a development of the mid-century pictorial, building-studded landscape towards the romantic and 'pictureque' taste of the later years of the century.

This ground-breaking book contains much new material and previously unpublished illustrations.

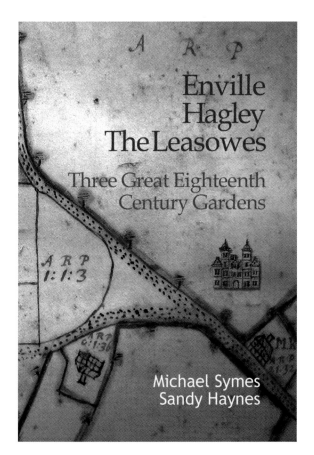

264pp
ISBN: 978-1-906593-53-7
Profusely illustrated with colour
and black and white illustrations
Softback
£14.99

'Mowl is determined to tramp over every piece of uneven grassland and through every bramble tangled woodland, looking for clues'
Ursula Buchan *The Spectator*

The Historic Gardens of England
from Redcliffe Press
buy online at: www.redcliffepress.co.uk
or call 0117 973 7207

Cheshire
the eighth title in Tim Mowl's celebrated series
Tim Mowl and Marion Mako
From the Duke of Westminster's Eaton Hall to Lord Leverhulme's Thornton Manor and his noted garden village at Port Sunlight, there is a swagger and grandeur about the landscape and garden experiments in Cheshire.

Staffordshire
the ninth title in Tim Mowl's celebrated series
Tim Mowl and Dianne Barre
Staffordshire is usually associated with the Potteries and the Black Country, the industrial heartland of the Midlands, yet it is also a county of gently rolling landscape with some of the most eccentric gardens in the country. Nothing is quite what it seems.

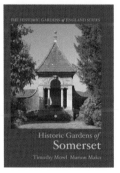

Somerset
the tenth title in Tim Mowl's celebrated series
Tim Mowl and Marion Mako
Somerset is still a county of deep-delved country lanes, textured manor houses and small market towns that remains agrarian and refreshingly old-fashioned. Rich in medieval deer parks, its period of greatest garden activity was the eighteenth century when a group of aesthetic rivals laid out circuits of exotic garden buildings in and around the Quantocks.

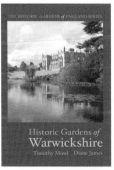

Warwickshire
the eleventh title in Tim Mowl's celebrated series
Tim Mowl and Diane James
Warwickshire is a county rich in history, one that has constantly recycled the legends of its heroes. It maintains a deep sense of nostaliga for the past and a traditional approach to garden design, yet modernism peeps briefly through.

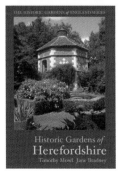

Herefordshire
the twelfth title, Tim Mowl and Jane Bradney
Herefordshire is a secretive border county of castles, small manor houses, farms, lush orchards, scattered villages and meandering rivers. It is the epitome of rural England before the onset of industrialisation. In 1794, two squires – Richard Payne and Uvedale Price –published their theories of Picturesque taste and initiated a 'style wars' campaign against Humphry Repton's suburban proposals.